Sunset
Trees &
Shrubs

BY THE EDITORS OF SUNSET BOOKS AND SUNSET MAGAZINE

Sunset Books Inc. ■ Menlo Park, California

Acorns of pin oak (Quercus palustris) *reveal unexpected beauty on close inspection.*

Research & Text
Philip Edinger

Coordinating Editor
Suzanne Normand Eyre

Design
Joe di Chiarro

Illustrations
Lois Lovejoy

Calligraphy
Sherry Bringham

Editorial Director: Bob Doyle

Third printing July 1997

Photographers

Scott Atkinson: 22, 25; **Dr. Ralph Byther:** 38 top right; **Scott Camazine:** 37 top center; **J.L. Castner:** 37 top left and bottom center; **Jack Clark/COMSTOCK, INC.:** 37 right; **Priscilla Connell/Photo/Nats:** 37 middle center; **Crandall & Crandall:** 7 top, 14 top, 39 bottom left, 48 left, 53 bottom right, 54, 68 bottom right, 84 top, 98 top, 99 bottom, 105, 113 top left, 117, 119 bottom right, 122, 123 top, 125, 127, 131, 132 top, 140; **Derek Fell:** 4, 38 left and bottom center, 39 right, 46 left, 48 right, 49 left, 50 top, 53 bottom left, 66, 68 top, 71 top, 74 center, 80, 83 right, 87 right, 88 bottom, 89, 90 bottom left and right, 91 bottom, 101, 106 top, 112 left, 113 bottom right, 119 bottom center, 123 bottom left, 124, 129 bottom, 136, 139 bottom; **Saxon Holt:** 8, 9 right, 14 bottom, 16 left, 20, 40, 43 bottom right, 45 left, 47, 53 top, 58 top right, 62, 64, 67 top, 69, 74 right, 77 right, 91 top, 96 bottom, 99 top, 102 bottom, 109, 112 right, 113 bottom left, 118, 121 top, 128 right, 132 bottom, 134, 141; **Horticultural Photography:** 15, 18 bottom, 43 bottom left and top right, 45 right, 46 right, 49 right, 50 bottom, 51 bottom, 52, 58 bottom right, 61, 63 right, 68 bottom center, 73 top right, 76, 79, 81 left and center, 84 bottom, 96 top, 97 top, 98 bottom, 102 top, 104 top right, 111, 114, 115 top; **Jerral Johnson:** 39 top center; **James MacDonald:** 39 bottom center; **Robert & Linda Mitchell:** 36 bottom center; **R. H. Molinar:** 38 bottom right; **Nelson-Bohart and Associates:** 36 top right; **Don Normark:** 18 top, 51 top, 55, 56, 71 bottom; **Arleen Olson:** 36 bottom right; **Anne Reilly/Photo/Nats:** 38 top center; **J. H. Robinson:** 37 middle left; **Michael S. Thompson:** 2, 6 left, 11, 12, 13, 16 right, 17, 21, 57 right, 59, 63 left, 75, 77 left, 83 left, 86, 88 top, 90 top left, 94, 97 bottom, 100, 104 bottom left, 106 bottom, 107, 108 right, 110, 119 top, 120, 128 left, 135, 138; **John Trager:** 8 top, 57 left, 74 left, 108 left, 130, 139 top; **Darrow Watt:** 29; **D. Wilder/TOM STACK & ASSOCIATES:** 37 bottom left; **Cynthia Woodyard:** 1, 6 right, 7 bottom, 9 left, 10, 19, 42, 58 top left, 67 bottom, 73 bottom right, 81 right, 87 left, 93, 103, 104 bottom center, 108 center, 115 bottom, 116, 121 bottom, 123 bottom right, 129 top, 133, 137; **Tom Wyatt:** 70, 73 top left.

Cover: Yellow cascade of *Laburnum watereri* 'Vossii' shelters *Rhododendron* 'Purple Splendour'. Cover design by Susan Bryant. Photography by Cynthia Woodyard.

Setting the Tone

More than any other plants, trees and shrubs determine the shape, mood, and character of the landscape. A sense of openness or enclosure, a casual air or one of formality, an impression of high drama or quiet simplicity—these are determined by trees and shrubs, in any setting from countryside to cityscape. Furthermore, these versatile and indispensable plants provide an almost endless variety of foliage, fruit, flowers—and even interesting bark. Small wonder, then, that trees and shrubs are so highly valued by gardeners.

In this book's four chapters, you'll become well acquainted with these plants. From the first chapter you'll learn their uses in the landscape, as well as important points to consider when choosing them. Chapter 2 presents easy-to-use information on all aspects of planting and care. Finally, in Chapters 3 and 4 you'll find descriptive encyclopedia entries for countless useful and popular trees and shrubs.

The information in these pages derives from experts in the world of trees and shrubs—beginning with the many contributors to the Sunset *Western Garden Book* and including more than a dozen specialists who reviewed copy for our earlier work solely on *Garden Trees*. For their valuable advice as we prepared this book's manuscript, we extend our thanks to Philip Normandy of Brookside Gardens in Wheaton, Maryland; Warren Roberts of the University of California Arboretum in Davis; and Lance Walheim of Exeter, California.

Our thanks also go to copy editor Pamela Evans, whose interest in gardening provided valuable insights in editing the manuscript, and to Kevin Freeland and Cynthia Overbeck Bix for their editorial assistance.

Contents

Arbutus unedo

Defining the Landscape

F *rom woodsy acre to well-mannered knot garden, most successful landscapes embrace a carefully planned framework of trees and shrubs. Sometimes these versatile plants shape the landscape in subtle ways. The curve of a low-growing shrub directs a visitor to a garden bench; a grove of trees forms a shady bower. But trees and shrubs may also take center stage, delighting the senses with a sunburst of autumn foliage or masses of fragrant flowers. To use these plants effectively in your own landscape requires only a little study and planning. This chapter helps you choose just the right ones for your garden.*

Confetti shower of blossoms drifts down from a classic springtime duo: flowering dogwood (Cornus florida) and azaleas (Rhododendron).

Acer palmatum
'Atropurpureum'

5

Trees & Shrubs in the Landscape

If you can imagine your familiar landscape without its trees and shrubs, you'll quickly grasp the importance of these plants in our daily lives. In the following 16 pages you'll learn the various functions trees and shrubs perform and meet good candidates for specific landscape situations.

Defining Trees & Shrubs

Trees and shrubs are woody plants that live for many years; new annual growth springs from a framework of established branches. In the case of trees, the annual growth forms a gradually enlarging structure, the trunk (or trunks) and branches gaining in girth while the foliage canopy grows larger. Many shrubs also follow this pattern, establishing a permanent woody framework in their youth and then building on it for the remainder of their lives. But a number of shrubs produce shorter-lived woody stems each year from the plant's base, a few to many new stems emerging as the older stems decline in their productive ability.

Separating the Trees from the Shrubs

Size alone doesn't reliably separate trees from shrubs. You'll find trees that reach no more than 20 feet at maturity and shrubs that will attain that height in a very few years. Better distinguishing characteristics are aspect and use. Think of a tree as having one or several trunks topped by a canopy of foliage; in mature specimens, trunks will be tall enough so that the foliage is carried above head height. A shrub, in contrast, usually carries its foliage to ground level, revealing little or none of its main branch framework. In simplest terms, you would walk *under* a tree but *around* a shrub.

To confuse the matter, some of these plants can be tree or shrub, depending on their training. Oleander *(Nerium oleander)*, smoke tree *(Cotinus coggygria)*, and hop bush *(Dodonaea viscosa)* are bulky shrubs by nature, but you also see them shaped into single-trunked tree specimens. Other large shrubs, such as strawberry tree *(Arbutus unedo)*, peegee hydrangea *(Hydrangea paniculata)*, and some rhododendrons, will become multitrunked trees as their canopies expand

Since ancient times, trees have offered shelter and shade. Among the best are the long-lived oaks (this is scarlet oak, Quercus coccinea).

Planted in soldierly formation, trees can direct sight lines and create perspectives. These Yoshino flowering cherries, Prunus yedoensis, *lead the eye down a frothy allée.*

Trees can soften hard architectural lines and link structures to the landscape. Here, a mature saucer magnolia, **Magnolia soulangiana,** *embraces a vintage home.*

at the expense of lower branches. Even the normally treelike crape myrtle (*Lagerstroemia indica*) will make a stunning shrub if you let several stems develop from ground level.

The Value of Trees & Shrubs

More than any other plants, trees establish the landscape's general character. They provide shade, give a feeling of shelter, establish perspective, and form the dominant focal point. They can also be used to frame special vistas as well as to block out unattractive ones.

Shrubs form the framework of a landscape—they're the stable plantings that influence views, direct circulation, and make a smooth transition from tree canopy to ground level. They can be used to punctuate the landscape in a less dominant manner than trees do; and, of course, they have a traditional use as a "foundation planting"—whether or not there's actually a house foundation to mask.

Among both trees and shrubs are countless individuals that will offer seasonal focal points such as showy flowers, fruits, and autumn foliage color. A smaller number offer decorative, other-than-green foliage throughout the growing season.

As you translate these generalities to your own practical situations, you'll find that trees and shrubs have a number of specific functions. Using trees, shrubs, or the two in conjunction, you can not only block unappealing views but create other sorts of barriers to make your garden more comfortable. With careful tree and shrub placement, you can block or divert prevailing winds. In the same manner, you can use a dense foliage barrier to absorb or moderate noises outside. And, of course, the most widely used barrier is the hedge—to define limits and ensure privacy within its confines.

Not the least benefit of trees is their role in energy conservation. The difference between a tree-shaded house in summer and one that is exposed to the sun's full force can be measured in dollars—and the money saved translates to reduced energy consumption. Shrubs, too, play a part in this conservation. They're capable of shading the sides of structures when the sun is at a low angle and, as windbreak plantings, shielding a structure from wind chill that would drain interior heating resources.

Selecting Trees & Shrubs

From the vast and sometimes bewildering array of available trees and shrubs, some will be good, some bad, and some indifferent choices for your particular garden. The factors discussed on the next pages will help you narrow your choices.

Don't overlook the subtle beauties that winter brings to deciduous shrubs and trees, such as this snow-frosted weeping white mulberry, **Morus alba** *'Pendula'.*

Landscape function. Choose the plant according to what you want it to do in the garden. If you want a shade tree, you can disregard a great many trees and just concentrate on those with a sizable canopy. If it's a screen you need, to block the sightline from your neighbor's second-story window, you'll seek out tall, dense shrubs (or even short trees) that will put foliage at the height you need. For a focal point plant to be enjoyed during most (or all) of the year, you'll look for trees and shrubs that not only fit the size of your site but also offer a display of flowers, fruits, unusually attractive foliage, and even a good-looking bare winter silhouette.

Climate adaptability. No matter what you prefer, your climate really makes the choices for you. So to avoid disappointment, operate within your climate's constraints. Choose plants that will accept the winter low temperatures you normally expect; this cold tolerance is given at the beginning of each tree and shrub description in the encyclopedia (pages 40–142). In mild-winter regions, be sure to choose plants that don't need winter chill. Summer is a factor, too: is yours hot, cool, dry, humid? Again, choose plants that accept your prevailing conditions or, if necessary, select planting locations where conditions will be moderated to their liking.

Shrubs are the preeminent "foundation plants"—whether the foundation is man-made or natural. Doublefile viburnum (Viburnum plicatum tomentosum), right, and V. opulus, left, link woodland to lawn.

In splendid isolation, this South African heath, **Erica canaliculata,** *displays its beauties as a showpiece specimen shrub.*

Cultural preferences. It is critical to match the needs of a tree or shrub with what your garden can offer it. Not only will you choose according to climate adaptability, you'll also select plants that will accept the sort of soil you have and the amount of water they'll receive naturally or that you are able to provide.

Deciduous versus evergreen. You'll find that trees and shrubs come in three types. Most *deciduous* kinds start their growth year in spring, with a burst of new leaves or flowers, and continue through summer fully clothed in foliage. In autumn, leaf color often changes from green to a warm autumnal yellow or red. Leaves then drop for winter's duration, revealing the structure of bare limbs. *Broad-leafed evergreens* have the same sort of foliage as deciduous plants, but their foliage clothes the plant all year round. Older leaves may fall intermittently or in one season, but there is always enough foliage to give plants complete cover. *Needle-leafed evergreens* include those with actual needles—pines, firs, and spruces, for example—as well as those like junipers and cypresses, whose leaves are merely tiny scales. They present a uniform appearance throughout the year, though some change color a bit during the coldest months.

To some extent, your climate will determine whether you choose a deciduous or an evergreen tree or shrub. The broad-leafed evergreens aren't, as a rule, able to survive in really cold-winter climates (a few exceptional ones may endure temperatures down to −20°F/−29°C). In such cold areas, you'll select from among the deciduous and needle-leafed evergreen plants. But where winters are mild to just moderately cold, your field of choice opens up. In the really mild-winter areas, you may prefer to avoid deciduous plants altogether, because their winter bareness may look out of place in a year-round lush landscape.

Growth rate and size. How quickly or slowly a tree or shrub reaches a significant size is always a vital factor whenever a landscape problem demands a quick resolution. The need for shade or privacy, for example, may push you toward selecting a fast-growing plant; but when the need is purely for beauty, you can afford to wait longer for fulfillment.

Visualizing the ultimate size—as well as calculating a plant's speed at reaching it—should be an early concern. The tree or shrub that overpowers its space is a testimony to poor choice. When excessive size becomes obvious, you have three unhappy options: pruning heavily (and thereby destroying the natural lines of the plant), removing the specimen, or

living with it. Better to avoid the problem through a bit of advance study.

Potential liabilities. Though a plant's potential liabilities are built in, they are not always a negative factor. Climate and garden location can make the difference. Plants with aggressive root systems or annoying quantities of litter may be superb choices for background locations where they won't interfere with your more delicate plants or spoil the neatness of your deck or patio. Trees with brittle wood may be accidents waiting to happen in wind- or stormswept areas, but supremely beautiful where no threat exists. A plant's susceptibility to some pests or diseases can also vary according to climate or geography. A classic example is European white birch *(Betula pendula)*—a poor choice east of the Rocky Mountains (where the bronze birch borer zeros in on it) but successful in western states (where the pest is absent).

Beauty. Although appearance is always uppermost in a gardener's mind—and preliminary plant lists may usually consist of aesthetic choices—beauty is the final point to consider while evaluating trees and shrubs for your garden. Once you've compiled a list of truly *suitable* plants, you can savor the pleasure of selecting for color, texture, and all the other nuances that will paint your garden canvas as you envision it.

What better plants than shrubs to clearly define boundaries? This tightly controlled hedge is made of the classic hedge plant, boxwood **(Buxus sempervirens)**. *Foreground color is* **Hamamelis intermedia 'Jelena'**.

Shrubs in mass plantings can screen or direct views, even echo distant land forms. Welcoming springtime are **Ceanothus 'Dark Star' (blue) and white C. thyrsiflorus 'Snow Flurry'**.

$\mathcal{A}$ Guide to Choosing Trees

Big Trees

The stereotypical tree is associated with two words: "shade" and "big." Choose from this list if you want to make a definite size statement.

NAME OF PLANT	PAGE	HARDY TO
Abies	42	varies
Acer macrophyllum	44	0°F/−18°C
Acer platanoides	44	−30°F/−34°C
Acer pseudoplatanus	44	−10°F/−23°C
Acer rubrum	44	−30°F/−34°C
Acer saccharinum	45	−30°F/−34°C
Acer saccharum	45	−30°F/−34°C
Aesculus hippocastanum	45	−20°F/−29°C
Alnus (most)	46	varies
Betula nigra	47	−20°F/−29°C
Betula papyrifera	47	−40°F/−40°C
Catalpa speciosa	49	−20°F/−29°C
Cedrus	49	varies
Celtis	50	varies
Chamaecyparis	52	varies
Cinnamomum camphora	64	20°F/−7°C
Eucalyptus (many)	59	varies
Fagus	59	varies
Fraxinus americana	62	−30°F/−34°C
Fraxinus excelsior	62	−30°F/−34°C
Fraxinus pennsylvanica	62	−40°F/−40°C
Ginkgo biloba	63	−20°F/−29°C
Gleditsia triacanthos inermis 'Majestic'	63	−20°F/−29°C
Larix kaempferi	68	−20°F/−29°C
Liquidambar styraciflua	68	−10°F/−23°C
Liriodendron tulipifera	68	−20°F/−29°C
Magnolia acuminata	69	−20°F/−29°C
Magnolia grandiflora	70	0°F/−18°C
Metasequoia glyptostroboides	73	−15°F/−26°C
Picea	75	varies
Pinus (many)	77	varies
Pistacia chinensis	77	−10°F/−23°C
Platanus	64	varies
Populus (some)	64	varies
Pseudotsuga menziesii	83	−10°F/−23°C
Quercus (many)	84	varies
Salix (many)	65	varies
Sequoia sempervirens	88	0°F/−18°C
Sequoiadendron giganteum	88	−10°F/−23°C
Sophora japonica	88	−20°F/−29°C
Tilia cordata	90	−30°F/−34°C
Tilia tomentosa	91	−10°F/−23°C
Tsuga	91	varies
Zelkova serrata	91	−10°F/−23°C

*For a dramatic landscape statement, nothing is grander than a truly large specimen tree. This arboreal patriarch, a cedar of Lebanon (**Cedrus libani**), has become a gigantic living sculpture with age.*

Carolina silver bell, **Halesia carolina,** *suspends graceful flowers from a tree small enough for close-up appreciation of their beauty.*

NAME OF PLANT	PAGE	HARDY TO
Halesia	66	−20°F/−29°C
Koelreuteria paniculata	66	−20°F/−29°C
Laburnum watereri 'Vossii'	67	−20°F/−29°C
Lagerstroemia indica	67	0°F/−18°C
Magnolia grandiflora (some)	70	0°F/−18°C
Magnolia kobus	69	−10°F/−23°C
Magnolia salicifolia	70	−10°F/−23°C
Magnolia soulangiana	70	−10°F/−23°C
Malus	71	varies
Melaleuca	73	20°F/−7°C
Palms (some)	76	varies
Pinus contorta	78	0°F/−18°C
Pittosporum (most)	79	20°F/−7°C
Prosopis	80	0°F/−18°C
Prunus	81	varies
Pyrus kawakamii	84	10°F/−12°C
Rhus	86	varies
Schinus terebinthifolius	93	25°F/−4°C
Sorbus hupehensis	89	−20°F/−29°C
Sorbus hybrida	89	−20°F/−29°C
Stewartia	89	−10°F/−23°C
Styrax	90	varies
Tabebuia chrysotricha	93	25°F/−4°C

Trees for Small Gardens & Patios

Small spaces don't need big trees. The following choices offer beauty, often delicacy of structure, and guaranteed modest stature.

NAME OF PLANT	PAGE	HARDY TO
Acer buergeranum	44	−10°F/−23°C
Acer griseum	44	−10°F/−23°C
Acer japonicum	44	−10°F/−23°C
Acer palmatum	44	−10°F/−23°C
Amelanchier	46	varies
Bauhinia	92	25°F/−4°C
Callistemon	48	20°F/−7°C
Cercidiphyllum japonicum	50	−30°F/−34°C
Cercidium	51	10°F/−12°C
Cercis	51	varies
Chionanthus	52	varies
Cladrastis lutea	53	−30°F/−34°C
Cornus	53	varies
Crataegus	56	varies
Davidia involucrata	58	−10°F/−23°C
Diospyros kaki	58	0°F/−18°C
Elaeagnus angustifolia	58	−40°F/−40°C
Erythrina (several)	92	25°F/−4°C
Eucalyptus niphophila	60	0°F/−18°C

Japanese flowering cherries, such as this **Prunus serrulata** *'Kwanzan', are among the best "conversation piece" specimen trees where space is limited.*

Flowers and fruits are conspicuous decorative features. **Cornus** *'Eddie's White Wonder' (left) and* **Crataegus** *'Autumn Glory' (right) provide convincing proof.*

Decorative Trees

Trees are far more than homogeneous big, leafy things. This chart sorts them out according to four decorative features: colorful flowers, showy fruits, telling autumn color, and good-looking bark that will add interest to a winter landscape.

NAME	PAGE	HARDY TO	FLOWERS	FRUITS	AUTUMN FOLIAGE	BARK
Acacia	43	varies	■			
Acer	43	varies			■	■
Aesculus	45	−20°F/−29°C	■			
Albizia julibrissin	45	0°F/−18°C	■			
Alnus	46	varies		■		■
Amelanchier	46	varies	■	■	■	
Bauhinia	92	25°F/−4°C	■	■		
Betula	47	varies			■	■
Callistemon	48	20°F/−7°C	■			
Carpinus	48	varies				
Catalpa	49	−20°F/−29°C	■	■	■	
Celtis	50	varies		■	■	■
Cercidiphyllum japonicum	50	−30°F/−34°C	■		■	
Cercidium	51	10°F/−12°C	■			■
Chionanthus	52	varies	■	■	■	
Cladrastis lutea	53	−30°F/−34°C	■		■	

NAME	PAGE	HARDY TO	FLOWERS	FRUITS	AUTUMN FOLIAGE	BARK
Cornus	53	varies	■	■	■	
Crataegus	56	varies	■	■	■	
Davidia involucrata	58	−10°F/−23°C	■	■		
Diospyros	58	varies		■	■	■
Elaeagnus angustifolia	58	−40°F/−40°C			■	■
Erythrina	92	varies	■	■		■
Eucalyptus	59	varies	■	■		■
Fagus	59	varies			■	
Fraxinus	61	varies	■		■	
Ginkgo biloba	63	−20°F/−29°C			■	
Gleditsia triacanthos inermis	63	−20°F/−29°C			■	
Halesia	66	−20°F/−29°C	■	■	■	
Jacaranda mimosifolia	93	20°F/−7°C	■	■		
Koelreuteria	66	varies	■	■	■	

NAME	PAGE	HARDY TO	FLOWERS	FRUITS	AUTUMN FOLIAGE	BARK
Laburnum watereri 'Vossii'	67	−20°F/−29°C	■	■		
Lagerstroemia indica	67	0°F/−18°C	■		■	■
Larix	67	varies		■	■	
Ligustrum lucidum	64	10°F/−12°C	■	■		
Liquidambar styraciflua	68	−10°F/−23°C		■	■	
Liriodendron tulipifera	68	−20°F/−29°C	■		■	
Magnolia	69	varies	■	■		
Malus	71	varies	■	■	■	
Melaleuca	73	20°F/−7°C	■			■
Morus alba	74	−20°F/−29°C			■	
Nyssa sylvatica	74	−20°F/−29°C		■	■	
Olea europaea	74	15°F/−9°C		■		■
Pinus	77	varies		■		■
Pistacia chinensis	77	−10°F/−23°C		■	■	
Pittosporum	79	20°F/−7°C	■	■		
Platanus	64	varies		■		■

NAME	PAGE	HARDY TO	FLOWERS	FRUITS	AUTUMN FOLIAGE	BARK
Populus	64	varies			■	■
Prosopis	80	0°F/−18°C	■	■		
Prunus	81	varies	■		■	
Pyrus	83	varies	■		■	
Quercus	84	varies		■	■	
Rhus	86	varies		■	■	
Robinia	87	varies	■			■
Salix	65	varies			■	
Sassafras albidum	87	−20°F/−29°C			■	
Schinus	65, 93	varies		■		
Sophora japonica	88	−20°F/−29°C	■			■
Sorbus	89	varies	■	■	■	
Stewartia	89	−10°F/−23°C	■		■	■
Styrax	90	varies	■			
Tabebuia chrysotricha	93	25°F/−4°C	■			
Tilia	90	varies	■		■	
Ulmus	65	varies				■
Zelkova serrata	91	−10°F/−23°C			■	

*Decorative accents may grace all plant parts. Paperbark maple, **Acer griseum** (below), flaunts its aptly named bark; American sweet gum, **Liquidambar styraciflua** (right), exemplifies the autumn foliage brigade.*

*Windbreak trees must be dense and tough, but not all are purely utilitarian. Rugged pink melaleuca, **Melaleuca nesophila,** offers a bonus of pleasant blossoms.*

Trees for Windbreak & Screen

When you need to deflect prevailing winds or mask a less-than-wonderful view, look to these trees for the solution.

NAME OF PLANT	PAGE	HARDY TO
Acer campestre	44	−20°F/−29°C
Callistemon	48	20°F/−7°C
Carpinus betulus	48	−10°F/−23°C
Cedrus deodara	49	5°F/−15°C
Chamaecyparis	52	varies
Crataegus monogyna	57	−20°F/−29°C
Cupressocyparis leylandii	57	−10°F/−23°C
Cupressus	57	varies
Elaeagnus angustifolia	58	−40°F/−40°C
Eucalyptus gunnii	60	5°F/−15°C
Ficus benjamina	92	30°F/−1°C
Melaleuca	73	20°F/−7°C
Pittosporum eugenioides	79	20°F/−7°C
Pittosporum tenuifolium	79	20°F/−7°C
Pittosporum undulatum	79	20°F/−7°C
Podocarpus	79	varies
Pseudotsuga menziesii	83	−10°F/−23°C
Rhus lancea	86	15°F/−9°C
Sequoia sempervirens	88	0°F/−18°C
Tsuga	91	varies

Fast-growing Trees

If you want to measure progress in feet rather than inches per year, these trees will give satisfaction.

NAME OF PLANT	PAGE	HARDY TO
Abies grandis	42	−10°F/−23°C
Acacia	43	varies
Acer rubrum	44	−30°F/−34°C
Acer saccharinum	45	−30°F/−34°C
Albizia julibrissin	45	0°F/−18°C
Alnus rhombifolia	46	−10°F/−23°C
Betula	47	varies
Callistemon	48	20°F/−7°C
Cedrus deodara	49	5°F/−15°C
Cercidium	51	10°F/−12°C
Cupressocyparis leylandii	57	−10°F/−23°C
Cupressus	57	varies
Erythrina	92	25°F/−4°C
Eucalyptus	59	varies
Ficus	92	varies
Fraxinus	61	varies
Gleditsia triacanthos inermis	63	−20°F/−29°C
Larix kaempferi	68	−20°F/−29°C
Ligustrum lucidum	64	10°F/−12°C
Melaleuca	73	20°F/−7°C
Metasequoia glyptostroboides	73	−15°F/−26°C
Morus alba	74	−20°F/−29°C
Palms (some)	76	varies
Picea abies	75	−40°F/−40°C
Pinus (some)	77	varies
Pittosporum (most)	79	20°F/−7°C
Platanus	64	varies
Populus	64	varies
Prunus (many)	81	varies
Pseudotsuga menziesii	83	−10°F/−23°C
Quercus (several)	84	varies
Rhus	86	varies
Robinia	87	varies
Salix	65	varies
Sassafras albidum	87	−20°F/−29°C
Schinus molle	65	15°F/−9°C
Sequoia sempervirens	88	0°F/−18°C
Sequoiadendron giganteum	88	−10°F/−23°C
Tabebuia chrysotricha	93	25°F/−4°C
Ulmus	65	varies

*When you need height in a hurry, turn to fast-growing trees for satisfaction. Scarlet oak, **Quercus coccinea,** towers over this fast-growing, red berried **Pyracantha** shrub.*

A Guide to Choosing Shrubs

Variegated foliage, as on this **Elaeagnus pungens 'Maculata'**, *introduces a decorative element to a functional hedge planting.*

Good Shrubs for Hedges & Screens

These dense shrubs will give you solid, leafy barriers in a variety of heights and widths; some can be sheared into formal walls.

NAME OF PLANT	PAGE	HARDY TO
Abelia grandiflora	96	0°F/–18°C
Berberis	97	varies
Buxus	98	varies
Callistemon	99	20°F/–7°C
Camellia sasanqua	101	5°F/–15°C
Chaenomeles	101	–30°F/–34°C
Choisya ternata	102	15°F/–9°C
Cotoneaster (some)	104	varies
Dodonaea viscosa	107	15°F/–9°C
Elaeagnus	108	varies
Escallonia	110	15°F/–9°C
Euonymus (many)	110	varies
Grevillea	113	15°F/–9°C
Heteromeles arbutifolia	141	5°F/–15°C
Ilex	116	varies
Juniperus (many)	105	varies
Leptospermum	118	20°F/–7°C
Ligustrum	119	varies

NAME OF PLANT	PAGE	HARDY TO
Lonicera	120	varies
Myrtus communis	122	15°F/–9°C
Nandina domestica	122	0°F/–18°C
Nerium oleander	123	15°F/–9°C
Osmanthus	123	varies
Photinia	125	varies
Pittosporum tobira	128	–5°F/–21°C
Prunus (evergreen)	129	varies
Pyracantha	131	varies
Rhamnus alaternus	131	0°F/–18°C
Rhamnus frangula 'Columnaris'	132	–40°F/–40°C
Rhaphiolepis	132	10°F/–12°C
Rosa (some)	133	varies
Rosmarinus officinalis	134	0°F/–18°C
Viburnum opulus 'Nanum'	138	–40°F/–40°C
Viburnum tinus	138	0°F/–18°C
Weigela	139	–20°F/–29°C
Xylosma congestum	139	10°F/–12°C

A mass planting of azaleas (Rhododendron) electrifies the spring landscape (left). Lacking a floral show, Chinese holly (Ilex cornuta, right) devotes its energies to showy fruits.

Colorful Shrubs

In the wonderfully varied realm of shrubs, you'll find beauty packaged in many ways. This chart lets you make preliminary choices to obtain conspicuous flowers, fruits, autumn foliage color, or other-than-green leaves.

NAME	PAGE	HARDY TO	FLOWERS	FRUITS	AUTUMN FOLIAGE	COLORED LEAVES
Abelia grandiflora	96	0°F/−18°C	■			
Arbutus unedo	96	5°F/−15°C	■	■		
Arctostaphylos	140	varies	■	■		
Aucuba japonica	97	0°F/−18°C		■		■
Berberis	97	varies	■	■	■	■
Brunfelsia	126	15°F/−9°C	■			
Buddleia	98	−20°F/−29°C	■			
Buxus	98	varies				■
Calliandra	126	28°F/−2°C	■			
Callistemon	99	20°F/−7°C	■			
Calluna vulgaris	99	−30°F/−34°C	■		■	■
Camellia	100	varies	■			
Caryopteris clandonensis	101	−20°F/−29°C	■			
Ceanothus	140	0°F/−18°C	■			
Cercis occidentalis	141	−10°F/−23°C	■	■	■	
Chaenomeles	101	−30°F/−34°C	■		■	
Choisya ternata	102	15°F/−9°C	■			
Cistus	102	15°F/−9°C	■			
Cornus	103	varies	■	■	■	■
Corylopsis	103	−10°F/−23°C	■			
Corylus	104	−20°F/−29°C				■

NAME	PAGE	HARDY TO	FLOWERS	FRUITS	AUTUMN FOLIAGE	COLORED LEAVES
Cotinus coggygria	104	−20°F/−29°C	■		■	■
Cotoneaster	104	varies	■	■	■	
Cytisus	106	varies	■			
Daphne	106	varies	■			■
Deutzia	107	−20°F/−29°C	■			
Dodonaea viscosa	107	15°F/−9°C				■
Elaeagnus	108	varies		■		■
Enkianthus	108	varies	■		■	
Erica	109	varies	■			
Escallonia	110	15°F/−9°C	■			
Euonymus	110	varies		■	■	■
Exochorda	111	−20°F/−29°C	■			
Fatsia japonica	112	5°F/−15°C	■	■		■
Forsythia intermedia	112	−20°F/−29°C	■			
Fremont-odendron	141	20°F/−7°C	■			
Gardenia	112	20°F/−7°C	■			
Grevillea	113	15°F/−9°C	■			
Hamamelis	113	varies	■		■	
Hebe	114	20°F/−7°C	■			■
Heteromeles arbutifolia	141	5°F/−15°C	■	■		

NAME	PAGE	HARDY TO	FLOWERS	FRUITS	AUTUMN FOLIAGE	COLORED LEAVES
Hibiscus	114	varies	■			
Hydrangea	115	varies	■		■	■
Hypericum	116	varies	■			
Ilex	116	varies		■		■
Juniperus	105	varies				■
Justicia	126	25°F/–4°C	■			
Kalmia latifolia	118	–20°F/–29°C	■			
Kolkwitzia amabilis	118	–30°F/–34°C	■			
Lantana	126	28°F/–2°C	■			
Leptospermum	118	20°F/–7°C	■			
Leucothoe fontanesiana	119	–20°F/–29°C	■		■	■
Ligustrum	119	varies	■	■		■
Lonicera	120	varies	■	■	■	
Lycianthes rantonnei	127	20°F/–7°C	■			
Magnolia	121	varies	■			
Mahonia	121	varies	■	■		
Myrtus communis	122	15°F/–9°C	■	■		■
Nandina domestica	122	0°F/–18°C	■	■	■	
Nerium oleander	123	15°F/–9°C	■			
Osmanthus	123	varies	■			■
Paeonia	124	–30°F/–34°C	■			
Philadelphus	124	varies	■		■	■

NAME	PAGE	HARDY TO	FLOWERS	FRUITS	AUTUMN FOLIAGE	COLORED LEAVES
Photinia	125	varies	■	■	■	
Pieris	128	varies	■			■
Pittosporum tobira	128	–5°F/–21°C	■	■		■
Platycladus orientalis	105	–10°F/–23°C				■
Plumbago auriculata	127	20°F/–7°C	■			
Plumeria rubra	127	30°F/–1°C	■			
Potentilla fruticosa	129	–40°F/–40°C	■			
Prunus	129	varies	■		■	■
Punica granatum	130	10°F/–12°C	■	■	■	
Pyracantha	131	varies	■	■		
Rhamnus	131	varies		■		■
Rhaphiolepis indica	132	10°F/–12°C	■	■		
Rhododendron	132	varies	■		■	
Rosa	133	varies	■	■		
Rosmarinus officinalis	134	0°F/–18°C	■			
Spiraea	135	varies	■		■	■
Syringa	136	varies	■		■	
Thuja	105	varies				■
Tibouchina urvilleana	127	25°F/–4°C	■			
Viburnum	137	varies	■	■	■	■
Weigela	139	–20°F/–29°C	■			■

Even leaves add color variety to the landscape. European cranberry bush, Viburnum opulus (below), offers autumn change; Weigela florida 'Variegata' (right) boasts variegated leaves throughout the growing season.

Growing wild in Southern California, **Ceanothus** *demonstrates that drought tolerance is a natural phenomenon. Such unthirsty shrubs are indispensable in dry-country landscapes.*

Shrubs That Tolerate Some Drought

If water is a scarce commodity—or if you simply refuse to be a slave to the hose—these less thirsty shrubs will accommodate.

NAME OF PLANT	PAGE	HARDY TO
Arbutus unedo	96	5°F/−15°C
Aucuba japonica	97	0°F/−18°C
Callistemon	99	20°F/−7°C
Ceanothus	140	0°F/−18°C
Cercis occidentalis	141	−10°F/−23°C
Chaenomeles	101	−30°F/−34°C
Cistus	102	15°F/−9°C
Cotinus coggygria	104	−20°F/−29°C
Cotoneaster	104	varies
Cytisus	106	varies
Dodonaea viscosa	107	15°F/−9°C
Elaeagnus	108	varies
Hypericum	116	varies
Mahonia (some)	121	varies
Myrtus communis	122	15°F/−9°C
Nandina domestica	122	0°F/−18°C
Nerium oleander	123	15°F/−9°C
Prunus besseyi	129	−50°F/−46°C
Prunus caroliniana	130	10°F/−12°C
Punica granatum	130	10°F/−12°C
Rhamnus	131	varies
Rosmarinus officinalis	134	0°F/−18°C

Fast-growing Shrubs

When you need it yesterday, you can confidently select from this list of proven performers.

NAME OF PLANT	PAGE	HARDY TO
Buddleia	98	−20°F/−29°C
Calliandra	126	28°F/−2°C
Callistemon	99	20°F/−7°C
Caryopteris clandonensis	101	−20°F/−29°C
Choisya ternata	102	15°F/−9°C
Cistus	102	15°F/−9°C
Cornus stolonifera	103	−50°F/−46°C
Cotoneaster	104	varies
Cytisus	106	varies
Dodonaea viscosa	107	15°F/−9°C
Elaeagnus	108	varies
Escallonia	110	15°F/−9°C
Forsythia intermedia	112	−20°F/−29°C
Hebe	114	20°F/−7°C
Hibiscus	114,126	varies
Hydrangea	115	varies
Kolkwitzia amabilis	118	−30°F/−34°C
Lantana	126	28°F/−2°C
Ligustrum	119	varies
Lonicera	120	varies
Lycianthes rantonnei	127	20°F/−7°C
Nerium oleander	123	15°F/−9°C
Philadelphus	124	varies
Plumbago auriculata	127	20°F/−7°C
Prunus (some)	129	varies
Rosa	133	varies
Tibouchina urvilleana	127	25°F/−4°C
Weigela	139	−20°F/−29°C

Molten gold **Forsythia** *is just one of a number of fast-growing shrubs that will reach full size in a satisfyingly short time.*

The challenge of shade is no obstacle to shrubs like this bigleaf hydrangea, Hydrangea macrophylla, *that revel in subdued light and cool temperatures.*

Shrubs for Shade

Shaded locations need not be a problem. The following shrubs all perform well in a bit of shade, and a few must have it to thrive.

NAME OF PLANT	PAGE	HARDY TO
Abelia grandiflora	96	0°F/–18°C
Aucuba japonica	97	0°F/–18°C
Berberis	97	varies
Buxus	98	varies
Camellia	100	varies
Choisya ternata	102	15°F/–9°C
Corylopsis	103	–10°F/–23°C
Corylus	104	–20°F/–29°C
Daphne	106	varies
Deutzia	107	–20°F/–29°C
Enkianthus	108	varies
Escallonia	110	15°F/–9°C
Fatsia japonica	112	5°F/–15°C
Hamamelis	113	varies
Hydrangea	115	varies
Hypericum	116	varies
Kalmia latifolia	118	–20°F/–29°C
Kolkwitzia amabilis	118	–30°F/–34°C

NAME OF PLANT	PAGE	HARDY TO
Leucothoe fontanesiana	119	–20°F/–29°C
Ligustrum	119	varies
Lonicera	120	varies
Mahonia	121	varies
Myrtus communis	122	15°F/–9°C
Nandina domestica	122	0°F/–18°C
Osmanthus	123	varies
Philadelphus	124	varies
Pieris	128	varies
Pinus mugo mugo	105	–40°F/–40°C
Platycladus orientalis	105	–10°F/–23°C
Rhamnus californica	132	0°F/–18°C
Rhaphiolepis indica	132	10°F/–12°C
Rhododendron	132	varies
Rosa (some)	133	varies
Taxus	105	varies
Thuja	105	varies
Viburnum	137	varies

Shrubs That Attract Birds

For the pleasure of "something extra" in your land-scape, plant these proven bird-attracting shrubs. Starred entries attract hummingbirds specifically; those with two stars attract hummingbirds and other birds as well.

NAME OF PLANT	PAGE	HARDY TO	NAME OF PLANT	PAGE	HARDY TO
*Abelia grandiflora	96	0°F/–18°C	Heteromeles arbutifolia	141	5°F/–15°C
Arbutus unedo	96	5°F/–15°C	*Hibiscus	114	varies
Arctostaphylos	140	varies	Ilex	116	varies
Berberis	97	varies	*Justicia brandegeana	126	25°F/–4°C
*Brunfelsia pauciflora	126	15°F/–9°C	*Kolkwitzia amabilis	118	–30°F/–34°C
*Buddleia	98	–20°F/–29°C	Lantana	126	28°F/–2°C
*Calliandra	126	28°F/–2°C	Ligustrum	119	varies
*Callistemon	99	20°F/–7°C	**Lonicera	120	varies
*Ceanothus	140	0°F/–18°C	Mahonia	121	varies
*Chaenomeles	101	–30°F/–34°C	Photinia	125	varies
Cornus	103	varies	Prunus	129	varies
Cotoneaster	104	varies	Pyracantha	131	varies
Elaeagnus	108	varies	Rhamnus	131	varies
*Erica	109	varies	Rosa (some)	133	varies
*Escallonia	110	15°F/–9°C	**Rosmarinus officinalis	134	0°F/–18°C
Euonymus	110	varies	Viburnum	137	varies
*Grevillea	113	15°F/–9°C	*Weigela	139	–20°F/–29°C

*As a red flag attracts bulls, bright **Pyracantha** berries lure hungry birds during autumn and winter.*

The Container Garden

A select group of trees and shrubs adapts well to life in containers. This amiable quality allows you to showcase them in patio and terrace settings, where their beauty can be appreciated at close range. The container option also lets you grow plants that might be ruled out by inhospitable local soil. If your soil is clay, for instance, you can grow in containers those plants that need well-drained soil; if it's alkaline, you can pot acid-loving azaleas, rhododendrons, pieris, and the like. And if you have a greenhouse or sheltered porch to give protection from winter freezes, you can enjoy plants normally too tender for your climate.

Soil for Containers

Container soil must drain rapidly to avoid waterlogging yet still retain moisture. This prescribes a loose, porous, well-aerated soil high in organic matter. Even the best garden soil, used alone, will be too dense and potentially soggy in a container. Special potting mixes—homemade or packaged—give the best rooting medium.

Nurseries and garden centers offer a variety of packaged potting mixes: their components vary, but none contains actual soil. Look for ingredients such as bark, sphagnum peat, vermiculite, forest products, and sand. Alternatively, mix your own potting soil by combining organic material (bark, peat moss, leaf mold, compost) and mineral matter (sand, perlite, vermiculite, soil). A basic formula, good for a broad range of plants, is one part good garden soil (not clay), one part sand (builder's or river, not ocean beach), and one part peat moss or nitrogen-stabilized bark. For an acid mix to suit azaleas and other acid lovers, add one more part peat moss or bark.

Superabsorbent polymers are a gel-like substance that absorbs hundreds of times its weight in water. Added to potting soil, the polymers retain water and dissolved nutrients without making the mix soggy; roots absorb moisture directly from them. Thus, you can lengthen the interval between waterings. Polyacrilimide gel is the longest lasting of those on the market. Mix the dry polymer material with water to expand the particles, then incorporate it into your potting mix in the manufacturer's recommended proportion—generally 1 pint polymer gel to 6 pints potting mix.

Watering

Because container soil is porous and because the root masses of container plants are dense, you must closely monitor watering, especially during warmer months. Use your fingers as a guide: water whenever the soil feels dry beneath the surface. Water thoroughly every time, covering the entire surface until water flows out the drainage holes.

Fertilizing

The frequent and thorough watering necessary for container gardening will inevitably leach the nutrients from potting soil. For best growth, therefore, you'll need to apply fertilizer during the growing season. Liquid or dry, granular fertilizers are your options; follow the label's directions. Best results come from a sustained nutrient supply at moderate to low strength. Liquid fertilizers give plants a quick tonic but are quickly used up or leached out; to compensate, apply diluted strengths more frequently. The slow-release dry fertilizers release nutrients over time; one application may suffice for a month or more.

Repotting

If you start your shrub or tree in a small- to moderate-size container, you'll need to move it to a larger size when its roots completely fill the soil mass. Replant in a container only slightly larger than the original—one that allows just 1 or 2 inches of fresh

Mahonia lomariifolia

soil on all sides. If you have a root-bound older specimen plant in a large container and want to maintain it in that container, you can root-prune the plant during its dormant period and replant it. Carefully removing the plant, shave 1 or 2 inches of root from all sides of the root mass with a sharp knife. Replant in the original container, using fresh potting soil beneath and around the root mass.

Trees for Containers

Acer japonicum	Ilex
Acer palmatum	Lagerstroemia indica
Citrus	
Ficus	Podocarpus

Shrubs for Containers

Arbutus unedo	Lantana
Aucuba japonica	Ilex
Camellia	Mahonia
Fatsia japonica	Nandina domestica
Gardenia jasminoides	
Hebe	Nerium oleander
Hibiscus rosa-sinensis	Potentilla
Hydrangea macrophylla	Punica granatum
	Rhododendron
	Rosa

Getting Started

*W*hen you plant trees and shrubs, you're planting—and planning—for the future. You envision them as they'll look when full-grown, but their progress to that point will take time. Along the way, you'll want to do all you can to help them reach maturity in good health and top form.

In this chapter, you'll learn the essentials of tree and shrub care, from soil preparation to pruning to pest control. With good care, your chosen plants will look beautiful and perform well at every stage of their development.

*Potentilla
fruticosa*

When grown in containers, trees and shrubs can be chosen at any time of year. Autumn is prime planting time in milder regions.

23

Groundwork

All good gardens start, literally, at ground level. You need to know the character of your garden soil before you attempt to ready it for planting.

The Basics of Soil

Although soil may appear to be an inert brown mass, it's really a lively, complex environment containing not just mineral particles (the bulk of all soils) but also organic matter, air, water, and a variety of organisms from earthworms to microscopic bacteria. The nature of the particles and the ratio of the components determine a soil's character and quality—and how hospitable it is to the plant roots that depend on it for sustenance.

Thus, a knowledge of your soil's character directs you to preparation, planting, and maintenance techniques that will encourage the best growth from the plants you ultimately select.

For good growth, plant roots need water, air, and nutrients. Water percolates from surface soil down through the pore spaces between soil particles, carrying with it dissolved nutrients in solution. At first water completely fills those spaces. But in time most of the water is diminished by gravity (carrying it downward), by wind and the sun's heat (evaporating it), and by plant roots (absorbing it to compensate for transpiration). During this process air gradually returns to the pore spaces, eventually leaving just a film of water on particles until the next watering occurs. Most plants need a balance of moisture and air: soil that is neither too dry for prolonged periods nor so continuously moist as to be waterlogged.

Generations of gardeners have spoken of soil as "heavy" or "light" (and gradations between the two). These are perfectly good layperson words for two opposing soil types properly known as clay (heavy) and sand (light). Differences in the size and shape of mineral particles account for the physical characteristics of these two soil extremes. Those characteristics, in turn, affect the growth of plants and influence soil management practices.

Clay particles are tiny and flattened, fitting closely together (rather like a pile of playing cards). Soils composed primarily of clay particles have so little pore space between particles that water soaks in slowly and percolates through slowly as well. Clay soils therefore retain water longest and retain dissolved nutrients well; but, because drainage is slow, they can be deficient in soil air if overwatered. They are also slow to warm up in spring. A clay soil feels slick to the touch; squeeze a ball of it in your hand, and it will ooze through your fingers in ribbons.

Sandy soils, the opposite of clay, have particles that are not only much larger but also irregularly rounded; they therefore fit together much more loosely (like marbles in a jar), leaving relatively large pore spaces between particles. Water percolates easily through sandy soils: they are well drained and well aerated, but they need frequent water and nutrient applications to maintain adequate moisture and fertility. A sandy soil is the first to warm up in spring. It feels gritty: compress a ball of it in your hand and watch it fall apart at the slightest prod.

The best soils contain a mixture of particle sizes and shapes, balancing clay's density with sand's permeability. The gardener's ideal, loam, contains a mixture of particle sizes plus organic matter so that 30 to 50 percent of a given volume consists of pore space. Roughly 20 percent of that pore space will contain soil air, the remainder water.

Fortunately, most garden soils fall somewhere between the absolute extremes of clay and sand and need little if any special treatment to grow most trees and shrubs well. If a tree or shrub has special soil needs, it will be noted in its encyclopedia description.

Soil Improvement

Unless you have a definite problem soil—compacted, shallow, or extremely acid or alkaline (see "Acid & Alkaline Soils" on the facing page)—you'll be able to grow a wide range of trees and shrubs adapted to your climate without significantly altering your soil. In fact, most trees and shrubs will outgrow any "improved" soil within a few years anyway. If you select those that are likely to grow well in the kind of soil you have, your only task may be to amend the soil right around the new plant's root system to encourage new roots to grow and establish the plant quickly.

Organic matter is the all-purpose soil amendment that will significantly moderate both the density of clay and the porosity of sand. When dug into the soil, organic soil amendments—compost, peat

Acid & Alkaline Soils

Your soil is one of three types: acid, alkaline, or neutral. This characteristic is measured in pH—short for potential hydrogen—with a pH of 7 representing neutral. Readings of less than 7 indicate acid soil; of more than 7, alkaline. The soil's reaction—that is, its degree of acidity or alkalinity—primarily affects the availability of certain nutrients. If readings are extreme in either direction, key nutrients are "tied up" in the soil and not available to roots. Fertilizers won't help, because their nutrients, too, will be tied up by the overacidic or overalkaline soil (see "Chlorosis," page 39).

A few favorite plants definitely prefer soil that is either acid or alkaline—acid-loving heaths, heathers, and rhododendrons are classic examples—but most trees and shrubs will pros-

A soil test kit is easy to use and gives you an immediate pH reading.

per in soils registering a pH of from 6.0 to 7.2. As a workable guide, you can assume that high-rainfall, humid-summer regions have acid soil, whereas low-rainfall, dry-summer regions have alkaline soil.

A soil test will disclose your soil's pH; the more sophisticated tests will also measure nutrient content and the amount of organic matter. The soil test kits sold at nurseries and garden centers will give you a ballpark reading—enough to indicate a potential problem. Professional tests will give you more precise results; look under "Soil Laboratories" in the Yellow Pages for agencies that run tests for a fee. In some states, tests can be made by county or state agricultural extension services, which can also suggest remedies for extreme pH imbalances.

---

moss, nitrogen-fortified wood by-products, and a host of others—lodge in the pore spaces between soil particles and groups of particles. In clay, this opens up the soil to improve drainage and aeration; in sand, organic matter acts as a sponge to slow the passage of water and dissolved nutrients. See "How to Plant" on page 26 for suggested soil preparation keyed to soil types.

Three soil conditions will require special treatment or consideration.

Compacted soil. In new housing developments, soil may have beencompressed by heavy equipment used during construction. This soil is poorly drained, difficult to dig, and nearly impossible for roots to penetrate. Special soil-loosening equipment may remedy the situation; contact a landscape contractor. The alternative is to construct raised beds and fill them with good soil.

Shallow soil. Shallow soil has many causes, but in all cases it is a shallow layer of good soil overlaying impermeable soil. It may be found on new homesites, where the developer has spread new soil over exist-

ing soil compacted during construction. Or it may occur naturally over a layer of dense hardpan; in the Southwest, gardeners must cope with an alkaline hardpan known as *caliche*.

If a hardpan layer is fairly thin, you may be able to dig full-width planting holes through it to more porous soil beneath. You may even be able to have your entire garden plowed or deep-ripped to break up the thin hardpan. With a thicker layer, you may be able to use a soil auger to drill a "chimney" from the bottom of each planting hole through the hardpan to porous soil beneath. If none of these schemes is practical, you'll have to resort to planting in raised beds.

Acid or alkaline soil. If your soil is distinctly acidic or alkaline (see above), you may be able to moderate its extremes with a particular soil treatment. But the effect won't be permanent, and in time you'll need to repeat the treatment—which is impractical among permanent tree and shrub plantings. Far simpler is to choose plants that will thrive in the normal acidity or alkalinity of your soil. Grow nonadapted plants in containers or raised beds where you can more easily control soil conditions.

Planting

Successful planting begins with choosing a healthy specimen and then carefully planting it at a time of year favorable to good root growth.

Selecting a Healthy Plant

Nursery plants are available bare-root, balled-and-burlapped, and container-grown.

Bare-root trees and shrubs have all the soil removed from their roots before being offered for sale; these are deciduous plants, available for planting only during their autumn-through-winter dormant period. First, look for healthy stems, preferably forming a well-balanced plant (though shrubs that frequently send up new stems from the base will probably correct any initial imbalance within a few years). Then check the root system: it should be well balanced and in good proportion to the top growth. Avoid buying plants whose roots have been broken or severely shortened during digging.

Balled-and-burlapped (commonly called "B-and-B") plants are dug from growing fields with sizable clumps of soil surrounding their root systems; the soil is wrapped in burlap or some other loose-woven material to secure it around the roots. Be sure the root ball is firm and moist, not dry. If the plant is evergreen—either broad-leafed or needle-leafed—look for a shapely plant with lustrous (not dull) foliage. If the plant is deciduous, apply the same guidelines mentioned for bare-root plants.

Container-grown trees and shrubs are sold growing in metal, plastic, or fiber pots, from a 1-gallon volume to 15-gallon (or larger) specimen sizes. Look for plants that appear vigorous and shapely; check for healthy foliage on evergreens and, during the growing season, on deciduous plants. Roots should not be seriously tangled or constricted, bespeaking an overlong life in the container. You can expect overcrowded roots: if a plant is unusually large for the size of its container; if a plant is especially leggy, with dead twigs and branches or short-jointed new growth; if roots show above soil level (particularly if they coil or spiral); and if husky roots grow through the container's drainage holes.

How to Plant

The illustrations on the facing page show procedures for planting bare-root, B-and-B, and container-grown trees and shrubs. How you treat the backfill soil (the soil you return to the planting hole) depends on your garden soil and the roots of the tree or shrub you're setting out. The object is to match the soil around the roots as closely as possible to that of your garden.

If your soil is medium to heavy in texture (that is, heavier loam to clay), you can plant bare-root plants in the soil you dug from the hole. The same applies to B-and-B plants, because they are usually grown in a fairly heavy soil. Plants in containers, though, will be growing in a lightweight, porous container soil mix that drains more freely than clay. When planting them, it is better to amend the backfill soil with organic matter to create a "transition zone" for roots to explore initially. This helps avoid the "bathtub effect," in which water collects in the porous container soil because it is absorbed so slowly by the heavy soil of your garden.

If your garden soil is medium (loam) to light (sandy) in texture, you can safely plant bare-root and container plants with unamended backfill soil.

Digging the Planting Hole

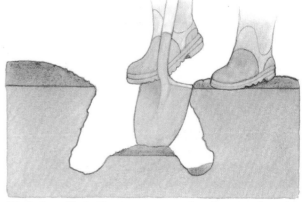

Dig hole so that sides taper outward and are roughened, not smoothly sculpted (use a spading fork to roughen shovel-dug sides); this lets roots penetrate more easily into surrounding soil. Make the hole a bit shallower than the root ball or root system of the plant it will receive; then dig deeper around edges of the hole's bottom. This leaves a firm "plateau" of undug soil to support the plant at proper depth without settling.

Planting Bare-root

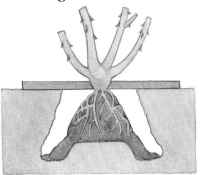

Make a firm cone of soil in hole. Spread roots over cone, placing plant at same depth (or a bit higher) as it was in the growing field. Use a stick to check depth.

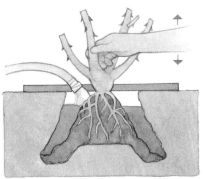

Fill in backfill soil nearly to top of hole, firming it as you fill. Then add water. If plant settles, move it up and down in saturated soil to raise it to proper level.

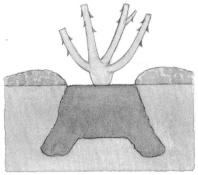

After plant is watered and correct level is established, add remaining soil. When the growing season begins, make a soil ridge around hole to form watering basin.

Planting Balled-and-Burlapped

Set balled-and-burlapped plant into planting hole, its root ball on plateau of undug soil; see that top of root ball is about 2 inches above soil grade.

Untie burlap and spread it out to uncover about half of root ball. Drive in stake alongside root ball before hole is filled; then add backfill soil.

After firming in backfill soil, create a watering moat by mounding soil. Gently water in plant; then loosely tie plant to stake.

Planting from Containers

Roots of container plants may have become coiled or matted. Spray soil off the outer few inches of root ball; then uncoil circling or twisted roots.

Spread roots out over a firm plateau of soil; then add unamended backfill soil. Top of the root ball should be about 2 inches above the surrounding soil.

Mound soil to form a watering moat. Irrigate gently—water should remain in moat rather than flood the basin; the objective is to keep trunk base dry.

But add organic amendments if you wish to enhance the quality of the soil that roots will grow into first. When planting B-and-B plants whose root-ball soil is fairly heavy, be sure to add organic amendments to the backfill soil to improve its water retention. Mix one shovelful of organic amendment (peat moss, ground bark, or nitrogen-fortified sawdust, for example) to every three shovelsful of backfill.

When to Plant

In milder regions, where soil seldom freezes during winter, you can plant trees and shrubs throughout the year. And even in the coldest areas, you can plant in spring, summer, and autumn. The best time of year to plant depends on your climate, the type of plant you will be setting out, and the mode in which it is offered for planting.

For the best first-year growth with the least stress on the new plant, you want to plant in advance of the spring growing season while the soil is cool. This gives roots a chance to grow into the new soil before foliage growth begins, placing demands on the root system. In milder climates, where soil freezes seldom or not at all, autumn through winter is the preferred period. In colder regions, late winter to early spring—the earliest point possible—will get most new plants off to the best start.

Some cold-climate gardeners prefer to set out deciduous plants in autumn, after dormancy sets in but at least a month before the soil freezes. With perhaps some slight protection to their branches over winter, these fall-planted specimens will produce some root growth in autumn that will continue immediately after the soil thaws in spring. In such climates, though, needle-leafed evergreens are best left to the late winter–early spring period; the combination of frozen soil and winter winds can fatally desiccate these plants if they're set out in autumn.

Bare-root trees and shrubs are available only during autumn and winter, while they are dormant. Even though bared of soil, the roots must be kept moist before planting. In the nursery, the roots are buried in a moisture-retentive medium such as sawdust; bare-root plants sold by mail-order nurseries may arrive encased in a plastic bag or with their roots packed in a moist material.

Balled-and-burlapped plants are available over a somewhat longer period than bare-root offerings: typically early autumn into the following spring. Their root balls must not dry out before planting—that's why many nurseries nestle these plants, too, in shallow beds of moist sawdust.

Container-grown plants are available for planting whenever the soil is not frozen. Though they're best planted in the cooler months, container plants may be set out during spring or summer if you water them during dry periods and, if necessary, shelter them from intense sun and wind.

Care after Planting

Any newly planted leafy tree or shrub may need to be protected from wind and heat until new roots have begun to grow. Without protection, leaves can transpire moisture faster than roots can replenish it.

If a newly planted tree will be exposed to intense heat or freezing cold, you would be wise to wrap the trunk with burlap or special trunk wrap. This also offers some protection against rubbing and scratching animals. If the unsupported trunk is not sturdy enough to stand upright, stake as shown below.

Staking a Young Tree

Stake top-heavy tree so that trunk will bend a bit in wind. Place two stakes in direction of prevailing wind, looping tie around trunk from each stake. Trunk wrap protects bark.

atering

Trees and shrubs need soil moisture to encourage root growth and to supply water to leaves so they can keep abreast of transpiration. Water needs differ: some plants tolerate prolonged dry periods (or even demand it), whereas others are at their best in nearly boggy soil. Young plants getting established in the garden need more attention to watering than do older specimens with extensive root systems.

When to apply water. No exact rule exists to tell you how often to water your trees and shrubs. Besides the plant's inherent needs and its age in your garden, soil type exerts a large influence. Water-retentive clay soils need less frequent water applications than do well-drained sandy soils. Remember, too, that clay absorbs water more slowly than sand, and that a clay soil needs more water than sandy soil for it to penetrate to any given depth. With any soil, a mulch will retard surface evaporation.

Your best guide to watering is a soil check. For newly planted and young trees and shrubs, water thoroughly when the top inch of soil has dried. For established specimens, you may be able to wait until the top 2 to 4 inches of soil have lost moisture. Check the individual plant descriptions on pages 40–141 for any special water guidelines that differ from this general recommendation.

If you want to know for sure just how deep your watering is penetrating, check with a soil sampling tube. This instrument can also help you determine when to water if you take soil samples to observe how moist the soil is at various depths.

How to apply water. Prolonged rainfall will apply enough water to penetrate deeply; but if you use sprinklers to duplicate rainfall, you must adjust water delivery to avoid wasteful runoff.

Some form of irrigation, from which water can soak into the soil over a period of time, will give the best penetration with the least waste through runoff and evaporation.

The simplest irrigation method requires only a low, circular earthen berm around each young tree and shrub to create a watering basin; then just add water. Soaker hoses will deliver water slowly and steadily to plants set out in a linear arrangement. Some are made of porous canvas or of plastic with

Soaker hoses deliver moisture efficiently to soil. Mulch hides hoses while keeping soil cool and moist.

numerous pinhole openings (place the holes toward the soil); others are made of recycled tires, the water oozing through porous rubber walls.

Drip irrigation comprises several low-volume water delivery options that offer great flexibility in terms of the planting schemes you can water at one time and the precise control of water quantity delivered. The basic system operates through ½-inch black polyvinyl tubing into which you insert emitters—either directly or via ¼-inch "spaghetti" tubing that leads to the emitters. Among emitters are those that actually do drip water (at a prescribed amount per hour), as well as a host of minisprinklers and minisprayers that will cover a greater area. All operate on the principle of gradual application: run over an extended period, drip emitters apply enough water to penetrate deeply with little or no waste from evaporation or runoff. Visit a well-stocked nursery, hardware store, or irrigation supply firm to see the array of possibilities. You need no special expertise or tools to assemble a drip irrigation system.

Don't forget that leaves as well as roots can absorb water, though not a major amount. You can help along newly planted trees and shrubs by sprinkling their leaves in early morning and on cloudy days.

In cold-winter regions where soil freezes during winter, you should water trees and shrubs well just in advance of hard freezes. Plants that enter winter in dry soil have no moisture reserves in the root zone to counteract drying winter winds; the result can be dehydrated, dead plants. All evergreen plants are especially vulnerable.

Fertilizing

In the wild, trees and shrubs obviously receive no fertilizer as we think of it. But the annual layer of fallen leaves plus the remains and deposits of animal life decompose to release a small but continuous supply of nutrients. In the garden we tend to tidy up and dispose of these natural nutrient sources and then rely on fertilizer applications to furnish necessary nutrients.

Some shrubs—notably roses—do best with a regular fertilizer regime so they can continue to produce new growth and bloom throughout spring and summer. And other shrubs, such as azaleas and camellias, are often included in an annual fertilizer program to produce optimal blossom quantity and size. But a great many trees and shrubs may continue to grow and produce well with no supplemental nutrients. With these plants, you'll have to observe their growth and judge for yourself. An annual output of strong new growth with good color tells you the plant is doing well without your assistance. But turn to a fertilizer supplement if new growth is scant or weak, has smaller or paler leaves than normal, or if the plant shows a significant amount of dieback. Pale or yellow leaves with dark veins, though, probably indicate chlorosis (see page 39).

Essential Nutrients

Plants need sixteen nutrients for growth, of which three are considered "primary": nitrogen (N), phosphorus (P), and potassium (K). Soil furnishes thirteen of the sixteen, including two of the three primaries, phosphorus and potassium. But nitrogen, the nutrient needed in greatest quantity, is a gas in its elemental form. It's therefore available to plants only from the air (both carried to the soil by rainfall and extracted from soil air by certain root bacteria), from decaying organic matter, and from fertilizers.

Aside from their different (but interrelated) functions in a plant's metabolism, the three major nutrients are available to plants in different ways. Phosphorus and potassium must be in the soil if they are to be useful; roots extract these two nutrients either from the films of water surrounding soil particles or from the particles themselves. The best time to apply fertilizer containing phosphorus or potassium is, therefore, before you plant, digging it well into the soil.

Nitrogen, however, is immediately to ultimately soluble (depending on its form), so it will leach into the soil. Because of this solubility, it will also leach right on past a plant's root zone with rainfall and

Nitrogen Conversion & Availability

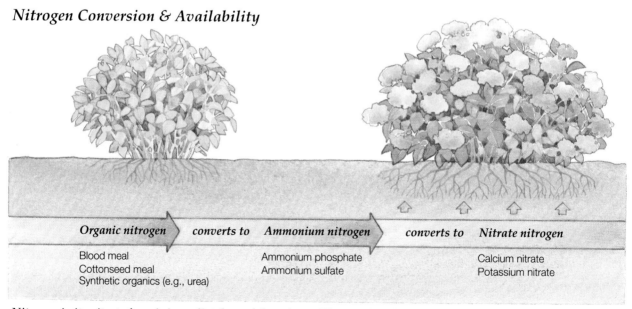

Organic nitrogen	converts to	Ammonium nitrogen	converts to	Nitrate nitrogen
Blood meal Cottonseed meal Synthetic organics (e.g., urea)		Ammonium phosphate Ammonium sulfate		Calcium nitrate Potassium nitrate

Nitrogen in its nitrate form is immediately useful to plants. Nitrogen in other forms must be converted to nitrate nitrogen before plants can benefit from it.

watering; this means that you'll need to resupply it periodically if you decide your trees or shrubs need it. For immediate availability, nitrogen must be in its soluble *nitrate* form; if a fertilizer's package label indicates that much or all of the nitrogen is in nitrate or nitric form, the fertilizer will be released quickly—but it will also be used up quickly. Nitrogen in other forms becomes available more slowly, having to be converted by soil organisms to a nitrate form before it's soluble. In the *ammonium* form (as in ammonium sulfate), release will be slower—anywhere from 2 weeks to 3 months—but should be more sustained once it starts. (*Note:* ammonium nitrate—its nitrogen half in ammonium form and half in nitrate form—offers both immediate and delayed availability.) Slowest to act are the organic and synthetic organic nitrogen forms: blood meal, urea, and IBDU (isobutylidene diurea), for example.

Fertilizer Choices

A fertilizer containing all three of the primary nutrients is called a "complete fertilizer." Its nutrients are in a guaranteed ratio to one another, expressed in numbers such as 5-10-5 that will be noted clearly on the bag, box, or bottle. The order of the numbers is always the same: nitrogen-phosphorus-potassium (expressed as potash). A 5-10-5 formula will contain, by weight, 5 percent nitrogen, 10 percent phosphorus, and 5 percent potassium. In addition to complete fertilizers, you can also buy some containing just one or two of the primary nutrients. The most familiar of these are the nitrogen-only types, such as ammonium sulfate (21-0-0).

When selecting a fertilizer, you'll find there are two different types, dry and liquid. The greatest range of choice is among the dry fertilizers. These are meant to be broadcast over the soil or dug into it; water then dissolves them, releasing the nutrients they contain. Most are simple granules, but you can also buy kinds that "package" the fertilizer in ways that offer certain advantages. The most popular of these are the controlled-release fertilizers, whose soluble granules are encased within a permeable coating. With each watering, small amounts of nutrients are released from the pellets until the fertilizer is eventually consumed. Some remain effective for several months. Other dry fertilizers come compressed into tablets or cylindrical sticks; you implant these in the soil, where they release nutrients slowly as they are contacted by water. These are most advantageous for getting phosphorus and potassium into the soil among established shrubs and trees.

Liquid fertilizers—either liquid concentrates or soluble granules—must be diluted with water and then applied as a soil drench or foliar spray. Because the dissolved nutrients are available immediately, liquids are good for giving plants a quick tonic. But because the nutrients are in solution, they quickly leach through the soil. Liquids are particularly useful for fertilizing container plants (see page 21). And because leaves as well as roots can absorb nutrients, liquid fertilizers can be sprayed on foliage for almost immediate effect.

Timing & Application

Plants need to have nutrients available when they are actively producing new growth. For trees and shrubs, prime growth time is late winter to midspring, depending on the climate. One good time to apply fertilizer, then, is about a month in advance of the spring growth flush—from mid- or late winter to early spring. If needed, you can follow up with later applications in spring and early summer.

In mild- and frost-free-winter regions, you can continue a fertilizer program through summer. But in cold-winter climates, cease applying fertilizer to plants in the ground by early summer; new growth stimulated by later applications will be at risk when freezes come. In these regions, though, your trees and shrubs can benefit from fertilizer applied just before the first frost is expected. Plants will have stopped making new growth, but their roots are still able to absorb nutrients and store them for the following spring's growth push.

How much fertilizer to use depends on the product's strength and the size of the plant. Labels on fertilizer packages will suggest amounts based on that product's formula. To determine how much actual nutrient a product contains, multiply its percentage by the package weight; thus, a 10-pound bag containing 5 percent nitrogen by weight contains half a pound (.5 pound) of actual nitrogen.

Some tree specialists determine the quantity of fertilizer to apply by measuring the trunk diameter. A moderate application would be 1 pound of a 10 percent nitrogen fertilizer for each inch of trunk diameter (measured at 4 feet above the ground). Another way to figure fertilizer quantity for trees is to apply about 4 pounds *actual nitrogen* over 1,000 square feet of soil surface. When fertilizing trees, broadcast the fertilizer beneath the outer two-thirds of branch spread plus a distance beyond equal to one-third the radius of the total spread. Then water thoroughly, so that you moisten at least the upper 6 inches of soil.

Pruning

Unless you're a grower of roses or fruit trees—or maintain a formal hedge—you won't need to consider pruning a part of your regular maintenance. Those specialty plants need yearly pruning to produce the best flowers and fruits (or to maintain a rigid, artificial shape), but the majority of garden trees and shrubs will meet shears or saw on only an occasional basis.

Pruning ranges from elective to emergency surgery. Here are the reasons you might need to prune a shrub or tree.

■ To enhance quality or quantity of flowers or fruit

■ To direct or control growth ("improving appearance" or "shaping")

■ To rejuvenate an overgrown or neglected plant

■ To remove broken stems and limbs (and perhaps reshape the damaged plant)

The one reason you should not have to prune (hedges excepted) is to limit a plant's size. If you find yourself doing so, you chose the wrong plant for the location; replace the overlarge plant with one that will fit the site naturally.

Remember that each kind of tree or shrub has its own natural shape: one may be bolt upright, another rounded and spreading; yet another may send up arching branches in a fountainlike pattern. Don't try to force-prune a shrub or tree into a shape contrary to its natural inclination; though you may temporarily achieve your goal, you'll have to repeat the process frequently as the plant tries to overcome your work—and the plant will never display its full beauty.

Basic Pruning Cuts & Techniques

All pruning redirects growth. At its simplest, pruning stops a branch from growing in one direction, forcing new growth to take another tack. Major limb removal, on the other hand, eliminates a major directional thrust; growth energies are channeled into the remainder of the plant.

Some needle-leafed evergreens need special pruning treatment. These trees and shrubs fall into two broad classes. Some produce branches that radiate from trunks and limbs in whorls; spruces, firs, and most pines are familiar examples. The other type—including arborvitae, hemlock, juniper, and yew—produce branches in a random manner, conforming to no distinct pattern.

A characteristic of whorl-branching evergreens is that growth buds appear at the tips of new stems,

Basic Pruning Techniques

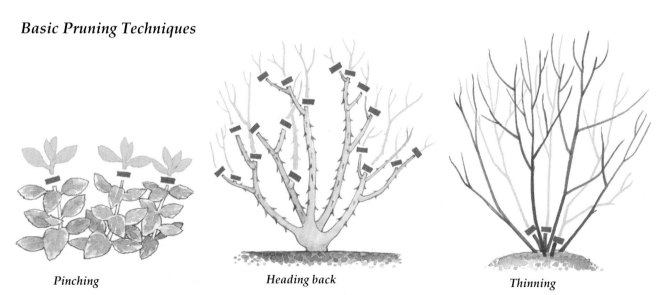

Pinching

Heading back

Thinning

Pinching (left) nips off tips of new growth to stimulate branching from below the pinch. Heading back (center) removes parts of stems to reduce plant size and encourage branching from below the cuts. Thinning (right) reduces plant's density but not size.

along the lengthening new growth, and at the bases of new shoots. These new growths are often referred to as "candles"; look at a pine to understand the metaphor. On these plants, you *must* make pruning cuts above these potential growth buds if you expect new growth to take place below the cut. This means you can cut back the candles about halfway to generate more branching, or you can cut out candles to their bases to force branches to grow from that point. If you cut into an older stem—even though it may bear foliage—it won't sprout new growth.

Random-branching evergreens, on the other hand, may be pruned much as other shrubs and trees are; new growth will sprout from branches below pruning cuts as long as the remaining branch bears some foliage. Other than yew, most kinds won't develop new growth from bare wood.

When to Prune

As a general rule, the best time to prune most trees and shrubs is during their dormant period, just before growth resumes. In mildest-winter regions, where it may be hard to tell one growing season from another, midwinter is probably the best choice. (However, deciduous tropical shrubs and trees may not be leafless and dormant then.) In cold-winter areas, late winter to early spring is the preferred range, depending on the severity of the climate.

You may prune during summer as well. But summer pruning, because it reduces the foliage mass that is working to supply energy to the plant, may slightly diminish vigor that year. Of course, you should prune to remove damage whenever it occurs.

Pruning Flowering Shrubs

Most flowering shrubs blossom but once a year, either in spring or in summer to autumn. It's important to know the flowering season of your shrub so you can prune at the point that will enhance flower production. Prune at the wrong time, and you simply throw away potential flowers for the coming season.

Spring-flowering shrubs such as forsythia and lilac produce flowers on stems that were formed following the last year's bloom. Prune these plants either while they are in bloom (for cut flowers) or just after flowers fade and before new shoots lengthen. Summer- and autumn-blooming shrubs (and the repeat-flowering roses) produce flowering stems in spring and then blossom later in the year. Prune those shrubs in winter, before spring's growth begins.

Making a Proper Pruning Cut

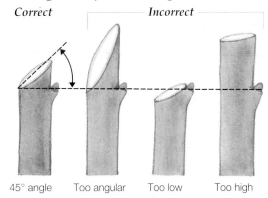

Correct   Incorrect

45° angle   Too angular   Too low   Too high

A correct pruning cut has its lowest point even with the top of the growth bud; it slants upward from that point at about a 45° angle.

Removing a Tree Limb

To remove a large limb, make first cut about one-third through beneath the branch. Next, cut off limb beyond first cut. Finally, remove limb stub, cutting just outside bark ridges at limb's base.

Training a Young Tree

The needle-leafed evergreen trees seldom need early training unless they develop more than a single leading shoot where just one should be.

With a deciduous or broad-leafed evergreen tree, though, you'll spend the first several years guiding its developing structure. You want growth to continue upward as a straight trunk. If the tree's leader was cut back before purchase, it will have to grow a new leader from a dormant bud (generally the topmost) beneath the cut. To maintain dominance of the leader, pinch or head back vigorous side branches that are below the height where you want permanent structure to develop. Leave those branches for the time being—their foliage shades the trunk and allows it to thicken faster than if you were to remove them entirely (see page 34). When the trunk is high enough for side branches to remain as permanent

Pruning

scaffold limbs, see that they develop at fairly evenly-spaced intervals, both up the trunk and spiraling around it. Remove badly placed and superfluous branches before they gain size; head back any overly vigorous branches that unbalance the tree's shape and any that threaten to usurp the leader's upward dominance.

Branches that form a narrow "V" angle to the trunk are attached less strongly than are those that make a wider angle. Whenever possible, favor the wider-angled limbs and remove those with a narrow "V" attachment.

Professional Tree Help

Professional arborists—popularly known as tree surgeons—are your friends in need whenever you face tree work that is beyond your equipment, know-how, or strength. They'll answer the simple What's wrong? question or contract for pruning and limb removal, pest control, fertilizing, moving a tree, or changing the soil level around a mature specimen. Most homeowners rely on these services for major pruning and damage repair, cabling to prevent limb splitting, and cavity cleaning and filling to prolong the life of "hollow" trees.

Forming a Strong Tree Trunk

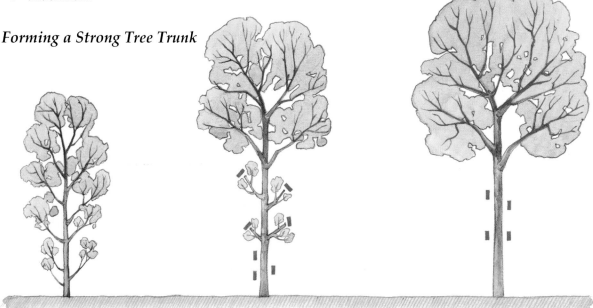

Young trees develop strong trunks faster if you remove trunk branches gradually. At first, leave all branches on trunk to develop thickness. As tree grows, head trunk branches back so that most growth is directed into height, finally removing them entirely.

Transforming a Shrub into a Tree

If an older shrub has become too bulky for its space, consider turning it into a small tree. Select major stems to become trunks, removing lower branches to the desired canopy.

Protecting Tree Roots

Healthy roots—receiving satisfactory amounts of water and air—are vital to a tree's well-being. Anything that alters that congenial root environment poses an adjustment problem for an established tree: the greater the alteration, the more adjustment—and risk.

The following four alterations in environment are potentially damaging to an established tree.

Compacted soil. The heavy equipment used on building sites can seriously compact soil, making it difficult if not impossible for air and water to penetrate a tree's root zone. If you know that heavy equipment will operate near valued established trees, surround them with sturdy barricades that, *at a minimum,* protect the ground beneath their branch spread.

Paved-over soil. If solid pavement is laid beneath a tree, it can totally prevent water and air from reaching established roots. Should you decide to install a paved surface beneath all or part of an established tree, be sure the soil coverage isn't total. First, leave as much open soil as possible around the trunk. Then select a paving design that will allow water to penetrate it. Bricks or other pavers should be set in a sand base with spaces between units; the spaces can then be filled with sand or gravel. If you pour concrete in rectangular modules, fill the spaces occupied by the form boards with sand or gravel after the concrete is set.

Added soil. If you need to add soil over ground containing established tree roots, follow these guidelines. If the fill will be no deeper than 4 inches, use a sandy, porous soil and don't pack it down. New roots will grow into the fill from old surface roots.

If you plan to add from 4 to 12 inches of soil, first encircle the tree's trunk with a retaining wall that will leave at least a 3-foot radius of soil at the original grade. Make the wall as high as the fill will be. Cover the soil outside the wall to within 4 inches of the new surface height with coarse gravel; then add a 1-inch layer of fine gravel followed by a 3-inch layer of new soil. Water (and air) will then be able to percolate through a shallow layer of soil and gravel to reach the roots beneath.

Whenever a grade change involves 1 to 2 feet of soil, you should supplement this operation with drainage pipes. Before spreading the gravel, place about eight perforated pipes (their holes facedown) or drainage tile radiating out from the well around the trunk and extending at least to the edge of the tree's canopy. The inner ends of the pipe should open into the tree well, and the outer ends should be either sealed off (to prevent clogging with soil) or connected to upright sections of pipe or tile that will vent them to slightly above the new soil surface. Venting will allow air and moisture to enter at both ends. After the pipes are in place, proceed to layer the gravel and soil.

For grade changes of greater than 2 feet, seek professional advice.

Removed soil. Any major soil removal from beneath and around a tree will include some roots that help sustain the tree. It may even remove roots that provide anchorage. The most successful regrading operations remove soil on one side of a tree only, and to a depth no greater than 2 feet. If possible, limit soil removal to beyond the tree's canopy; the closer to the trunk you excavate, the greater the risk.

When you have carefully removed soil to the point where the grade is to change, build a retaining wall to separate the two levels. Fill in behind the wall (on the tree's side) with good soil liberally enriched with organic matter to encourage new roots to grow. Be sure to provide drainage holes in the retaining wall to let water seep through.

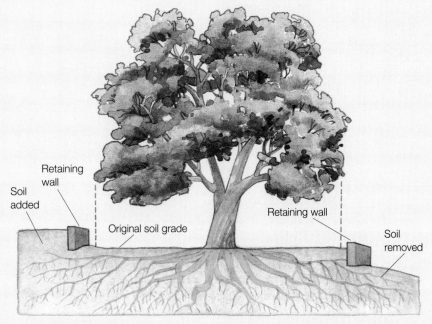

To change the soil level around an existing tree, try to preserve the original grade beneath the tree; making elevation changes beyond the branch spread.

$\mathcal{P}$lant Problems

The nemesis of gardeners, pests and diseases are simply a fact of garden life. But their mere presence does not always merit a call to action. Many insect visitations come in short-lived waves triggered by weather and season; the first aphids of spring are a familiar example. And some fungal diseases are active during particular weather conditions (usually damp), so they appear only in particular seasons or years that favor their increase.

The object in pest and disease control is to combat only those problems that may stay and increase. Faced with a problem that will in all probability soon be gone, you'd best relax and accept some chewed leaves or mildew. In the case of many insect pests, natural predators may do the work for you (and might be eliminated by sprays). But if you decide that you must intervene, choose the least toxic control as your first offensive. Suggested controls* for each pest and disease are listed in order of increasing toxicity, or from narrow-spectrum to broad-spectrum targets. Read and follow all cautions and directions on product labels.

Before you spray with an insecticide or fungicide, be sure to water your plants thoroughly a day or two in advance. A water-stressed plant may be damaged by any spray other than water. Spray in the early morning or late afternoon, when the air is likely to be still and the temperature lower; avoid the hottest part of the day, as high temperatures combined with some spray materials can cause leafburn.

Mature trees are too large for homeowner treatment. If you have a tree that needs pest or disease control, have it done by a professional arborist.

New control products continue to be developed and marketed, while existing products may be withdrawn from sale for home use if research reveals possible hazards to health or the environment. For up-to-the-minute control recommendations, check with your Cooperative Extension agent or the personnel at a reputable nursery.

Pests

These are the creatures that crawl—at least in some part of their life cycle. In popular terms they are known as "insects."

Sucking insects. These creatures have sucking mouth parts, through which they extract vital juices from stems and leaves.

Aphids

■ *Aphids* are tiny green, yellow, black, or pink insects—soft and sometimes winged. They cluster thickly on new growth; heavy infestations will stunt growth. In trees, the secretions of sticky "honeydew" they produce will drip on everything beneath the branches.
Controls: Hose them off or spray with insecticidal soap, diazinon, malathion, or acephate.

Mealybugs

■ *Mealybugs* are small, waxy, white, nearly immobile insects that form colonies at stem joints or toward leaf bases (usually on the undersides).
Controls: Spray with insecticidal soap, diazinon, malathion, or acephate.

Scale

■ *Scale* insects begin life as tiny crawlers but in their adult stage attach themselves to stems and leaves, covering their bodies with protective waxy shells. Typically they congregate in colonies.
Controls: Adult scale can be hand-picked (for light infestations) or sprayed with a dormant oil (for deciduous plants, in winter only); for the juvenile, crawler stage in summer, spray with summer oil, diazinon, carbaryl, malathion, or acephate.

* Control products are listed by their generic names—the names you will find under "active ingredients" on product labels.

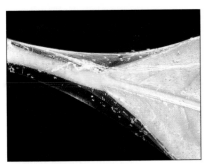

Spider mites

■ **Spider mites** are active during the warm summer months. They work on leaf undersides but are almost too small to see. Look for a stippled appearance on leaf surfaces; a heavy infestation will show silvery webbing on leaf undersides.

Controls: Hose them off (on three consecutive days, or every other day for a week), or spray with insecticidal soap or acephate three times at 7- to 10-day intervals.

Chewing insects. All kinds of caterpillars and worms belong here, including leaf miners that chew away the tissue between leaf veins but not the outer leaf surface.

Japanese beetle

Cucumber beetle

■ **Beetles** are hard-shelled insects that chew holes in leaves and flowers;

in the larval phase, they're ground-dwelling grubs (worms). Japanese beetles are a major summer foliage pest in the eastern United States.

Controls: Hand-pick, use pheromone traps, counter with milky spore disease (for Japanese beetles), or spray with carbaryl or malathion.

Gypsy moth caterpillar

Pine saw larvae

■ **Caterpillars and worms** include a wide range of many-legged, crawling larvae of moths and butterflies. They range in seriousness from the relatively innocuous inchworm to the voracious, highly destructive gypsy moth caterpillar.

Controls: Hand-pick or spray with *Bacillus thuringiensis*, carbaryl, or acephate.

Leaf miners

■ **Leaf miners** are the larvae of various sawflies. Your earliest chance to control them is when leaves emerge

in spring—when you can target adult flies before they lay eggs—and a bit later, when larvae have hatched but have not yet tunneled into leaves. Once they're inside the leaves, only the systemic acephate will reach them.

Controls: Spray with diazinon or malathion, in three applications about 10 days apart, or spray with acephate.

Burrowing insects. These invisible pests go to work on twigs, limbs, and trunks.

Shothole borer

■ **Borers.** Telltale signs may be small holes in a branch accompanied by bits of sawdust nearby; those that tunnel beneath bark will show no entry holes but may leave bits of sawdust in bark crevices. Young trees of softwood types are particularly vulnerable. For prevention, wrap tree trunks of newly planted specimens with special trunk wrap. Adult moths lay eggs on bark, so the best time to intervene is when the larvae are newly hatched and before they have entered the wood.

Controls: Spray with diazinon at 10-day intervals from early spring to midspring; for adult moths, use pheromone traps starting in midsummer.

Diseases

The heterogeneous category of diseases includes problems of foliage, stems, and roots. Most leaf and stem diseases are caused by fungi and bacteria; the most prevalent soil diseases are caused by fungi.

Leaf problems. When climatic conditions are particularly favorable, you may need to intervene to prevent a debilitating infection.

Anthracnose

■ **Anthracnose.** This fungus attacks new shoots and leaves in spring, causing them to turn brown and die; in older leaves it causes large, irregular brown patches and premature leaf drop. Spores are spread by rainfall and sprinkling, so the disease is severe in wet springs but disappears during warm, dry weather. It overwinters, to reinfect next spring, in cankers on twigs it has killed. Therefore, prevention means cutting out all dead twigs and branches.

Controls: Spray with chlorothalonil as leaves unfold, then two or three times more at 2-week intervals.

Rose black spot

■ **Leaf spots.** This heading covers a range of diseases from black spot on roses to the "shot hole" fungi that infect *Prunus* species. The organisms thrive in warm, wet weather from spring through summer; they're most damaging where summer rainfall occurs. Spores will overwinter to begin infection anew in plant refuse (leaves, fruits) and on stems. A thorough cleanup of potentially diseased refuse is a start at prevention.

Controls: Spray the foliage with folpet, triforine (favored by rose growers), or chlorothalonil; repeat as long as weather favors fungus development.

Powdery mildew

■ **Powdery mildew.** Starting as gray or white circular patches on foliage, this fungus spreads to become a powdery coating on leaves and stems. It thrives when humidity is high (but not in wet weather; water will kill the spores), especially wherever plants are too shaded or crowded. Warm days and cool, moist nights encourage it.

Controls: Spray with triforine or folpet.

Scab

■ **Scab.** Apples, crabapples, and hawthornes are notoriously scab-prone, but resistant kinds are available and should be planted in preference to susceptible sorts. Several kinds of scab exist, some infecting pyracantha and even willow. Symptoms are scablike lesions on fruits and foliage; severe infestation causes defoliation.

Controls: Spray with captan or wettable sulfur, starting just before flower buds show color, reapplying when they do, and again when three-quarters of the petals have fallen.

Stem diseases. Dead branch tips and leaves—sometimes entire branches—betray the presence of one of these diseases. Another symptom is oval, discolored areas on branches.

Fireblight

■ **Fireblight.** This bacteria starts in blossoms and progresses down branches, blackening leaves and stems until they look as though they were scorched by fire. Once present, it can also enter through cracks in bark and via pruning cuts. It thrives during moist spring weather, targeting a number of plants in the rose family. In areas where it is an ongoing problem, avoid growing susceptible plants.

Controls: Remove blighted branches (cutting below the infected part) and disinfect shears between cuts by dipping in rubbing alcohol for 30 seconds; to prevent infection, spray blossoms at 4- to 5-day intervals with a fixed-copper-based spray or (if available) agricultural streptomycin.

Root diseases. These are the most difficult diseases to combat, because roots are hidden from sight and access. By the time the top growth shows symptoms, it may be too late to attempt a remedy. And in most cases, remedial measures are beyond the home gardener's capacity. If a cherished specimen is afflicted, consult a professional tree service or arborist for diagnosis and advice. If any of these diseases is a serious problem in your area, plan to grow only non-susceptible plants. Check with your county agricultural office or state university agricultural extension service for lists of resistant plants.

Armillaria root rot

■ **Armillaria root rot.** Known in western states as oak root fungus (after its most conspicuous victim), this fungus also favors a number of other plants. It invades root tissue, forming black, shoestringlike threads just beneath the roots' bark. The final stage of infection produces clusters of mushrooms at the plant's base. The fungus lives for many years in the dead root systems of its victims; if these contact roots of other susceptible plants, infection can occur.

Texas root rot

■ **Texas root rot.** This fungus is found in the semiarid Southwest, particularly in alkaline soils having low organic content. The fungus destroys the outer portion of roots, eliminating their ability to take up water; the result is a sudden wilting. Standard controls involve acidifying the soil and adding organic matter—no easy task among permanent plantings.

Verticillium wilt

■ **Verticillium wilt.** This fungus invades and plugs water-conducting root tissue, shutting off the water supply to top growth. Common symptoms are wilting of just part of a shrub or tree, the leaves turning yellow, then brown, then dying upward from the base of the plant or branch. A cut branch will show discolored sapwood: olive green, dark brown, or black. The fungus develops in moist, cool soil during spring, but symptoms may not appear until summer warmth causes leaves to transpire more rapidly than the infected roots can handle. Mildly affected plants may go into remission—aided by infrequent but deep irrigation—but nothing will kill the fungus once it has invaded a plant. And the fungus will live for years in the soil even without plants to infect.

Chlorosis

Chlorosis

Symptoms of chlorosis show as yellow new growth. In milder cases, areas of yellow show up between the dark leaf veins; in severe or prolonged cases, the entire leaf turns yellow. Chlorosis usually indicates an iron deficiency; in rare instances, it results from lack of another mineral, such as zinc. Usually this iron deficiency occurs in an alkaline soil pH (see "Acid & Alkaline Soils," page 25) that renders existing iron unavailable to plants. To correct chlorosis, you can use iron sulfate to reduce the soil pH or iron chelate which is able to hold iron in a form available to plants regardless of soil alkalinity. You can also use foliar sprays containing iron for a quick, temporary remedy.

Selecting Your Trees

C hoosing a tree, like making a friend, is something you do with the long view in mind.
You want to find that perfect individual—
one you can get along with on both practical
and aesthetic terms for a lifetime.

To make a well-considered choice, combine the practical guidelines of this book's opening chapter with the
descriptions in the encyclopedia that follows. Whether
you select a stalwart redwood or an
effervescent flowering cherry,
you're certain to find a tree
that will be a welcome garden
presence for years to come.

Quercus rubra

Ablaze in autumn, Japanese maples
(Acer palmatum) *enliven the
prevailing green of this tree-shaded
garden.*

41

Using Our Encyclopedia

The descriptions that follow are organized in an easy-reference format. Each entry begins with the plant's botanical name, followed by its common name and the plant family to which it belongs. Some entries contain references to a number of species and hybrids, so the entry is headed simply by the plant genus name—Crataegus, for example. Other entries cover just one plant, so they appear listed by genus name followed by the species—such as Liriodendron tulipifera.

Following the plant and family names, five points of information serve as a quick selection guide: whether the tree is evergreen or deciduous and its hardiness to cold; color and season of flowers (if they're an important feature); its preferred sun or shade exposure; its moisture needs expressed in watering frequency; and its growth rate.

Finally, the text offers descriptive profiles of the tree or trees: verbal portraits of shape and structure, foliage, and flowers (see the glossary on page 142 for illustrations of descriptive terms). Potential weak points, liabilities, or cautions are mentioned along with the assets. Cultural information includes soil preference, climate restrictions if they apply, any special pest or disease cautions, and advice on any pruning that may be needed on a regular or recurring schedule.

ABIES
Fir
Pinaceae

Evergreen (conifer): Hardiness varies; most need some winter chill
Flowers: None
Exposure: Sun
Water: Regular to moderate
Growth: Varies

Symmetrical is the word for firs. Densely foliaged, almost perfectly cone-shaped trees are formed by evenly spaced branches that radiate, layer upon layer, around straight, single trunks. Firs might be confused with spruces *(Picea)*, but they have

Abies concolor

softer needles that fall directly from the stems (whereas spruces leave short pegs behind), and their cones grow up rather than down.

With few exceptions, firs grow best in cool, humid climates; none will thrive in polluted city air. In the wild, most firs are majestic timber trees, and though they seldom reach forest size in gardens, they still take up considerable space.

Give firs well-drained soil; nearly all species prefer acid soil, as well. With good humidity they can get by with moderate watering, but they'll accept regular water given good drainage. Aphids and spider mites may be occasional pests.

A. amabilis, CASCADE OR SILVER FIR, is hardy to −20°F/−29°C. This Pacific Coast native does best in the cool, moist air from Alaska down to the central California coast. Glossy, dark green needles curve upward to show silvery undersides. Although taller in the wild, in the garden these firs will reach about 50 feet. Their branches droop gracefully, a departure from the stiff horizontality of most firs.

A. concolor, WHITE FIR, is hardy to −20°F/−29°C. This is the most adaptable North American fir. Although native to drier mountain reaches of the West and Southwest, it succeeds in the humid-summer North and Northeast. Given shelter from summer heat and drying winds, it will also thrive in the lower Midwest and

in some lower-elevation areas of the interior West. Moderate to fast garden growth reaches 50 to 75 feet high and about 25 feet wide. Typical needles are bluish green and 2 inches long, but color varies; the selection 'Candicans' has bluish white foliage.

A. grandis, LOWLAND OR GRAND FIR, is hardy to −10°F/−23°C. In Northern California and Northwest gardens, this fast-growing fir can reach 100 feet or more. Deep green, 1½-inch needles are lined white on their undersides and arranged horizontally along the branches. This fir needs regular moisture, but the soil need not be acid.

A. homolepis, NIKKO FIR, is hardy to −20°F/−29°C. This Japanese fir adapts well to the warm humidity of the northeastern to north-central United States. Moderate growth rate produces a conical tree to 80 feet high and about 20 feet across; the basic color is dark green, but trees can appear silvery because their needles angle upward to reveal silver-white banding.

A. nordmanniana, CAUCASIAN OR NORDMANN FIR, is hardy to −20°F/−29°C. From the mountains of Armenia, Asia Minor, and the northeastern Mediterranean comes this sturdy, dense, dark green fir. Garden size is 50 to 60 feet high and 20 feet across, with horizontal to downward-sweeping branches. Growth rate is slow at first but then moderate after the tree is established. It adapts well to the warm- and dry-summer western United States and humid mid-Atlantic and Southeastern states but does best with regular watering.

A. pinsapo, SPANISH FIR, is hardy to −10°F/−23°C. This species flourishes in warm, dry regions without acid soils as well as in cool, moist "fir country." Growth is slow, to 50 feet only after many years. Dark green, stiff needles less than an inch long are densely set around the branches. The selection 'Glauca' has blue-gray needles.

A. procera (A. nobilis), NOBLE FIR, is hardy to −10°F/−23°C. Though it will grow satisfactorily—if slowly—in the Northeast, this species is at its best within its native Washington to northernmost California territory. There growth is fairly rapid, forming a narrow yet graceful tree to well over 100 feet in gardens. Blue-green needles clothe short, stiff branches.

ACACIA
Leguminosae

Evergreen: Hardiness varies; only for western United States
Flowers: White to yellow; late winter, spring
Exposure: Sun
Water: Moderate
Growth: Fast

Australians know many of these trees as "wattles," and florists may sell their blossoms as "mimosa." Among the earliest trees to blossom in mild-winter regions, their blossoms typically are small, fluffy balls of stamens grouped into clusters.

No acacia has a long life expectancy (20 to 30 years is a good average), but all grow so rapidly that they soon reach good tree size. Not too particular about soils, acacias are also quite drought tolerant when established. For the best results, plant a small tree (1-gallon size or smaller) and stake it until the roots are well anchored. Water deeply but infrequently to discourage their tendency to shallow rooting.

Large, older trees may need occasional thinning to admit light into the crown (shaded branches will die) and to decrease wind resistance. Bare wood will not produce new growth, so always remove any twig, branch, or limb back to its point of origin.

A. baileyana, BAILEY ACACIA, is hardy to about 15°F/–9°C. In California and

Acacia baileyana

Arizona, Bailey acacia is often the first tree to flower in the new year, presenting a spectacle of brilliant yellow in January. A mature tree will be 20 to 40 feet high and wide with a soft-looking canopy composed of finely cut blue-gray to gray-green, pinnately compound leaves. The selection 'Purpurea'—purple-leaf acacia—has lavender to purple new growth that later pales to gray-blue. You can also grow this species as a multitrunked specimen.

A. decurrens, GREEN WATTLE, is hardy to 15°F/–9°C. Visualize this species as a taller, more upright, greener version of *A. baileyana;* the dark green leaves are slightly larger but still feathery. Its flowering time is 3 to 4 weeks later, its blossoms also bright yellow but with a greenish tinge. Ultimate size can reach 50 feet, with equal spread. For a silvery gray–leafed version, look for *A. dealbata* (hardy to 10°F/–12°C), formerly known as *A. decurrens dealbata.* Compared with Bailey acacia, green wattle is a longer-lived tree tolerating more wind and water. Its roots, however, are more invasive and its leaf, flower, and seed-pod litter more profuse.

ACER
(see chart on pages 44–45)
Maple
Aceraceae

Deciduous: Hardiness varies
Flowers: Not showy
Exposure: Varies
Water: Regular to moderate
Growth: Moderate (generally)

The word "maple" may bring to mind a large, round-headed tree with broad, lobed leaves. Some of these beloved shade tree species match that description, but maples embrace a broad spectrum of size, shape, and foliage character. You can also find almost shrubby or sinuously irregular maples. Their foliage, too, ranges from simple ovals to deeply lobed and finely dissected shapes. One element common to all but one species is the fruit: each seed has two wings, one on either side, resembling a hardware store wing nut.

Acer platanoides

Acer palmatum

Maples of one kind or another will grow over much of the country. Heat, dryness, and lack of winter cold are the limiting factors. Southern California and low-elevation southwestern deserts are inhospitable to nearly all species; and only those identified as tough or drought tolerant are worth a try in the lower Midwest. All maples prefer well-drained soil but must have moisture available in the root zone throughout their leafy period. Most have shallow, fibrous, competitive roots, and the sizable ones cast dense shade; it's not easy to maintain a garden beneath them.

(Continued on next page)

Acer

Name	Growth	Characteristics
A. buergeranum TRIDENT MAPLE −10°F/−23°C	To 25 feet Moderate Rounded, spreading	Leaves are three-lobed (trident-shaped), glossy green with paler undersides; autumn color is usually red but may be orange to yellow. The natural tendency is for several trunks, branching low, to form a spreading canopy; however, it can be trained to a single-trunked, narrower tree.
A. campestre HEDGE MAPLE −20°F/−29°C	To 35 feet Slow to moderate Rounded	Dense, compact growth makes this a good tree for screen and high hedge planting. Each tree is upright and round headed; dull green leaves have three to five lobes, reach 4 inches across, and turn yellow in autumn. 'Queen Elizabeth' has more upright branches, glossier foliage; 'Postelense' has golden yellow leaves.
A. circinatum VINE MAPLE −20°F/−29°C	To 35 feet Moderate Variable	In shaded West Coast forests, vine maple has a crooked, almost vinelike habit; in the open or at forest's edge, it becomes nearly symmetrical and upright, with one or several trunks. Leaves are nearly circular in outline, to 6 inches across, with five to eleven lobes; autumn color is yellow in shade and warm regions, red in the open given distinct chill. Needs some shade in hot-summer areas. 'Monroe' is a dissected-leaf seclection.
A. davidii DAVID'S MAPLE −10°F/−23°C	To 40 feet Moderate Rounded, spreading	Distinctive bark is shining green, striped white. Leaves are 5 to 7 inches long, heart shaped with serrated margins. New growth is bronze tinted; autumn color is bright yellow, orange-red, and purple. Branches tend to layer in horizontal tiers. In eastern states, needs some shade and regular moisture.
A. griseum PAPERBARK MAPLE −10°F/−23°C	25 to 30 feet Slow Upright, rounded	The unique feature is cinnamon brown bark that peels from the trunk in paper-thin sheets, exposing smooth, bronzy bark beneath. Each leaf is three leaflets (about 2½ inches long), dark green with a silvery underside; autumn color is bright red. Habit is rather open, with branches that angle outward and then upward from the trunk.
A. japonicum FULLMOON MAPLE −10°F/−23°C	20 to 30 feet Slow Rounded	Suggests a larger Japanese maple (*A. palmatum*) in its graceful, tiered branching. Leaves are nearly circular in outline, to 5 inches across, with seven to eleven lobes; autumn color is orange to bright red. 'Aconitifolium' has palmately lobed, dissected leaves; 'Aureum' has yellow spring foliage that matures to chartreuse.
A. macrophyllum BIGLEAF MAPLE 0°F/−18°C	40 to 90 feet Moderate to fast Rounded, spreading	On the West Coast, this becomes a magnificent tree with three- to five-lobed leaves that reach 6 to 15 inches across; autumn color is bright yellow to orange. Seeds are conspicuous, hanging in long, chainlike clusters. Young trees tend to irregular shapes.
A. negundo BOX ELDER −30°F/−34°C	30 to 35 feet Moderate Rounded, spreading	The basic species is a poor garden tree, but two selections are outstanding. Leaves are divided into separate leaflets. 'Variegatum' has green leaflets irregularly bordered with creamy white; hanging seed clusters are also white. Foliage of 'Flamingo' emerges pink and white, becoming green and white with pink tints.
A. palmatum JAPANESE MAPLE −10°F/−23°C	20 feet Slow to moderate Rounded, spreading	The basic species has five- to nine-lobed leaves 2 to 4 inches across, with foliage carried in horizontal layers. Autumn color is yellow through orange to red shades. This exceptionally graceful tree branches low or has several trunks. Countless named selections are sold, encompassing these variations: dissected and variantly lobed foliage; smaller and larger leaves than normal; foliage color variations, including dark red, bronze, and variegated; colored bark; and variant growth habits, including mop-headed shrubs. Where summer is hot and dry, give trees even moisture, some shade, and shelter from wind.
A. platanoides NORWAY MAPLE −30°F/−34°C	50 to 90 feet Moderate to fast Rounded	A majestic, dense, and widely adapted tree, its size and greedy roots rule it out for small gardens. Five-lobed leaves reach 4 to 7 inches across and turn yellow in autumn. Chartreuse flowers are conspicuous on bare branches before leaves emerge. Nurseries offer many named selections. Smaller growers are 'Cavalier', 'Cleveland' and 'Cleveland II', and 'Globosum'; a narrow one is 'Columnare'. Also look for purple-leafed 'Crimson King', 'Faassen's Black', 'Royal Red Leaf', and 'Schwedler' (all are smaller than the basic species) and for white-variegated 'Drummondii'.
A. pseudoplatanus SYCAMORE MAPLE −10°F/−23°C	40 to 70 feet Moderate to fast Broadly rounded	This is another large, dense maple with a showy display of yellow flowers. Five-lobed, dark green leaves reach 5 inches across, are thick and prominently veined, and lack autumn color. 'Atropurpureum' ('Spaethii') has dark leaves with purple undersides. Sycamore maple will thrive in salt-laden seashore winds.
A. rubrum RED MAPLE −30°F/−34°C	50 to 70 feet Fast Upright	Red tints the spring growth buds, flowers, leafstalks, young fruits, and autumn foliage. Glossy leaves are five lobed, to 5 inches across, on a tree oval in profile. Named selections include those with notable autumn color ('Autumn Radiance', 'October Glory', 'Red Sunset', 'Shade King', and 'V. J. Drake') and several with columnar or narrow growth ('Armstrong' and 'Armstrong II', 'Bowhall', 'Columnare', 'Karpick', and 'Scarlet Sentinel').

Name	Growth	Characteristics
A. saccharinum SILVER MAPLE −30°F/−34°C	40 to 100 feet Fast Upright, rounded	The main limbs ascend sharply, but the side branches droop gracefully, forming a somewhat open canopy of five-lobed, 3- to 6-inch leaves. Upper leaf surfaces are light green, undersides silver (like all but the oldest bark); when breezes flutter leaves, silver is always evident. Autumn color is usually yellow. 'Silver Queen' is a more upright-growing, seedless selection; 'Wieri' has dissected leaves. Roots are shallow, aggressive, and will lift pavement; weak wood and narrow branch crotches make trees subject to breakage by wind, storms, snow, and ice. Susceptible to aphids, cottony scale, and chlorosis in alkaline soil.
A. saccharum SUGAR MAPLE −30°F/−34°C	60 to 75 feet Moderate Rounded to oval	Maple syrup comes from this stout-trunked tree with upward-sweeping branches and a dense canopy of three- to five-lobed leaves 3 to 6 inches across. Autumn color is spectacular: yellow, orange, or red. The root system is shallow and greedy. This is not a good city tree (and it is intolerant of road salt), nor is it adapted to the humid heat of the lower South. Named selections include 'Arrowhead' (pyramidal); 'Green Mountain' and 'Legacy' (fast growing, more tolerant of summer heat); and 'Monumentale' and 'Seneca Chief' (narrower and more upright than the species).

AESCULUS
Horsechestnut
Hippocastanaceae

Deciduous: Hardy to −20°F/−29°C
Flowers: White, pink, red; spring
Exposure: Sun
Water: Regular
Growth: Moderate

There's nothing subtle about these horsechestnuts. Their large, bold leaves and gingerlike flower spikes seem to have been plucked straight from the tropics. Both species become large, dense trees that produce a moderate litter of fallen flowers and then large (and slightly toxic) seeds. Roots can be invasive and shallow.

These trees are not culturally demanding, but they do need regular moisture to support their full canopies of foliage. In warm-humid climates, both are susceptible to leaf scorch.

Aesculus hippocastanum **'Baumannii'**

A. carnea, RED HORSECHESTNUT, reaches an ultimate 40- to 50-foot height and 30-foot spread—a round-headed to gumdrop-shaped affair clothed in palmate leaves whose segments may be 10 inches long. Midspring flower spikes (also to 10 inches) bear soft pink to red flowers. 'Briottii' is a bluish red–flowered selection; 'O'Neill' has bright red blossoms.

A. hippocastanum, COMMON HORSECHESTNUT, is similarly dense and bulky but larger— to 60 feet high and 40 feet across. Its spring flower show is all delicacy in pink-tinted white, the blossoms carried in foot-long spikes. 'Baumannii' is a double-flowered selection that bears no seeds.

ALBIZIA JULIBRISSIN
Silk tree
Leguminosae

Deciduous: Hardy to 0°F/−18°C
Flowers: Pink; summer
Exposure: Sun
Water: Regular to moderate
Growth: Fast

To describe a silk tree, the word "feathery" is perfection. Each light green, pinnately compound, 8- to 16-inch-long leaf contains countless tiny leaflets, and the flowers are fluffy powderpuffs of stamens. With training, a single-trunked specimen can be obtained, but the natural form is multitrunked. Either way you get a broad, flat-topped canopy to 40 feet with horizontally layered foliage that

Albizia julibrissin

merely filters the sunlight; you can use it as a lawn or patio tree if you don't mind some litter from fallen flowers, seedpods, and leaves. Because flower clusters dot the top of the canopy, silk tree is attractive to look down upon. Leaves are light sensitive, folding up at night.

Nurseries may offer named selections, most commonly *A. j.* 'Rosea' (also sold as 'Ernest Wilson'), which has darker pink flowers and is a bit hardier—perhaps to −10°F/−23°C. In southern states a wilt disease can be fatal; there, choose the resistant selections 'Charlotte' and 'Tryon'.

Silk trees are easy to grow and revel in summer heat, both dry and humid. Good garden soil and regular water coax the most rapid growth, but trees will adapt to moderate watering and to poor, sandy, or alkaline soils. Trees establish best when planted as small specimens from containers. However, in regions that approach their hardiness limit, either plant a good-size specimen (6 feet tall or more) in spring or carefully protect a smaller tree for the first two winters.

ALNUS
Alder
Betulaceae

Deciduous: Hardiness varies; most need some winter chill
Flowers: Small catkins; winter
Exposure: Sun, light shade
Water: Regular
Growth: Moderate to fast

The different alder species vary in ultimate size, but all are recognizably similar. Like their birch relatives, alders look good in grove plantings and often grow as multitrunked specimens. Autumn foliage color is not remarkable—rusty gold to brown—but the gray-barked winter silhouette is good-looking with tassel-like male catkins and conelike female ones as subtle decoration.

Alders are not particular about soil so long as it is moist. Their roots are shallow and invasive, suggesting their use as background, grove, screening, and stream- or pondside planting.

Alnus rhombifolia

A. cordata, ITALIAN ALDER, is hardy to –10°F/–23°C but will grow where there is no winter cold. This is the smallest (to 40 feet) and neatest appearing of the alders and also the least demanding of damp soil. Its habit is upright, somewhat broader than half its height, with branches that tend toward the horizontal. The dense foliage canopy consists of heart-shaped leaves to 4 inches long, glossy rich green with pale undersides; the leafless period is brief. In the Northwest, leaf miners may be troublesome.

A. glutinosa, BLACK ALDER, is hardy to –30°F/–34°C but will also thrive without winter chill. Sticky new growth and upper leaf surfaces distinguish this species; dark green leaves are 2 to 4 inches long, rounded to pear shaped. Specimens tend to grow several trunks to as high as 70 feet, the dense foliage touching the ground unless you remove lower branches. The selection 'Laciniata' has deeply lobed leaves.

A. rhombifolia, WHITE ALDER, is hardy to –10°F/–23°C. Very rapid growth carries this gray-barked alder up to 90 feet and out about half as wide. Nevertheless, trees appear graceful due to branches that spread out, then droop at the tips. Coarsely toothed oval leaves, to 4½ inches long, are dark green with lighter undersides and appear early in spring. Within its native western states, it may be plagued by tent caterpillars and borers.

AMELANCHIER
Shadblow, Serviceberry
Rosaceae

Deciduous: Hardiness varies; all need a definite period of winter chill
Flowers: White; early spring
Exposure: Sun
Water: Regular to moderate
Growth: Moderate

The shadblows offer the winning combination of four-season beauty, good garden behavior, and easy culture. All species are lightweight, delicate trees, often with multiple trunks. In early spring they put on a show of small flowers, followed in early summer by edible (blueberry-flavored) fruits; glowing autumn foliage color rounds

Amelanchier grandiflora

out the growing season. Then leaf drop reveals an attractive tracery of limbs and twigs throughout winter.

Give shadblows neutral to acid soil. Their noninvasive roots and light shade make them good trees to garden under. Spider mites and fireblight may be occasional problems.

A. canadensis, SHADBLOW OR DOWNY SERVICEBERRY, is hardy to –30°F/–34°C. A profusion of slender-petaled, single white flowers mantles the tree in early spring, giving way to new growth covered with gray down. Mature leaves are dark green, 1- to 2-inch ovals that in autumn turn brilliant yellow, orange, or red. In cultivation this natural 60-footer seldom reaches 30 feet, making a slender specimen, often with several trunks. Small fruits are dark red.

A. grandiflora, APPLE SERVICEBERRY, is hardy to –20°F/–29°C. This hybrid of the other two species described here bears larger flowers than its parents on a smaller tree—to 20 to 25 feet with about equal spread. Following the white blossoms, new leaves emerge bronzy red, turning green at maturity; autumn color ranges from yellow to red. Fruits are purplish black.

A. laevis is hardy to –20°F/–29°C. This 30-foot tree (with equal spread) puts on a spring display of white blossoms in drooping clusters. Then bronzy purple new growth emerges, the small, oval leaves maturing to dark green and finally changing to yellow or red in autumn. Fruits are red. Its hybrid 'Cumulus' has a narrower habit, light green new spring foliage, and brilliant red-orange autumn color.

Bauhinia (see page 92)

BETULA
Birch
Betulaceae

Deciduous: Hardiness varies; most need some winter chill
Flowers: Small catkins
Exposure: Sun, partial shade
Water: Regular
Growth: Fast

Although some birch species may reach 100 feet, these trees are light-weights of the forest, never appearing massive. During the growing season they provide clean green foliage that changes in autumn to a glowing yellow. After leaf drop, the delicate limb structure, handsome bark, and hanging seed tassels provide a winter display. All species feature thin bark that peels in layers.

A steady supply of moisture is the key to success with birches. Roots are competitive and tend to be shallow, even with deep watering. Although birches are at their best where they receive some winter chill, the European white birch (*B. pendula*) is a landscape staple in mild-winter Southern California. If you need to remove limbs, wait until late spring, after leaves have formed; if pruned while dormant, birches will bleed profusely when sap starts to flow.

A few insect pests are widespread. Aphids can be a nuisance anywhere on any birch; in heavy infestations, the honeydew they secrete drips on anything beneath the tree. East of the Sierra Nevada–Cascade ranges—and especially of the Rocky Mountains—the bronze birch borer is a threat to some species. This small grub tunnels into stems, frequently girdling and killing upper limbs; a heavy infestation can kill an entire tree. Plants under stress—in poor soil and lacking sufficient water—will be the first victims. A problem in the northern latitudes is the birch leaf miner, which eats the tissue between leaf surfaces, disfiguring leaves; severe attacks cause leaves to turn brown.

B. jacquemontii is hardy to 0°F/ –18°C. In its best forms it shows the brilliant white bark you'd expect of a birch. Its habit is tall and narrow, with smooth, ovate leaves to 2½ inches long. Youthful rapid growth will carry it to about 40 feet; then the pace slows to reach an ultimate 60 feet.

B. lenta, CHERRY OR SWEET BIRCH, is hardy to –30°F/–34°C. The common names derive from its smooth, lustrous, red-brown bark and the wintergreen flavor of its young branches. Trees grow from a youthful pyramid to a mature rounded canopy—to 75 feet in the wild but generally less in gardens. Oblong, dark green leaves reach 5 inches. This is a good landscape tree in moist soil within its native eastern North America.

B. maximowicziana, MONARCH BIRCH, is hardy to –10°F/–23°C. It boasts the largest birch leaves, heart shaped and up to 6 inches long, which reliably turn golden yellow in autumn even in mild-winter regions. Peeling, flaking, orange-brown bark eventually becomes gray to nearly white on old specimens, which may attain 80 feet. Fast growth produces an open, more stiffly upright tree than other birches. It is resistant to the bronze birch borer.

B. nigra, RIVER OR RED BIRCH, is hardy to –20°F/–29°C. Native to stream banks and lowlands over a vast area of eastern and central North America, this species thrives wherever it receives plenty of moisture. Youthful fast growth guarantees a tree in a hurry; then the pace slows a bit, leading to a pyramidal specimen 50 to 90 feet high and 40 to 60 feet wide. Diamond-shaped leaves to 3 inches long are glossy green with silvery undersides. Young bark is apricot to pinkish white and peels in shaggy strips; on older trees, bark becomes dark silvery gray to black and peels less. This is a better species than *B. pendula* for hot-summer areas, but it is subject to chlorosis in alkaline soil. 'Heritage' has longer-lasting bark color and darker leaves.

B. papyrifera, CANOE OR PAPER BIRCH, is hardy to –40°F/–40°C. Traditionally, the creamy white bark of this birch was used by some Native Americans to cover their dwellings and canoes.

Betula nigra

Multiple trunks and branching close to the ground are common. Height ranges from 50 to 90 feet; width is about half that. The see-through canopy consists of oval, 4-inch leaves. Compared with white-barked *B. pendula*, this is taller, more open and upright, and more resistant to leaf miners and bronze birch borer.

B. pendula (B. alba, B. verrucosa), EUROPEAN WHITE BIRCH, is hardy to –40°F/–40°C; performance is poor in medium and low desert areas and in humid summers of the lower South. Many would say this is the loveliest of all birches. Growth is upright and somewhat pyramidal, the branches angling upward but drooping at their ends to create a slightly weeping effect. Diamond-shaped leaves are glossy green and about 2½ inches long, each with a slender, tapered point. Bark on twigs, branches, and trunks of young trees is golden brown, but the trunk and main limbs later develop white bark marked with black clefts. Eventually, trunks become dark gray. This tree is *the* favorite of the bronze birch borer.

Nurseries offer several selections. Cutleaf weeping birch, *B. p.* 'Dalecarlica' ('Laciniata'), has strongly weeping branches and deeply cut foliage. Young's weeping birch, *B. p.* 'Youngii', has normal foliage on branches that hang straight down. Stake the tree, as it grows, to the height you want; branches then hang from that point. Both weeping forms will sunburn in hot, dry weather.

In contrast, the pyramidal white birch, *B. p.* 'Fastigiata', sends branches upright to form a broadly columnar tree. For striking foliage variation, the purple birch, *B. p.* 'Purpurea', has maroon-purple foliage (fading to purplish green in summer) on nearly black twigs; it performs best in cool-summer, chilly-winter regions.

B. platyphylla japonica, JAPANESE WHITE BIRCH, is hardy to –30°F/–34°C. This is another white-barked birch that will grow in both cold- and warm-winter climates (except for the desert) but that resists incursions by the bronze birch borer. Rather narrow but open growth is fast, to 50 feet. Glossy, 3-inch leaves are shaped like arrowheads, yellowing in autumn.

CALLISTEMON
Bottlebrush
Myrtaceae

Evergreen: Hardy to 20°F/–7°C
Flowers: Red, cream; spring, summer, some throughout the year
Exposure: Sun
Water: Regular, but tolerates drought
Growth: Fast

Callistemon citrinus

When you see the flower spikes, you'll understand *Callistemon*'s common name: flowers consist mostly of long, brushlike stamens tightly circling the stems. Woody seed capsules follow the flowers and remain attached to branches for several years; new growth continues on from the tops of flower clusters. Narrow leaves are linear to lance shaped. These *Callistemon* species are by nature giant shrubs that need some training to become single-trunked trees. All can be planted as high hedges or screens.

Bottlebrushes grow best in well-drained soil; they prefer regular watering, but they'll tolerate drought at some expense to appearance. They'll also grow in alkaline and saline soils, though plants may need treatment for chlorosis.

C. citrinus (C. lanceolatus), LEMON BOTTLEBRUSH, is the species most tolerant of poor soils and temperature extremes. Trained to a single trunk, it becomes narrow and lollipop shaped to about 25 feet; grown with several trunks, the crown is broader and the effect less stiff. Narrow 3-inch leaves are copper colored at first, becoming bright green at maturity. Flaming red "bottlebrushes" in 6-inch-long clusters appear in spring and in bursts throughout the rest of the year. For especially good flower quality, choose the selections 'Improved' or 'Splendens'.

C. salignus, WHITE BOTTLEBRUSH, makes a dense, fairly slender specimen to 25 feet. Narrow, 3-inch, willowlike leaves emerge bright pink to copper and mature to green. Despite its common name, flowers are cream to pale yellow, in 3-inch-long clusters.

CARPINUS
Hornbeam
Betulaceae

Deciduous: Hardiness varies
Flowers: Insignificant
Exposure: Sun, light shade
Water: Regular to moderate
Growth: Moderate

No one will ever exclaim, "Look at that hornbeam!"—but these trees' neat appearance, good garden habits, and moderate size add up to valuable if

Carpinus betulus

undramatic landscape specimens. They're dense and pyramidal to round headed, clothed in oval, sawtooth-edged leaves that color agreeably in autumn. Their fruits (actually small nuts) are carried in attractive, drooping clusters, each nutlet encased in a three-winged leafy structure.

Give hornbeams ordinary garden soil (neutral to acid for *C. caroliniana*) and a climate with some winter chill. They don't thrive in the warm-winter, arid Southwest and Southern California. Scale insects may bother *C. betulus*.

C. betulus, EUROPEAN HORNBEAM, is hardy to –10°F/–23°C. For many years this tree remains a dense pyramid to 40 feet tall; but with age the outline becomes broader, with drooping outer branches. Dark green, oval leaves, to 5 inches long, turn yellow in autumn and remain on trees (as dead leaves) into winter. You can use European hornbeam as an individual specimen, planted in a row for screening, or even as a sheared high hedge. Its selection 'Fastigiata' has many upright branches that form a narrow column in youth but spread to a pyramid at maturity. In contrast, the tall, narrow *C. b.* 'Columnaris' has a single trunk with short branches radiating from it.

C. caroliniana, AMERICAN HORNBEAM, is hardy to –40°F/–40°C. It is also known as blue beech and ironwood in its native southeastern to southcentral

United States, where it often grows at forest edges or even beneath taller trees. Its dome-shaped canopy will reach 30 to 40 feet high and about 20 feet wide, clothed in dark green, oval leaves to 3 inches long; autumn color is red to mottled red and yellow. Multitrunked specimens are fairly common. The trunk bark is smooth and blue-gray, with undulations that have been described as looking like muscles flexing beneath the surface.

CATALPA
Catalpa, Indian bean
Bignoniaceae

Deciduous: Hardy to –20°F/–29°C
Flowers: White with yellow and brownish purple; spring to early summer
Exposure: Sun, light shade
Water: Regular to moderate
Growth: Moderate to fast

The catalpas are among a few select trees (see also *Aesculus*, page 45) that can bring a tropical touch to cold-winter regions. Their large, fuzzy, heart-shaped leaves are the perfect complement to the upright pyramidal clusters of trumpet-shaped, ruffled blossoms in late spring to early summer. After flowers fade, long, beanlike pods develop that mature to brown or black and may remain on the tree after leaf drop. Despite a dense foliage canopy, catalpa's branch structure is actually fairly open and uncomplicated.

Catalpas are especially amenable to climate extremes and will grow in virtually any soil. Young trees tend to

Catalpa speciosa

grow irregularly; you may need to train them to a single trunk and shorten wayward branches for a symmetrical head. Where spring and summer winds are strong, locate a catalpa in the lee of taller trees or buildings to protect the large leaves from damage. In eastern states, the catalpa sphinx moth larva (a caterpillar resembling tomato hornworm) can defoliate trees unless controlled.

C. bignonioides, COMMON CATALPA OR INDIAN BEAN, is native to the southeastern United States and is the smaller of the two North American species. Heart-shaped leaves are 4 to 8 inches long on a tree that reaches 25 to 50 feet high and nearly as wide. Leaves of its selection 'Aurea' are a soft yellow color.

C. erubescens is a hybrid between common catalpa and a Chinese species. In the form 'Purpurea', new stems and leaves are dark purple, becoming dark green by midsummer; some leaves are shallowly lobed. The tree resembles its *C. bignonioides* parent.

C. speciosa, WESTERN CATALPA, hails from the central and southern Midwest. Leaves to a foot long deck a round-topped tree of 40 to 70 feet high with narrower spread.

CEDRUS
Cedar
Pinaceae

Evergreen (conifer): Hardiness varies
Flowers: None
Exposure: Sun
Water: Moderate
Growth: Varies

Needles grouped in tufted clusters distinguish true cedars from the somewhat similar cone-bearing firs *(Abies)* and spruces *(Picea)*. Like firs, though, cedars carry their barrel-shaped cones upright on their branches. Male cedar catkins disperse copious amounts of yellow pollen in late winter or early spring.

These are stately specimen trees, looking best where their branches have space to spread widely without crowding (though for an exceptional use, see *C. deodara,* at right). The cedars tend to

Cedrus deodara

form heavy limbs low on their trunks; in time, these become almost secondary trunks as they arch upward and outward. Soil type or quality is not an issue, though trees do best where they can root deeply. Established specimens tolerate considerable drought.

C. atlantica, ATLAS CEDAR, is hardy to 0°F/–18°C. Young plants are usually open, angular, and straggly—giving little indication of their mature beauty. Horizontal branches tilt upward at their extremities in comparison with the other two species. On young trees these limbs may get too long and heavy unless you pinch tips or cut them back slightly to encourage compactness; limbs can break under a heavy snow load. Needles are under an inch long and bluish green to light green (color varies among seed-raised plants). Named selections include silvery blue 'Glauca' (the blue Atlas cedar) and yellow-tinted 'Aurea'; 'Pendula' is a curiosity whose branches droop vertically.

C. deodara, DEODAR CEDAR, is hardy to about 5°F/–15°C. It has the softest and lightest texture of the three cedars and is readily identified by the graceful droop to its branches and a nodding tip silhouetted against the sky. Even young trees appear fairly dense, due to the combination of semipendulous growth and needles that can reach 2 inches long. Needle color may be green, gray-green, blue-green, or bluish gray; lighter-colored new growth in spring contrasts pleasingly with the older, darker needles. Color, density, and droopiness vary among seed-raised plants.

Rapid growth carries deodar's pyramid shape ever higher to 80 feet or more, with an ultimate ground-level spread of 40 feet; lower branches tend to sweep down to the ground and then curve upward. Named selections include the distinctly blue-gray 'Glauca'; 'Aurea', which has yellow new growth that matures to golden green; and 'Descanso Dwarf' ('Compacta'), which grows slowly (to 20 feet in 15 years).

In contrast to the other two cedars, you can control a deodar's spread and increase density by cutting back the new growth of side branches in late spring by half. This treatment, combined with an annual topping, lets you maintain a line of deodars as a high hedge or screen. Chlorosis may occur in alkaline soils. This is the best cedar for hot, humid climates.

C. libani, CEDAR OF LEBANON, is hardy to 0°F/−18°C. This is the most famous of cedars, mentioned in biblical texts and featured on the Lebanese flag. Slow and rather irregular growth (15 feet in 15 years) eventually produces a picturesque specimen to 80 feet high. Needles under an inch long are bright green on young trees, dark gray-green on old. Youthful individuals are dense and pyramidal, but maturity reveals horizontally spreading branches, an irregularly open canopy, and a flat-topped profile.

CELTIS
Hackberry
Ulmaceae

Deciduous: Hardiness varies
Flowers: Insignificant
Exposure: Sun, light shade
Water: Moderate
Growth: Moderate

The overall aspect of these trees suggests their near relatives, the elms, but in all details the hackberries are smaller. They're also better garden

trees, because of their deep roots: you can grow lawn beneath a hackberry or place one near pavement without fear of roots lifting or cracking it. Oval to lance-shaped leaves form a canopy that casts moderate shade during spring and summer, turning yellow in autumn. Mature trees have picturesque bark with corky warts and ridges. Small, berrylike fruits (usually purple) are relished by birds. An established tree is tough, taking desert heat, strong winds, and dry, alkaline soil.

Because large bare-root specimens sometimes fail to leaf out, plant from containers or install a small bare-root tree with a large root system. In desert and intermountain regions, a leaf gall may disfigure foliage, though it does no harm to the tree. All but common hackberry (*C. occidentalis*) need some winter chill.

C. australis, EUROPEAN HACKBERRY, is hardy to 0°F/−18°C. This Mediterranean native reaches 40 to 70 feet with less spread than its round-topped height. Dark green, lance-shaped leaves are 2 to 5 inches long, with coarsely toothed margins.

C. laevigata, MISSISSIPPI HACKBERRY OR SUGARBERRY, is hardy to −10°F/−23°C. In the wild, this species can reach 100 feet, but garden specimens are usually about half that. The canopy is somewhat open: broad and rounded with semipendulous, spreading branches. The thin, 4-inch oval leaves usually have smooth edges. This species resists the witches' broom affliction that can disfigure *C. occidentalis.*

C. occidentalis, COMMON HACKBERRY, is hardy to −30°F/−34°C. Like the Mississippi hackberry, this tree attains a garden height of about 50 feet—just half of its capability in the wild. In outline it is rounded to a bit irregular, the canopy spreading about as wide as the tree's height. The 4- to 5-inch ovate leaves have smooth to lightly toothed margins.

Throughout its native region (a large area extending from the Rocky Mountains to the Atlantic, north to Quebec and south to Alabama), it may be afflicted by a witches' broom: thick clusters of tiny twigs growing where just one shoot should. Though not life-threatening, the condition is unattrac-

Celtis occidentalis

tive; throughout much of this area, Mississippi hackberry and Chinese hackberry are better garden choices.

C. sinensis, CHINESE HACKBERRY, is hardy to −10°F/−23°C. The general effect is of a smaller common hackberry (*C. occidentalis),* up to 60 feet high, clothed in glossy, scalloped-edged leaves. This Asian species resists the witches' broom condition and differs from the other hackberries in that its mature fruits are orange-red.

CERCIDIPHYLLUM JAPONICUM
Katsura tree
Cercidiphyllaceae

Deciduous: Hardy to −30°F/−34°C
Flowers: Red-purple; early spring
Exposure: Sun, light shade
Water: Regular
Growth: Slow to moderate

Given ample water and shelter from intense sun and wind, a katsura tree will become a landscape focal point: elegantly refined, graceful, and pest

Cercidiphyllum japonicum

Cercidium floridum

free. In early spring, the bare branches cover themselves with a reddish purple haze of tiny flowers. Then the leaves emerge, in an attractive bronze color. When mature, they're nearly round with heart-shaped bases, 2 to 4 inches long, and a rich blue-green color; but throughout the growing season they'll show tints of red. In autumn, foliage changes to brilliant yellow or red.

Young katsura trees grow at a moderate rate but slow the pace when well established. In time, a tree may attain 50 feet with equal spread, always well foliaged but fairly open so that it filters breezes. A single-trunk specimen will remain narrow and upright for many years before spreading out; but if you let several trunks develop, the shape will become broadly spreading with branches angling upward and outward, holding foliage in nearly horizontal layers.

Give katsura tree a good, deep, neutral to slightly acid soil and regular garden watering. For enhanced autumn color, water less frequently starting in late summer.

CERCIDIUM
Palo verde
Leguminosae

Deciduous: Hardy to 10°F/–12°C
Flowers: Yellow; spring
Exposure: Sun
Water: Moderate to little
Growth: Fast

Desert dwellers know the palo verdes as trouble-free, tough-as-nails trees that will give welcome light shade under any condition—from total neglect to ordinary garden care. Shade is cast by the intricate canopy of twigs rather than by the tiny, ephemeral leaves. Clusters of bright yellow, sweet pea–shaped flowers nearly hide the branches in spring. With garden watering and fertilizing, trees are more dense, attractive and rapid growing.

Three species are commonly available. Blue palo verde (*C. floridum*, sometimes sold as *C. torreyanum*) reaches 25 feet high and wide with spiny, blue-green branches. Tiny leaves come in pairs along leafstalks; the leaves are short lived, but the leafstalks remain to contribute additional sun filter.

Littleleaf palo verde (*C. microphyllum*) is similar but with more plentiful leaflets, a yellowish green color, and pale yellow blossoms. It is the more drought tolerant of the two. Sonoran palo verde (*C. praecox*) forms an umbrella-shaped canopy carried aloft by a lime green trunk and branches.

CERCIS
Redbud
Leguminosae

Deciduous: Hardiness varies
Flowers: Pink, red-purple, white; early spring
Exposure: Sun, light shade
Water: Regular to moderate
Growth: Moderate

The redbuds dramatically announce their presence with a lavish preleaf spring display of purplish pink blossoms. The small, sweet pea–shaped flowers literally cover the tree, appearing on twigs, branches, main limbs—even on the trunk. Flattened, beanlike seedpods follow; they're evident during summer and autumn and then are decorative during winter as red-brown pendants. All redbuds feature broad, rounded leaves with distinctive heart-shaped bases; autumn color is yellow.

Give redbuds well-drained soil. The Judas tree, *C. siliquastrum*, is fairly drought tolerant; in dry-summer regions, be sure to give the other species supplemental watering.

C. canadensis, EASTERN REDBUD, is hardy to –20°F/–29°C and needs some winter chill. You can tell this redbud from the others by its leaves: each 3- to 6-inch leaf has a pointed tip. Fairly rapid growth produces a round-headed, slightly irregular tree 25 to 35 feet high; mature specimens tend to carry branches in horizontal tiers. Several named selections are available, including 'Rubye Atkinson', with pure pink blossoms; 'Plena' ('Flame'), with rosebudlike double flowers; and 'Forest Pansy', which has purple foliage borne on reddish branches.

C. reniformis is hardy to 0°F/–18°C and will thrive where there is little or no winter cold. Except for its thicker, glossier leaves—which have rounded to notched tips and grow just 2 to 3 inches across—it is the Southwest native equivalent of eastern redbud. White-flowered 'Alba' ('Texas White') and wine red 'Oklahoma' are sometimes listed as selections of *C. canadensis* (above).

C. siliquastrum, the JUDAS TREE, is hardy to –10°F/–23°C and performs best where there is at least some win-

Cercis canadensis

ter chill. Multiple trunks are its natural inclination, but you can train it to a single trunk. In either case it will reach about 25 feet, bearing purplish pink flowers and 3- to 5-inch leaves with rounded or notched tips.

CHAMAECYPARIS
False cypress
Cupressaceae

Evergreen (conifer): Hardiness varies
Flowers: None
Exposure: Sun
Water: Regular
Growth: Moderate to slow

If you were to glance quickly at the foliage, you might mistake many false cypresses for arborvitae *(Thuja)*; but the former has white lines on its leaf undersides, whereas the latter's are entirely green. Most false cypresses have two distinct types of foliage: juvenile and mature. The juvenile phase—short, needlelike leaves that are soft but often prickly—appears on very young plants, on some new growth of larger trees, and on many of the dwarf selections. Mature foliage consists of tiny, scalelike leaves that overlap one another on thin twigs. Cones are small and round.

Of four commonly available species, two hail from the Pacific Coast of North America and two are native to Japan. The American species perform best in their native regions and in other parts of the world that offer similar cool, humid conditions. The Japanese species, on the other hand, will succeed in humid and warm parts of eastern North America. No false cypress will prosper in windy locales or where summer is hot and dry.

Be sure to plant in well-drained soil to avoid problems with root rot. Some dead foliage toward a tree's interior is commonplace, due to shading by the dense foliage cover; an unusual amount of dead material, though, may indicate spider mite infestation.

C. lawsoniana, Port Orford cedar or Lawson cypress, is hardy to –10°F/–23°C. In the forest, this tree can top 100 feet, but its garden height may be only 60 feet with a spread of one-quarter to one-third its height; it grows at a

Chamaecyparis lawsoniana

moderate rate. These dense, columnar to conelike or pyramidal trees have flat foliage sprays that droop gracefully. Blue-green is the typical color, but seed-raised plants vary greatly.

Among numerous named selections, 'Allumii', the blue Lawson cypress, forms a narrow, slow-growing, 30-foot pyramid of blue to blue-green foliage carried in vertical rather than drooping sprays. For upright, pyramidal growth and yellow new foliage, choose 'Lutea' or 'Stewartii'. 'Lutea' has distinctly stiffer foliage that matures to blue-gray; 'Stewartii' is a broader-based pyramid with drooping foliage sprays that mature to dark green.

Their pyramidal to columnar habit makes Port Orford cedars a good choice for grove or screen planting. These are not good city or highway trees, as foliage is damaged by dust and air pollution.

C. nootkatensis, Nootka cypress or Alaska yellow cedar, is hardy to –10°F/–23°C. Compared with *C. lawsoniana*, this is a slower-growing, smaller tree (to about 80 feet) with coarser-textured blue-green foliage and distinctly pendulous branches. Because it comes from high elevations farther north, it's the better choice for cold, exposed locations; it will prosper in poor (but well-drained) soil.

C. obtusa, Hinoki false cypress, is hardy to –30°F/–34°C. Although its eventual height may be 50 feet or more, growth is so slow that its garden function is chiefly that of an ever-enlarg-

ing, broadly pyramidal shrub. Foliage is glossy dark green on a somewhat irregular, open plant. Compared with *C. pisifera* it's more compact, denser, and will retain lower limbs longer.

C. pisifera, Sawara false cypress, is hardy to –30°F/–34°C. This species is better known for its named selections than for the wild plant, which is a fairly slow-growing, loose pyramid of dark green, 50 to 75 feet high. Leaves are tiny and scalelike, each with a spiny tip. Lower branches die while the tree is fairly young, exposing the trunk and its attractive red-brown, peeling bark.

Several selections grow slowly to become 30-foot-high trees. 'Plumosa', the plume false cypress, forms a bright green, cone-shaped tree with upright branches; 'Plumosa Aurea' features bright yellow new growth that ages to green. Foliage is short, soft needles that create a fluffy appearance. 'Squarrosa', the moss cypress, also looks soft and feathery, but its needles are longer and silvery gray-green. Horizontal branches give a much broader pyramidal outline; older specimens become picturesque as open patches develop. 'Squarrosa Veitchii' has blue-green needles and a filmier garden effect.

CHIONANTHUS
Fringe tree
Oleaceae

Deciduous: Hardiness varies; needs some winter chill
Flowers: White; midspring to early summer
Exposure: Sun, partial shade
Water: Regular to moderate
Growth: Moderate to slow

When most other spring-flowering trees have already blossomed and leafed out, fringe trees suddenly do both almost simultaneously. Individual flowers are unimpressive—about an inch long, composed of four threadlike petals—but the sheer quantity of lacy clusters makes for a first-rate show. Male and female flowers appear on separate trees, the male blossoms slightly larger and more profuse. If trees of both sexes grow in proximity, female trees will produce clusters of dark blue berries. In autumn, leaves turn bright yellow.

Chionanthus retusus

Plant fringe trees in good soil and give them regular garden care. Scale insects and borers may be occasional problems.

C. retusus, CHINESE FRINGE TREE, is hardy to –10°F/–23°C. In all but tree size, this species suggests a smaller version of *C. virginicus*. Smaller flowers in 4-inch clusters decorate the new growth in late spring or early summer. Glossy green, elliptic leaves reach 4 inches long on a small tree that ultimately may be 20 feet tall.

C. virginicus, FRINGE TREE, is hardy to –20°F/–29°C. In its native eastern North America, it can attain 30 feet, but in cultivation it's usually shorter—from 12 to 20 feet high. Flowers and flower clusters are twice the size of *C. retusus*; oblong leaves reach 8 inches.

Cinnamomum camphora
(see page 64)

Citrus (see page 54)

Cladrastis lutea

CLADRASTIS LUTEA
Yellowwood
Leguminosae

Deciduous: Hardy to –30°F/–34°C; needs some winter chill
Flowers: White; late spring
Exposure: Sun
Water: Regular
Growth: Moderate

Even if it lacked a showy flower display, yellowwood still would be a valued garden tree. Its appearance is neat and refined: a smooth, gray trunk supports a canopy of foliage that seems light textured even though each leaf may be up to a foot long and contain seven to eleven oval leaflets. In autumn the bright green foliage changes to an intense yellow before falling. And this tree roots so deeply that you can grow other plants beneath it; ultimate height may reach 35 feet.

In late spring to early summer, yellowwood attracts all eyes with its footlong clusters of fragrant blossoms resembling white wisteria. Flowering is erratic: heavy bloom occurs every 2 or 3 years, but some years may be skipped altogether. Young trees may not even flower until their 10th year.

Yellowwood grows best in good, deep, nonalkaline soil given average garden watering. Established trees, though, are fairly drought tolerant. Young trees may develop narrow, weak branch crotches; correct by pruning while trees are young. Prune in summer or early autumn; if you prune earlier, the cuts will bleed profusely.

CORNUS
Dogwood
Cornaceae

Deciduous: Hardiness varies; all need some winter chill
Flowers: White, pink, near-red; spring
Exposure: Sun, partial shade
Water: Regular
Growth: Varies

Throughout the year, dogwoods are superlatively good-looking trees. In all species, the spring bloom makes a good show: the massive display from *C. florida* equals that of the various *Prunus* species and goes them one better by lasting nearly twice as long. After flowering, trees appear fresh and well groomed throughout spring and summer, then change color before autumn leaf drop. During winter, you can appreciate the considerable beauty of their limb structures.

What appear to be flowers in many dogwoods are petal-like modified leaves called "bracts." These bracts surround the inconspicuous true flowers, which come into their own later in the season when they develop decorative fruits. You can easily recognize dogwood leaves by their vein pattern: secondary veins branch from the midvein out toward the edge, but just before reaching it bend and extend down to the leaf tip.

Give dogwoods well-drained, slightly acid soil; most need regular watering. In the wild, these trees inhabit forest fringes; in the garden, they like the same sort of high shade to moderate the hottest sun. If you plant a dogwood in lawn, be sure to avoid bumping it during mowing: dogwood trunks are easily bruised, leading to infection and borer attack.

C. controversa, GIANT DOGWOOD, is hardy to –10°F/–23°C. Fast growth builds a broadly pyramidal 40- to 60-foot tree composed of layers of horizontally arranged branches. In spring,

(Continued on page 55)

Cornus florida

Citrus

Oranges, lemons, limes, and their varied kin are all good-looking, relatively small or shrubby trees with glossy oval leaves, thorny stems, fragrant white flowers, and conspicuous, edible fruits. Most nursery plants are budded or grafted onto rootstock; many popular sorts are also available grafted onto dwarfing rootstocks that produce smaller trees or large shrubs.

Lack of hardiness (kumquats are the most cold tolerant) limits their landscape use to parts of California and the Southwest, Texas, and the Southeast. In colder-winter regions, grow citrus in containers and take plants indoors or into a greenhouse over winter. Where occasional freeze damage is a possibility, plant citrus where trees will be sheltered from winds and close to south-facing walls.

Because citrus is an important commercial crop, the specific climate needs of the various types are well documented. Your county agricultural agent or farm advisor will be able to recommend the best kinds of citrus—even specific varieties—for your area.

Grapefruit is hardy to about 25°F/ –4°C. Trees reach about 30 feet high. Fruit ripens 1½ years after bloom and needs high heat for best quality.

Kumquat is hardy to about 18°F/ –8°C. Height will vary from about 6 to 25 feet. Small fruits have sweet rind and sour-tart flesh; warm to hot summers are needed for fruit production.

Lemon is hardy to about 25°F/–4°C. Tree size, fruit size, and overall character vary by variety; all bear well in cool-summer regions. 'Lisbon' and 'Villa Franca' grow to about 25 feet; 'Eureka' reaches about 20 feet. 'Improved Meyer' bears sweeter, thin-skinned fruits on a slightly hardier, spreading tree to 15 feet.

Lime trees' hardiness varies. 'Mexican', the standard green lime, is safe only in frost-free regions, a slender and shrubby tree to 15 feet. Yellow-fruited

'Sanguinelli' blood orange

'Bearss' makes a dense, rounded tree to 20 feet and will grow where oranges succeed. 'Rangpur'—with orange skin and flesh—is not a lime; it's more akin to the mandarin oranges. The dense, bushy tree reaches 15 feet.

Mandarin orange (tangerine) is hardy to about 20°F/–7°C. Most varieties ripen in winter on 12- to 20-foot trees. Orange fruits are loose-skinned with sweet, orangelike flavor.

Orange is hardy to about 25°F/–4°C. Trees form dense globes to about 25 feet tall. A host of varieties are available that ripen at various times of year and grow in diverse climates ranging from cool coast to desert. Follow local agricultural advice. Blood oranges 'Moro', 'Sanguinelli', and 'Tarocco' have red flesh.

Sour orange (Seville orange) is hardy to 20°F/–7°C. Dense tree to 30 feet high, 20 feet wide makes a good hedge or tall screen. Clusters of 3-inch bitter fruits are used to make marmalade.

Tangelo is hardy to 25°F/–4°C. Tangelos are hybrids of mandarin oranges and grapefruits—sweet-flavored, but differing in character among the varieties. Trees are smaller, less dense than the grapefruit parent.

Citrus trees need well-drained soil to avoid root rot. If you have slow-draining soil, plant in raised beds or containers. But they also need consistent moisture. To establish new trees, water regularly. Thereafter, water thoroughly about every other week during warm weather: let the top several inches of soil dry out between waterings. With each watering, you should moisten the entire root zone—as deep as 4 feet for mature trees. Flood irrigation and drip irrigation are the best methods. For flood irrigation, make a doughnut-shaped basin with the inner ridge about 6 inches from the tree's trunk to keep trunk dry; build the outer ridge a bit beyond the branch spread. A mulch spread in the basin will keep soil and surface roots cool.

For best performance, citrus trees need nitrogen fertilizer. Start new trees with 2 ounces of actual nitrogen (see page 31) the first year, then increase that amount by 4 ounces each year. Mature trees need 1 to 1½ pounds of actual nitrogen a year in dry-summer regions, 1½ to 2 pounds in summer-rainfall areas. Spread the total yearly amount over three applications: in late winter, June, and August. Scatter it beneath the tree and just beyond the branch spread, then water in deeply.

Aphids, mealybugs, scale, and spider mites can afflict citrus. Slugs and snails can be thwarted by bait or by encircling the trunk with a copper band. Chlorosis (see page 39) can stem from either iron deficiency or excessive water; determine the cause to choose a remedy. Zinc deficiency (yellow blotches between green leaf veins) can be overcome with foliage sprays. Bark of young trees—and of any branches exposed by pruning—is subject to sunburn. Wrap trunks with paper trunk wrap or paint bark with whitewash or cold-water wall paint.

Prune citrus as needed to remove twiggy growth and weak or dead branches. You can leave a tree branched to the ground or train it to a canopy of foliage atop a bare trunk.

Cornus kousa

. . . *Cornus*

before leafing out, branches cover themselves with flat clusters of creamy white, bractless flowers. Each one is small, but clusters can be 7 inches across and so profuse that the tree looks like a floral snowfall. After blossoms finish, the tree clothes itself in broadly oval leaves to 6 inches long, each one dark green with a silvery underside. Birds flock to the late-summer crop of ½-inch blue-black fruits. Autumn foliage is glowing red.

C. florida, FLOWERING DOGWOOD, is hardy to −20°F/−29°C; many named selections are less cold tolerant. This has been called the most beautiful native tree of North America. Spring finds it covered with four-petaled, 4-inch "flowers," each bract having a characteristic notch at its tip. White is the usual color in the wild, but named selections offer pink shades to nearly red. Oval, bright green leaves grow to 6 inches long; they change to flaming red in autumn, coinciding with the ripening of clustered, berrylike, red fruits. The branch pattern is fairly horizontal, with upturned branch tips. Old trees are broadly pyramidal but rather flat-topped. Exceptional trees may reach 40 feet high and wide, but 20 to 30 feet is more common.

As flowering dogwood's native range extends from New England to central Florida, the species varies in climate adaptation over that range.

Ideally, gardeners in the eastern United States should plant trees grown from stock native to their climate.

Throughout the native range, an anthracnose fungus has been infecting and destroying trees. Dieback symptoms show up first in lower branches and can spread to an entire tree. Consult your county agricultural agent for recommended controls in your area. Borers will attack trunks and limbs of drought-stressed trees.

Nurseries offer a number of named selections; consider all but 'Rubra' and 'New Hampshire' hardy only to about −10°F/−23°C. 'Rubra' has pink to rose bracts; 'Cherokee Chief' has rosy red bracts and red new foliage that fades to green. Among white-flowering kinds, 'Cherokee Princess' offers especially profuse flowering. 'Cloud Nine'—a good choice in mild-winter areas—begins flowering as a young specimen and is smaller than the others. 'Fragrant Cloud' has scented flowers; 'Mystery' blooms earlier in the season than do most others. 'New Hampshire', selected from the northern part of the species' range, is the most cold tolerant and retains its flower buds undamaged over winter.

Several selections feature variegated foliage. Among white-flowered kinds, 'Daybreak' has cream-and-green leaves; 'First Lady' offers yellow-and-green shades; 'Rainbow' leaves combine yellow, chartreuse, and green. 'Pink Flame' features pink flowers and leaves that start out cream and light green and then deepen to dark green and red. 'Sunset' has nearly red flowers, with green and yellow leaves. 'Welchii', the tricolor dogwood, features leaves that are creamy white, pink, deep rose, and green; in autumn, they turn a deep rosy red. Its pinkish white flowers are neither conspicuous nor profuse. For a totally different aspect, white-flowered 'Pendula' forms a canopy of stiffly drooping limbs.

Hybrids between flowering dogwood and *C. kousa* flower in late spring after leaf-out. Flower bracts of 'Aurora' (white) and 'Stellar Pink' resemble the *C. florida* parent, whereas 'Constellation' is more *kousa*-like. Trees are slow growing and broadly pyramidal to 20 feet or more; they resist anthracnose.

C. kousa, KOUSA OR JAPANESE DOGWOOD, is hardy to −10°F/−23°C. Without assistance, kousa dogwood may become a bulky, multistemmed shrub. But with early training, it develops into a 20-foot tree with delicate limb structure and a dense, spreading, horizontally branched habit. Flowering (a few weeks later than *C. florida*) occurs after the leaves have emerged, but the display is still showy because the flowers appear above the branches, whereas the leaves hang below them. Bracts are creamy white, to 2 inches long, and sharp tipped. The edible red fruits that follow ripen in autumn, hanging below the branches. Lustrous medium green leaves are 4-inch ovals, coloring red (occasionally yellow) in autumn. The pure-white blooms of 'Milky Way' are especially profuse. This species resists both borers and anthracnose.

C. nuttallii, PACIFIC OR WESTERN DOGWOOD, is hardy to 0°F/−18°C, but only within its native range: from British Columbia to the mountains of Southern California. This is the tallest and most particular dogwood. Single or multiple trunks ascend to 50 feet or more, the branches spreading horizontally only about 20 feet, in a narrow pyramid. Gleaming white bracts appear on bare branches in early to midspring, each "flower" up to 6 inches across and containing four to eight bracts. Often there will be a second flowering during August and September. Oval, rich green leaves grow to 5 inches long; they turn yellow to red in autumn. Fruits in dense, button-like clusters ripen to orange or red starting in late summer.

Nurseries offer two selections and one similar hybrid. 'Colrigo Giant' makes a robust, stocky specimen with an abundance of flowers. 'Goldspot' (its leaves are splashed creamy yellow) has slightly larger flowers, a fuller autumn flower display, and better tolerance of regular garden conditions. 'Eddie's White Wonder' is a hybrid between Pacific dogwood and the eastern *C. florida,* hardy to perhaps −10°F/−23°C. Taller, more upright, and larger-flavored than the eastern species, it bears four- or five-bracted white flowers in May; it's more successful in gardens than its *C. nuttallii* parent.

(Continued on next page)

Pacific dogwood prefers a fairly cool atmosphere and, unlike other species, does not want regular garden watering once established. Locate a specimen out of reach of sprinklers, under high-branched trees or otherwise shaded during the hottest hours. Bark is especially sensitive to sunburn and injury from bruising. Climate adaptation varies a bit: northwestern trees need a cool, moist regime, but trees from California mountains will take warmer, drier conditions. Cool, wet weather fosters anthracnose.

CRATAEGUS
Hawthorn
Rosaceae

Deciduous: Hardiness varies; all need some winter chill
Flowers: White, pink, red; spring
Exposure: Sun
Water: Moderate
Growth: Moderate to fast

Despite differences in details, hawthorns are dense, usually thorny, small trees to about 25 feet with angular branching and a tendency to multiple trunks. Profuse flowering occurs after leaves have formed; single blossoms (most are white) are held in branched, flattened clusters and followed by pendant clusters of small fruits (usually red) that resemble tiny apples. Fruits ripen from summer into autumn; in many cases they remain on the tree after leaf drop. Leaves range from simple to lobed. American species usually color red in autumn, European ones some shade of yellow.

If soil is well drained, hawthorns will grow in good or poor, acid or alkaline soil. In fact, they're better grown on the lean side—good soil, regular water, and fertilizer promote succulent new growth that is most susceptible to their nemesis, fireblight. The rust stage of cedar-apple rust can be a problem in eastern states wherever red cedar (*Juniperus virginiana*) grows nearby. Aphids and scale are widespread potential pests.

Countless hawthorn species are native to the United States. If you find attractive wild hawthorns in your area, they may be good garden subjects.

C. 'Autumn Glory' is hardy to –10°F/ –23°C. This vigorous hybrid is dense and twiggy, to about 25 feet high and 15 feet wide. White flowers produce red fruits that color in early autumn (and last into winter) before the 2-inch, lobed leaves turn yellow to red; fruits last well into winter. It's fairly susceptible to fireblight.

C. crus-galli, COCKSPUR THORN, is hardy to –20°F/–29°C. Density, horizontal branching, and the ever-present thorns make this species a natural hedge candidate. Grown as a tree, it reaches 35 feet with a distinctive flat top that spreads to about 25 feet. Glossy, 3-inch oval leaves turn orange to red-orange in autumn; white spring blossoms form tiny, bright red fruits that remain far into winter. Despite rust problems, this is the most successful hawthorn for Oklahoma and the adjacent Southwest.

C. laevigata (C. oxyacantha), ENGLISH HAWTHORN, is hardy to –20°F/ –29°C. The common wild type has white single flowers (followed by conspicuous red fruits) on a round-headed dense tree to 25 feet high and 15 feet wide. More widely grown, though, are several named selections that offer variations in flower color or form.

All have 2-inch lobed leaves that lack outstanding autumn color. The most widely planted is 'Paul's Scarlet' ('Paulii'), for its eye-catching, double, rosy red blossoms; other double-flowered named selections offer pink or white blossoms. All double-flowered kinds concentrate on blossoms only: fruit production is scant or lacking. 'Crimson Cloud' ('Superba') has single red flowers, each with a star-shaped, white center; it forms glossy red fruits that last well beyond leaf drop.

English hawthorn is poorly adapted to the hot, humid summers of southern states and much of the Midwest. There foliage is subject to leaf spot, which can defoliate trees and shorten their life.

C. lavallei (C. carrierei), LAVALLE OR CARRIERE HAWTHORN, is hardy to –20°F/ –29°C. Compared with other hawthorns, this tree is more erect and open, with a less twiggy framework. White spring flowers form loose clusters of ½-inch or larger fruits that change to flaming orange-red in autumn and remain on branches well into winter. Leathery, dark green, oval leaves to 4 inches long turn bronzy red with frost, remaining past autumn. Ultimate height is about 25 feet with nearly equal spread.

C. mollis, DOWNY HAWTHORN, is hardy to –20°F/–29°C. This is a large, applelike tree to 30 feet high and wide clothed in 4-inch lobed, toothed, down-covered leaves. Its inch-wide white flowers form 1-inch red fruits that ripen in summer while leaves are green; they make a good jelly.

Crataegus laevigata **'Paul's Scarlet'**

C. monogyna, SINGLE-SEED HAWTHORN, is hardy to –20°F/–29°C. This, the familiar hawthorn of English hedgerows, becomes a round-headed tree to 30 feet tall. Its less showy fruits and lack of autumn color in the 2-inch lobed leaves make this species less decorative than the other hawthorns listed here. However, the selection 'Stricta' is useful for its narrow, upright habit to 30 feet high but only 10 feet wide—a good accent specimen or (planted in a row) high, narrow screen.

C. phaenopyrum, WASHINGTON THORN, is hardy to –20°F/–29°C and is not successful in the hot-summer lower Midwest. Wherever it will grow well, it's regarded as one of the choicest hawthorns. The head is less twiggy than many others, forming a more open, graceful structure. Trees reach about 25 feet high by 20 feet wide, clothed in 2- to 3-inch, maplelike lobed leaves that turn orange and red in autumn. Masses of white spring flowers are transformed into clusters of ½-inch fruits that turn brilliant Chinese red in autumn and hang on through winter.

C. 'Toba' is hardy to –30°F/–34°C. This round-headed, 20-foot Canadian hybrid resembles English hawthorn (*C. laevigata*) and is a good stand-in for it in colder climates. Double flowers open white but turn pink as they age; only a few fruits form. The dense, glossy foliage on sparsely thorned branches is disease resistant.

CUPRESSOCYPARIS LEYLANDII
Leyland cypress
Cupressaceae

Evergreen (conifer): Hardy to –10°F/–23°C
Flowers: None
Exposure: Sun
Water: Regular to moderate
Growth: Fast

From a cross of *Chamaecyparis nootkatensis* and *Cupressus macrocarpa,* this tree exhibits true hybrid vigor: plants can reach 20 feet high in just 5 years! From a columnar youth, it becomes narrowly pyramidal to 50 feet or more, the long, slender, upright branches bearing flattened foliage sprays of

Cupressocyparis leylandii

gray-green scales. Where summer is warm to hot, trees become broader and more open. Usually Leyland cypress is planted not as a specimen tree but as a high hedge (sheared or natural) or screen plant; grove plantings are also attractive. Named selections include 'Naylor's Blue', with blue-gray foliage, and 'Castlewellan', which has a particularly narrow form and bright yellow new growth (that fades in heat).

Leyland cypress is not particular about soil and thrives in diverse climates, from hot and dry to cool and moist. It takes strong winds in stride, though trees in rain-soaked soil have been blown over. Where summer is warm to hot as well as dry, trees are very susceptible to coryneum canker fungus; bagworm can be a problem in the East.

CUPRESSUS
Cypress
Cupressaceae

Evergreen (conifer): Hardiness varies
Flowers: None
Exposure: Sun
Water: Moderate
Growth: Fast

These two commonly available cypresses hail from areas where winter is mild and summer is dry and even hot. Their leaves are tiny and scalelike, closely set on cordlike branches; the profusion of branches gives trees their dense appearance. Small, round to oval cones are composed of "plates" (as on a basketball) that separate when ripe.

Cupressus arizonica glabra

C. arizonica, ARIZONA CYPRESS, is hardy to 0°F/–18°C. This species, and its form *C. a. glabra* (smooth Arizona cypress), not only endures but prefers regions where summer is hot and dry. Fast growth will take an individual to 40 feet high and 20 feet wide in a roughly pyramidal shape; more often, though, Arizona cypress is planted in groups or rows as a windbreak or screen. Trees tolerate drought and should receive no more than moderate water. They're shallow rooted and may blow over in saturated soil.

Arizona cypress has rough, furrowed bark, whereas smooth Arizona cypress's bark is smooth and cherry red. Seed-grown plants vary a bit in growth habit and in color: from green to blue-green to gray. Named selections include 'Gareei', with silvery blue-green foliage, and symmetrical, compact 'Pyramidalis'.

C. sempervirens, ITALIAN CYPRESS, is hardy to 0°F/–18°C. You seldom see—or would recognize—this species in its normal form as a horizontally branched, dark green tree. But the form *C. s.* 'Stricta' (*C. s.* 'Fastigiata'), the columnar Italian cypress, is familiar even if just from photographs of Mediterranean gardens and hillsides. This columnar selection nearly defies classification: it's much too tall to be a shrub yet not nearly bulky enough to count as a tree. To some 60 feet high but only a few feet across, it is the landscape's finest exclamation point.

The original form is a somber dark green color, but 'Glauca' has blue-green foliage, and 'Swane's Golden' features golden yellow new growth.

Davidia involucrata

DAVIDIA INVOLUCRATA
Dove tree
Nyssaceae

Deciduous: Hardy to –10°F/–23°C; not suited to the lower South or deserts
Flowers: White; spring
Exposure: Sun
Water: Regular
Growth: Moderate

Another common name — "handkerchief tree"—captures the appearance of the dove tree's floral display. The actual flowers are tiny and grouped in inch-wide spherical clusters, but surrounding each cluster are two white, petal-like bracts (one about 6 inches, the other 4 inches long) that hang like pieces of cloth draped from the branches. Fruits that follow dangle from branches like green golf balls, later turning brown and lasting into winter. The backdrop for these unique blossoms is a spreading, round-headed, 35- to 45-foot tree bearing bright green, heart-shaped leaves that have no autumn color change.

Plant dove trees in good garden soil, located where they'll be sheltered from strong or frequent wind. In mid-Atlantic states and dry-summer areas of Pacific Coast states, give trees partial or afternoon shade.

DIOSPYROS
Persimmon
Ebenaceae

Deciduous: Hardiness varies; needs a bit of winter chill
Flowers: Inconspicuous
Exposure: Sun
Water: Moderate
Growth: Moderate

An edible fruit crop is part of the persimmon's yearly life cycle, but many gardeners plant these trees for their beauty alone. From a neat, tailored spring and summer aspect, through autumn foliage and fruit color to winter branch pattern, persimmon trees are good-looking in all seasons.

Plant persimmon trees in soil that is at least moderately well drained, preferably neutral to slightly acid. Prune only to shape an irregular structure or to thin a crowded interior.

D. kaki, ASIAN OR JAPANESE PERSIMMON, is hardy to 0°F/–18°C. In spring, the young leaves are a fresh light green but mature to dark green, leathery, broad ovals to 7 inches long. In autumn—even where winter is mild—the foliage will change to brilliant yellow, orange, or scarlet. By leaf drop, the apple-size orange fruits are conspicuous, and they remain hanging on bare branches like holiday ornaments for many weeks. Trees can reach 30 to 40 feet high and wide.

Named selections differ in their fruit characteristics. 'Chocolate' ('Maru') is self-fertilizing; the others—'Fuyu', 'Gosho' ('Giant Fuyu'), 'Hachiya', 'Tamopan', and 'Tanehashi'—will produce more (and more flavorful) fruits with another tree nearby as a pollenizer. Trees need warmth (but not excessive heat) for good fruit production. In both cool-summer regions and desert areas within the hardiness range, trees may fail to bear.

D. virginiana, AMERICAN PERSIMMON, is hardy to –10°F/–23°C. Smaller fruits, larger tree sums up the differences between this tree and its Asian counterpart. In the wild, American persimmon can reach 75 feet, though garden size is about the same—30 to 40 feet—as the Asian type's. But its aspect is different: this one has a broadly oval

Diospyros kaki

canopy that spreads just about half as wide as its height. Wide, oval leaves reach 6 inches long and turn yellow, pink, and red in autumn. Yellow to orange fruits on female trees are about the size of large walnuts; for fruit production you'll need a male tree as well for pollination.

ELAEAGNUS ANGUSTIFOLIA
Russian olive
Elaeagnaceae

Deciduous: Hardy to –40°F/–40°C; needs winter chill
Flowers: Yellow; summer
Exposure: Sun
Water: Moderate to little
Growth: Moderate to fast

Drought, poor soil, hot summers, bitterly cold winters—these conditions will vanquish many trees, but not the Russian olive. Yet where winters are mild or summers either cool or especially humid, it falters. This is a good-looking tree with plenty of character.

Elaeagnus angustifolia

The single or multiple trunks are usually angular and covered with dark brown, shredding bark; branches may be thorny. Narrow, willowlike 2-inch leaves are a contrasting silvery gray. Small greenish yellow flowers fall far short of showy but offer fragrance in compensation; these are followed by yellow fruits that resemble miniature olives.

Easiest to cultivate in a large area extending eastward from the Sierra Nevada–Cascade ranges to the central Midwest, Russian olive needs only relatively well-drained soil. Though it makes an attractive small specimen tree to 35 feet, it also serves well as a windbreak or barrier planting—even as a clipped hedge. Some nurseries may offer thornless selections.

Erythrina (see page 92)

EUCALYPTUS
(see chart on pages 60–61)
Eucalyptus, Gum tree
Myrtaceae

Evergreen: Hardiness varies
Flowers: White, cream, yellow, pink, red, orange; season varies
Exposure: Sun
Water: Generally, moderate to little
Growth: Fast

In parts of California and Arizona, eucalyptus trees are such a familiar part of the landscape—both in gardens and as escapees into the wild—that it's hard to believe all species have been introduced from Australia, beginning in 1856. Much of their native Australian territory has a desert, Mediterranean (dry summer and mild, wet winter), or subtropical climate that is reproduced in Arizona, California, and Hawaii. A few species will endure enough cold to succeed in the Northwest.

The many eucalyptus species are such a varied lot that few recognizably common features can be isolated. Growth habits range from modest-size shrubby and almost vinelike plants to trees that are towering skyscrapers; leaf shape and flower form show equally wide variation. Yet there is a certain character that makes a euca-

Eucalyptus niphophila

lypt easy to recognize once you've seen a number of different types. Regardless of size, shape, or color, look for these three features: leaves that are crisp, leathery, and often aromatic; fluffy flowers composed of prominent stamens surrounding the edge of a cup- or chalicelike structure; and woody, rather flat-topped seed capsules. Most eucalyptus trees have two distinct leaf types: juvenile and mature. The juvenile leaves—found on seedlings, some vigorous young trees, and new branches that sprout from cut trunks and limbs—are softer, often broader, and bluer than the mature or "adult" foliage described in the chart for each species.

Rapid growth is usual, though unlike most fast-growing trees, eucalypts usually live to a ripe old age. But because of their fast growth, you need to select and plant these trees carefully. You want to buy the smallest healthy plant you can find so that it won't be rootbound in the container. Look for gallon-container (or smaller) plants; sometimes nurseries display flats of small seedling plants. Avoid buying large plants and specimens with many leafless twigs or that evidence severe pruning; these are likely to have spent so much time in containers that their roots are thoroughly tangled and contorted, needing the special handling described as follows.

If you must plant a rootbound specimen, wash all soil from the roots and spread them out as straight and evenly as you can in a premoistened hole. Set the plant so that the trunk's old soil line will be ½ to 1 inch below

the final soil level. Fill in moist soil around the fanned-out roots; then water thoroughly.

Chlorosis may affect some species growing in alkaline soil; soil treatment with iron chelates should remedy the condition. Until recently, eucalypts were totally pest free. But now the eucalyptus longhorn beetle is established in California, inflicting damage and death—especially on drought-stressed trees. Signs of infestation are oval holes in trunks and branches; limbs or entire trees die with their leaves attached. At present, management is our only weapon. Beetles are attracted to freshly cut wood, so avoid pruning from May to October and thoroughly seal any cuts made then, to prevent sap flow. If you have infested wood—as firewood or felled dead trees—bury it or cover it tightly with a tarpaulin for 6 months.

FAGUS
Beech
Fagaceae

Deciduous: Hardiness varies; best with some winter chill; not for hot, dry regions
Flowers: Insignificant
Exposure: Sun
Water: Moderate
Growth: Slow to moderate

The majestic, imposing beeches bring elegant grandeur to the larger landscape. Smooth gray bark covers a sturdy trunk that supports horizontally layered branches clothed in glossy, dark leaves. Autumn foliage is rusty yellow to ruddy brown and clings to the branches into winter. The inconspicuous flowers produce bristly burrs containing two or three edible nuts enjoyed by birds. Trees can reach 90 feet high, taller than wide, in outline a broad, round-topped pyramid. Their lowest branches will sweep the ground unless you remove them.

Beeches thrive in average to good soil but will show leafburn and stunted growth with insufficient water and where there are salts in the soil or water. Mature beeches' dense shade and mass of shallow roots rule out planting anything (including lawn) beneath them.

(Continued on page 61)

Eucalyptus

Name	Growth	Characteristics
E. calophylla 25°F/–4°C	50 feet Moderate Rounded	Flower show is a major feature here. Foot-long clusters of white, pink, or red blossoms appear on and off throughout the year. For guaranteed colors, 'Hawkeyi' is rose pink, 'Rosea' light pink. Dark green leaves with pale undersides are broadly oval, to 7 inches long; rough, fissured, corky bark distinguishes it from similar *E. ficifolia*. This species is drought tolerant.
E. citriodora LEMON-SCENTED GUM 25°F/–4°C	75 to 100 feet Fast Upright	Tall but far from massive, this eucalypt is suitable for average-size properties. Its powdery white to pinkish trunk is usually bare for one-half to two-thirds of its height but is then crowned by feathery billows of narrow, golden green 7-inch leaves. Roots are deep, so won't lift pavement or outcompete nearby plants; it will tolerate regular to little water. This is a fine tree for planting in groves. Young trees are weak trunked and need staking until they gain strength.
E. cornuta YATE 22°F/–6°C	35 to 60 feet Fast Rounded, spreading	The dense, spreading canopy is composed of shiny, lance-shaped leaves to 6 inches long. Three-inch clusters of greenish yellow flowers bloom in summer. It's a good shade tree, growing under a variety of conditions: regular or little water, alkaline soil, and diverse climates. Takes wind without limb breakage.
E. ficifolia RED-FLOWERING GUM 25°F/–4°C	40 feet Moderate Rounded	Where adapted, this is a choice flowering tree. Foot-long clusters of flowers appear throughout the year, especially in midsummer. Red shades are common, but orange, salmon, and pink shades—even cream—are possible. Woody, chalice-shaped seed capsules follow flowers. Handsome, dark green foliage (like a rubber plant's) is glossy, broadly oval to 7 inches long. Bark varies from red and stringy to gray and fibrous. Does best in a coastal climate.
E. gunnii CIDER GUM 5°F/–15°C	40 to 75 feet Fast Upright	This vigorous, dense eucalypt makes a good windbreak or screening tree. Trunks covered in smooth green and tan bark support a canopy of 3- to 5-inch lance-shaped leaves. Small, creamy white flowers appear throughout spring.
E. leucoxylon WHITE IRONBARK 15°F/–9°C	20 to 80 feet Fast Upright	An upright, open structure of pendulous branches makes this a particularly graceful eucalypt. Gray-green leaves are sickle shaped, to 6 inches long, and attractive against the mottled white, tan, and yellowish trunk. White flowers appear from winter into spring; 'Rosea' has pink blossoms. Grows well in heavy to light soils, heat, and wind; good planted in groves.
E. mannifera maculosa RED-SPOTTED GUM 20°F/–7°C	20 to 50 feet Fast Upright	Tall, slender growth supports gracefully drooping branches that sway in the wind. Narrow, 6-inch leaves are light gray-green; flowers are not showy. Bark on young trees is brown and gray; on mature trees, it flakes off in summer to show a powdery white surface beneath.
E. melliodora 20°F/–7°C	30 to 100 feet Fast Upright	A dense canopy with slightly weeping branches casts good shade and provides a good windbreak. Grayish green leaves are sickle shaped, to 6 inches long. White flowers in late winter are not showy but have a sweet, honey scent, attracting bees; 'Rosea' is a pink-flowered form.
E. microtheca COOLIBAH 5°F/–15°C	40 feet Moderate Rounded	Tolerating drought and wind, this is one of the best eucalypts for the low desert. One or several smooth-barked trunks support a bushy canopy of 8-inch, ribbonlike, blue-green leaves. Small, nearly white flowers are insignificant.
E. nicholii NICHOL'S WILLOW-LEAFED PEPPERMINT 15°F/–9°C	40 feet Fast Spreading	A billowing canopy of weeping branches displays very narrow, light green juvenile leaves to 5 inches long and coarser, gray-green mature foliage; when crushed, the leaves smell of peppermint. The upright trunk is covered in deeply furrowed, red-brown bark. Nearly white summer flowers are inconspicuous. It becomes chlorotic if kept too moist.
E. niphophila SNOW GUM 0°F/–18°C	20 feet Slow Spreading	A picturesque "character" tree, snow gum is a study in silver and white. Smooth white, peeling bark clothes a usually angular trunk supporting an open canopy of silver-blue, lance-shaped leaves to 4 inches long. Flowers are creamy white; seed capsules are gray. Tolerates drought and wind.
E. pauciflora GHOST GUM 10°F/–12°C	40 feet Moderate Spreading	A ghostly whiteness accounts for its common name: trunk and branches are entirely white, complemented by narrow, 6-inch gray-green leaves. Flowers are insignificant. Height and width are about equal, and growth is so open you can see through the foliage canopy. This tree grows well in nearly all soils, tolerating drought as well as heavy, wet soil and growing well in lawns.
E. polyanthemos SILVER DOLLAR GUM 15°F/–9°C	20 to 60 feet Fast Upright	Its nearly round, 2- to 3-inch gray juvenile leaves are the "silver dollars": mature foliage is lance shaped. Seedling trees vary: select for roundest, grayest leaves. Creamy white flowers come in spring and summer but are not a showy feature. Grow tree as a single- or multitrunked specimen; it is widely adapted but does poorly in damp soil.

Name	Growth	Characteristics
E. pulchella WHITE PEPPERMINT 20°F/–7°C	20 to 50 feet Moderate to fast Irregular, upright to rounded	A willowy grace characterizes this eucalypt. Weeping branches carry a dense canopy of long, very narrow, dark green, drooping leaves that make a telling contrast with the light tan trunk's peeling bark. Small, creamy white flowers appear in summer and early autumn. Tolerates drought and poor soil.
E. sideroxylon RED IRONBARK, PINK IRONBARK 15°F/–9°C	20 to 80 feet Fast Variable	Great variability among seedling plants suggests selecting a tree larger than usual, so you can choose characteristics you want. Height varies, and habit may be slender or squat, upright or weeping, open or dense. Flowers are light pink to nearly red (but occasionally white) and showy, in pendulous clusters from autumn to late spring. A strongly furrowed, blackish brown trunk contrasts with slim, blue-green leaves that become bronzed in winter. Adapts to a wide range of climates but becomes chlorotic in wet, heavy soil. Specimens that grow upright are handsome planted in groves.

. . . Fagus

F. grandifolia, AMERICAN BEECH, is hardy to –30°F/–34°C. This is just as worthy a tree as the more common European beech, but it is less used because it is slower to establish and lacks the assortment of fancy-leafed selections. Slow to moderate growth produces a narrower specimen than its European counterpart, and its lighter gray bark shows irregular, dark, horizontal bands. Prominently veined leaves are pointed ovals to 5 inches long with distinctly serrated edges.

F. sylvatica, EUROPEAN BEECH, is hardy to –20°F/–29°C. A thicker trunk (with darker gray bark) and greater branch spread distinguish this species from American beech. Too, its glossy dark leaves are about an inch shorter and lack the serrated margins. An assortment of named selections differ in leaf color or shape and in growth habit.

'Atropunicea' (also sold as 'Riversii' and 'Purpurea') retains deep red to purple leaf color throughout the leafy period. Plants labeled 'Cuprea' may be selected forms of 'Atropunicea', having lighter, bronzier new foliage. The purple leaves of 'Rohanii' are lobed in oaklike fashion. 'Spaethii' ('Spaethiana') has the darkest black-purple foliage of all and retains the color until autumn. The weeping copper beech, 'Purpurea Pendula', offers purple leaves on a much smaller tree with strongly weeping branches. When purple and copper beeches are raised from seed, there is some color variation among seedlings; usually such unnamed seedlings become bronzy green in summer.

'Zlatia', the golden beech, has yellow new growth that matures to yel-

Fagus sylvatica **'Tricolor'**

lowish green; because leaves are subject to sunburn, it needs a cool climate. Another sun-sensitive selection is 'Tricolor', the tricolor beech: this slow-growing, fairly small tree (to 40 feet) has green leaves variegated with white and edged in pink. Green-leafed selections with variant leaf shapes include 'Asplenifolia', with narrow, deeply lobed leaves, and 'Laciniata' (cutleaf beech), with broader but deeply cut foliage. 'Fastigiata', the Dawyck beech, is a narrowly upright tree that broadens a bit with age. 'Dawyck Purple' and 'Dawyck Gold' are foliage variants. The weeping beech, 'Pendula', has long branches that sweep to the ground in an irregular, spreading form; unless you stake the trunk to gain height, the tree will become broader than tall.

Ficus (see page 92)

FRAXINUS
Ash
Oleaceae

Deciduous, evergreen: Hardiness varies
Flowers: Inconspicuous
Exposure: Sun
Water: Moderate
Growth: Fast

Undemanding, tough, fast-growing—ashes are understandably widely planted. They're first-rate shade producers, and many grow particularly well where climate extremes limit tree choices. Most ashes have oval, pointed leaflets growing opposite one another along a leafstalk, with a single leaflet at the end. The foliage of most colors well in autumn.

Most ash species bear male and female flowers on separate trees. Whenever both sexes are close enough for pollination, you'll get a crop of winged fruits (each containing a single seed) that can be a litter problem initially and a weeding problem the next year, when ash seedlings germinate in quantity. This nuisance can be avoided by planting a male tree; named male selections are available for most of the species.

The ashes are not particular about soil. In general, they'll even grow well with poor drainage and in the alkaline soils of the arid Southwest. Most will tolerate summer heat. In interior California, ashes are susceptible to an array of major pests (anthracnose, ash whitefly, lilac borer, mistletoe).

(Continued on next page)

F. americana, WHITE ASH, is hardy to −30°F/−34°C. A broadly oval form and a height of 80 feet or more make this a fine shade tree for larger properties. Leaves grow 8 to 15 inches long, their five to nine leaflets dark green with paler undersides; leaf margins will burn in hot, windy regions. Autumn color is purplish yellow, the purple tone increasing in colder climates.

Male and female flowers are on separate trees. You take your chances when buying seedling trees, but several named selections are seedless males: 'Autumn Applause' and 'Autumn Purple' both have purple to wine red autumn foliage. 'Champaign County' has a dense canopy of glossy leaves that turn purple in autumn. 'Rosehill' offers bronzy red autumn color on a narrower, more pyramidal tree; 'Skyline' has similar autumn color on an upright, narrowly oval tree.

F. excelsior, EUROPEAN ASH, is hardy to −30°F/−34°C. This ash suffers in comparison with white ash only in its lack of autumn color and borer susceptibility; otherwise, European ash is a round-headed tree of similarly majestic height. Leaves to a foot long contain seven to eleven dark green leaflets with toothed margins and pale undersides. 'Kimberly' is a seedless male selection. 'Pendula', the weeping European ash, forms a stiffly drooping, irregular umbrella with ground-sweeping branches.

F. 'Fan West', hardy to −10°F/−23°C, is a seedless hybrid between *F. pennsylvanica* and *F. velutina* 'Modesto'. This is a 40-foot, oval-shaped tree with light green leaves that is particularly good where winds and desert heat are limiting factors.

F. holotricha 'Moraine' is hardy to −10°F/−23°C. This nearly seedless selection of the species is considerably smaller than most ashes, growing upright and rather narrowly to 35 or 40 feet. Each leaf consists of nine to thirteen dull green, 3-inch toothed leaflets that turn bright yellow in autumn; fallen leaves dry and disintegrate.

F. ornus, FLOWERING ASH, is hardy to −10°F/−23°C. In this species, the ordinarily insignificant flowers are transformed by their petals into a showy

Fraxinus velutina coriacea

display. In midspring the small, fragrant, greenish white blossoms appear in 3- to 5-inch branched clusters, highlighted against the dense canopy of glossy, bright green leaves. But this floral beauty has a price: nondecorative seed clusters remain on the tree into the following winter. In autumn, the 10-inch leaves (composed of seven to eleven leaflets) become soft yellow and lavender before falling. The tree may reach a round-headed 50 by 30 feet. Borers may be a problem in the East.

F. oxycarpa 'Raywood' is hardy to −10°F/−23°C. Smaller size and finer-textured foliage give this ash an air of refinement. This round-headed tree reaches 25 to 35 feet; each leaf contains seven to nine lance-shaped leaflets to 2½ inches long. Autumn color is purplish red.

F. pennsylvanica, RED ASH, is hardy to −40°F/−40°C. It and its subspecies *F. p. lanceolata* (green ash) differ in only minor details. Both become dense, compact, oval-shaped trees about 60 feet tall and 30 feet wide. Leaves are up to 12 inches long, composed of five to nine narrow, bright green, 4- to 6-inch leaflets; autumn color is usually bright yellow.

To avoid heavy seed crops, choose one of the seedless selections: 'Bergeson', 'Emerald', 'Newport', and 'Summit' all have an oval profile, 'Patmore' a more rounded canopy. All turn yellow in autumn. 'Marshall' (yellow in autumn) and 'Urbanite' (bronze) are pyramidal. 'Wandell', with red-bronze autumn color, forms a narrowly pyramidal tree.

F. uhdei, EVERGREEN, SHAMEL, OR MEXICAN ASH, is hardy to about 20°F/−7°C. Sharp frosts will cause partial to total leaf drop; in milder climates the tree remains evergreen. Fast growth produces a fairly narrow and upright youthful specimen; the shape becomes more rounded and spreading as the tree matures, to a height of around 70 feet. Leaves are divided into five to nine glossy, dark green, 4-inch leaflets. 'Majestic Beauty' is more reliably evergreen than the species and bears much larger leaves. 'Sexton' also has larger leaves on a compact, rounded tree. 'Tomlinson' grows at a moderate rate into a more upright and dense specimen.

Evergreen ashes are shallow rooted, but you can correct for this somewhat by watering deeply. Foliage will burn in hot winds, but otherwise this ash performs well in the low desert. In the West, this ash has fewer pest problems than the other species.

F. velutina, VELVET ASH, and *F. v. glabra,* ARIZONA ASH, are hardy to 0°F/−18°C. A gray fuzz covering young twigs and leaves distinguishes the former from the latter. Otherwise, they are identical trees: pyramidal in youth, becoming more rounded and open as they reach a mature height of 40 to 50 feet. Leaves consist of three to five narrowly oval leaflets to 3 inches long; in autumn they become bright yellow. These are useful shade trees for arid regions where summers are long, hot, and dry and soil is alkaline.

The Montebello ash, *F. v. coriacea,* is native to Southern California and has broader and more leathery leaflets. Its best-known selection is 'Modesto'—the Modesto ash—which makes a rounded, spreading tree to 50 feet. Though a lovely and useful tree, anthracnose fungus may attack foliage following a wet spring, causing a scorched appearance. Roots are vulnerable to verticillium wilt and, in the desert, to ash decline syndrome (a little-understood disease). Because branches tend to form narrow, V-shaped crotches, these trees break more readily in winds than do other ashes. The selection 'Rio Grande'—the Fan-Tex ash—thrives in the heat and alkaline soils of the desert Southwest; its foliage is resistant to windburn.

Ginkgo biloba

GINKGO BILOBA
Ginkgo, Maidenhair tree
Ginkgoaceae

Deciduous: Hardy to –20°F/–29°C
Flowers: None
Exposure: Sun
Water: Regular to moderate
Growth: Moderate

If trees could talk, this one would tell tales of dinosaurs. Along with just one other tree (*Metasequoia glyptostroboides*), it originated in the Jurassic period and survived—just barely—into modern times in China. Ancient fossils clearly show the same unique leaf of today's tree. Each one is shaped like an open paper fan on a stick, looking just like the "leaflets" of maidenhair fern (or, as one Chinese account claimed, like a duck's foot). Each leathery leaf is wavy margined and shallowly to deeply cleft at the midpoint, ranging in width from 1 to 4 inches. During spring and summer, the foliage canopy is a fresh light green, but in autumn, leaves suddenly turn a pure, dazzling yellow, remain for a while on the tree, and then fall—virtually all at once.

A ginkgo's growth habit—unless you plant one of the named selections—is irregular and unpredictable; at maturity, the tree may be upright and fairly narrow, rounded, spreading, or even umbrella shaped. Young trees may go through an awkward period of asymmetrical growth, but as a tree matures its outline becomes more regular. In general, a ginkgo will grow upright 60 to 80 feet but no more than half to two-thirds as wide.

Male and female reproductive parts are borne on separate trees, and when trees of both sexes grow in the same vicinity the females produce quantities of ½-inch, plum-shaped, yellowish fruits that enclose an edible nut. Unfortunately, when fruits drop and their fleshy coating bursts, they emit a powerful, repulsive odor. Therefore, it's best to plant a guaranteed male tree such as one of the named selections. (Seedling trees are a gamble, as they may not reach reproductive age for over two decades.) Named male selections include 'Autumn Gold', eventually a broad and spreading tree; 'Fairmount', a fast-growing, broadly pyramidal tree with a particularly straight trunk; and 'Lakeview' and 'Princeton Sentry', both of which become fairly narrow, conical specimens.

The adaptable ginkgo thrives in a variety of climates and soils, asking only good drainage. Growth rate varies according to culture: with casual care, it will be slow. But given regular watering and fertilizer, a tree may put on as many as 3 feet in a year. To encourage self-sufficiency, water a young tree during dry periods until it reaches about 20 feet; after that, it should get by on casual watering at most. Stake young trees to encourage a straight trunk; in hot-summer regions, protect the bark of young trees from sunburn.

GLEDITSIA TRIACANTHOS INERMIS
Thornless honey locust
Leguminosae

Deciduous: Hardy to –20°F/–29°C; needs some winter chill
Flowers: Insignificant
Exposure: Sun
Water: Moderate
Growth: Fast

The virtues of the native honey locust for garden use were long outweighed by its formidable array of thorns on both trunk and branches and by its annual litter of seedpods. With the advent of this thornless form and its numerous named fruitless selections, gardeners can now take advantage of

Gleditsia triacanthos inermis

the locust's outstanding qualities. Honey locusts grow quickly, tolerate both acid and alkaline soils, and endure some drought once established. They're not bothered by hot summers or cold winters, performing better where seasonal differences are sharp.

Each fernlike, twice-pinnate leaf of up to 10 inches long consists of opposite pairs of small oval leaflets. Leaves appear in late spring, cast filtered shade (allowing growth of lawn or other plants beneath), turn yellow and drop early in autumn, and then dry and disintegrate. The trees' chief liabilities are several pests, especially prevalent in humid-summer regions east of the Mississippi but also in interior California. Mimosa webworm chews leaves, and pod gall midge deforms foliage; both pests can cause partial defoliation. Honey locust borer may attack limbs and trunks, especially of trees under stress. Roots of mature specimens can lift and crack pavement.

Named selections offer specific characteristics; seedling trees are unpredictable. 'Moraine', the Moraine locust, is the original selection, featuring upward- and outward-angled branches that form a vase-shaped, somewhat spreading tree to 50 feet high. 'Majestic' is even taller—to 60 feet—whereas 'Imperial' reaches only about 35 feet, with a dense canopy of dark green leaves. Both 'Shademaster' and 'Skyline' grow to 45 feet, but the former has a vase-shaped profile and foliage that remains longer in autumn; the latter forms a compact, dark green,

(Continued on page 66)

Good Trees with Bad Habits

The nonexistent "perfect tree" would never need water, fertilizer, pest control, or pruning—and it would never drop anything you'd need to rake up. Some widely sold trees, however, fall so far short of perfection that you should seriously consider the impact of their drawbacks.

CINNAMOMUM camphora. CAMPHOR TREE. *Lauraceae.* Evergreen; hardy to 20°F/–7°C. Camphor tree gives you year-round beauty. The heavy, dark-barked trunk and sturdy structure of oaklike, spreading limbs support a canopy of glossy, light green, pointed-oval leaves; showy new spring foliage is pink to red or bronze.

But among camphor's drawbacks are its ultimate 50-foot height and greater spread. The root system is shallow and competitive; it can raise and crack paved surfaces. Old leaves drop in spring; they demand removal because they resist decomposition (when dry, they feel almost artificial). A litter of flowers, fruits, and twigs comes later. Trees are susceptible to verticillium wilt, especially if soil is poorly drained.

Platanus

LIGUSTRUM lucidum. GLOSSY PRIVET. *Oleaceae.* Evergreen; hardy to 10°F/ –12°C. Handsome foliage, showy flowers and fruits, moderate size, ease of culture: this accurately encapsulates glossy privet's good points. Lustrous, dark green, 4- to 6-inch oval leaves clothe a dome-shaped to round-headed tree of one or several trunks. A lavish froth of small white flowers in clusters produces a display of blue-black, pea-size fruits.

This beauty, however, masks liabilities. Some people find the flower odor disagreeable; many are allergic to the blossoms. The gargantuan fruit crop stains whatever it falls upon; birds feast on the fruits and distribute seeds widely—which then germinate and create a weed problem. The root system is shallow and on the greedy side.

PLATANUS. PLANE TREE, SYCAMORE. *Platanaceae.* Deciduous; hardiness varies. Many people who count plane trees among their favorites have seen them mainly in parks and along avenues. And that's where these trees belong: where their structure and majesty have ample elbow room—and where someone else does the litter cleanup. All feature heavy trunks and sculptural branch pattern, and most have unusually handsome bark that sheds in patches to disclose pale to white inner bark. Big leaves (up to 10 inches) are rough surfaced and lobed like maples'; their yellowish to brown autumn color rules them out of the showy category. Inconspicuous flowers produce ball-shaped seed clusters that hang on threadlike stalks and are decorative when branches are bare.

Size is the chief problem for home garden planting; all range from 80 to over 100 feet. Foliage and young stems (particularly of *P. racemosa*) are susceptible to the anthracnose fungus (see page 38), which causes leaf drop and twig dieback.

London plane tree, *P. acerifolia*, is hardy to –20°F/–29°C. This is a stan-

dard street and park tree in cities, where it rises above the indignities of smog, soot, dust, automobile exhaust, and reflected heat from pavement and buildings. It can reach 80 feet high by 40 feet wide. The London plane's parent, *P. occidentalis* (American sycamore), is also hardy to –20°F/–29°C. In contrast, this tree has greater size (to 120 feet in the wild), whiter bark, and no tolerance of urban conditions. California sycamore, *P. racemosa*, is hardy to 0°F/–18°C. This species is likely to assume an irregular shape, with a leaning trunk or multiple trunks. Its height ranges from 50 to 100 feet; its spread depends on the tree's shape.

POPULUS. POPLAR, COTTONWOOD, ASPEN. *Salicaceae.* Deciduous; hardiness varies; needs winter chill. All *Populus* species are fast-growing, tough trees especially suited to rural areas and the fringes of large properties, where these qualities are virtues. Poplars and cottonwoods are almost signature trees in semiarid plains regions and westward into desert and intermountain territory. But planted in the smaller garden, their network of aggressive surface roots vanquishes other plants, raises pavement, and—because roots seek out water—clogs sewer and drainage lines. Most poplars will sucker profusely if their roots are cut or disturbed.

Several poplars are beautiful or distinctive enough to be widely sold despite their liabilities; all have considerable autumn color value. White poplar, *P. alba*, is hardy to –30°F/ –34°C. Lobed leaves flutter in the slightest breeze, showing off the contrast between their dark green upper surface and white underside. Mature trees can reach 60 to 80 feet high and wide; 'Pyramidalis', the Bolleana poplar, forms a narrow column. Lombardy poplar, *P. nigra* 'Italica', is hardy to –30°F/–34°C. This is the best-known columnar poplar, a 40- to 100-foot exclamation point in the landscape. In cold-winter, dry climates it may be fairly trouble free. In other regions it can be attacked by a canker disease that will soon kill it; best use in these areas is as a quick, temporary screen.

Quaking aspen, *P. tremuloides*, is hardy to –40°F/–40°C. Native to mountains and northern latitudes, this species needs winter cold and cool to mild summers. Leaves flutter with any provocation and turn brilliant yellow in autumn. Trunks and limbs are a smooth, light gray-green to nearly white. Height ranges from 20 to 60 feet, but the tree always seems lightweight. This species often grows with several trunks or in a clump, the trunks arising from a single root system.

SALIX. WILLOW. *Salicaceae*. Deciduous; hardiness varies. Wherever there's water, you're likely to find willows. In farm country and on semiarid plains, these trees line the courses of streams and rivers. But, like their poplar and cottonwood relatives, willows are not high-quality trees. Their wood is brittle and breaks easily. All have shallow, invasive roots that will foul nearby water pipes and septic tanks; and because of roots and continual leaf drop, gardening beneath them is difficult. Further, most are subject to a variety of foliage, twig, and branch pests.

The most popular willows are the various weeping kinds, all with strongly pendulous branches and narrow leaves. These are best planted as specimens near lakes or streams; all need to be staked and trained to form canopies high enough to walk beneath. Golden weeping willow, *S. alba* 'Tristis', is hardy to –40°F/–40°C. A mature tree may be 70 feet high with a greater spread; a special feature is the golden yellow of its year-old twigs. Weeping willow, *S. babylonica*, is hardy to 0°F/–18°C. This is the most famous—and most pendulous—of these weeping sorts; it's also the smallest tree (30 to 50 feet high, with greater

spread). Wisconsin weeping willow, *S. blanda*, is hardy to –20°F/–29°C. This hybrid of *S. babylonica* is less strongly weeping, grows a bit larger, and has distinctly bluish green leaves. The selection 'Fan' is resistant to borers and blight. The Thurlow weeping willow, *S. elegantissima*, is another *S. babylonica* hybrid, as hardy as Wisconsin weeping willow but with longer, more decidedly weeping branches.

SCHINUS molle. CALIFORNIA PEPPER TREE. *Anacardiaceae*. Evergreen; hardy to 15°F/–9°C. The California pepper tree (which is actually from Peru) offers a beguiling fusion of beauty and character. Trunk and branches are heavy, gnarled, and knobby, early giving the impression of great age. Supported by this rugged structure is a cascade of fine-textured, light green foliage in the style of a weeping willow. Pendant clusters of rose-colored berries make a good autumn and winter show. Trees will grow in virtually any (even poorly drained) soil and will tolerate drought once established; where hardy, they thrive in deserts.

Consider, however, the following negative points. Greedy surface roots preclude growth of all but lawn beneath (and that will take some effort). They'll raise and crack nearby pavement, seeking out and penetrating water and sewer lines. Root rots, especially Texas root rot, can be fatal where present. Falling leaves and berries make for considerable litter. Infestations of aphids and scale may require treatment. Finally, some people are allergic to the flowers' pollen. Best use is in noncultivated garden areas where nothing will be expected to grow underneath. Stake young trees to establish an upright trunk.

ULMUS. ELM. *Ulmaceae*. Deciduous; hardiness varies. The near-legendary American elm once graced the lawns and streets of countless "hometown America" communities, its distinctive

vase shape creating vaults of foliage over tree-lined streets and offering a large and graceful silhouette off on its own. Unfortunately, a phloem necrosis virus and the Dutch elm disease (spread by a bark beetle) have stalked the American elm throughout North America, making it a risky choice anywhere. And as all elms are more or less susceptible to Dutch elm disease, planting them is especially worrisome wherever the disease has occurred.

Aside from diseases, elms have other problems. Their root systems are shallow and aggressive. Various pests—leaf beetles, bark beetles, leafhoppers, aphids, and scale—find elms desirable. Branch crotches are often narrow, splitting easily in storms or even from the weight of foliage. Some produce quantities of seed, which germinates to become a weed problem.

One elm can be valuable in mildwinter and desert regions of the West. Chinese elm (Chinese evergreen elm), *U. parvifolia*, is hardy to about 10°F/–12°C. Often sold as *U. p.* 'Sempervirens', it may be evergreen in mild winters but lose leaves briefly during cold periods. Long, arching, semipendulous branches can give you a tree 40 to 60 feet high with a spread of 70 feet. Growth is extremely fast: up to 30 feet in 5 years. Older trees have handsome, sycamorelike bark that sheds in patches to produce a mottled effect.

Glossy, oval, toothed leaves to 2½ inches in length color well in autumn: yellow in mildest areas, reddish orange where cold is more intense. The selection 'Brea' has larger leaves on a tree of more upright habit; 'Drake' has small foliage and weeping branches; the rounded canopy of 'True Green' is more reliably evergreen.

Stake all young trees to gain height and lend trunk strength to support the canopy; head back overly long branches to strengthen and balance it. For an elm, this species is remarkably free of pests and diseases, but Texas root rot can be a problem in the desert.

pyramidal tree. For a broadly pyramidal outline (to 45 feet) and light green leaves, choose 'Trueshade'.

'Halka' forms a sturdy trunk early, which supports a rounded head to 40 feet with horizontal branches; unlike other selections, it can bear a heavy crop of seedpods. 'Rubylace' has distinctive, deep red new growth that fades to a bronzed green by midsummer; this 40-foot tree is slower growing than other selections and more subject to wind damage. Bright yellow new foliage is the hallmark of 40-foot 'Sunburst'. Its leaves gradually turn green, but new growth is produced into midsummer for a long period of gold-on-green contrast. Fast temperature changes or drought can cause foliage drop, and strong winds will break its limbs. This is the most susceptible to foliage pests.

HALESIA
Silver bell
Styracaceae

Deciduous: Hardy to –20°F/–29°C; best with some winter chill
Flowers: White; spring
Exposure: Sun, partial shade
Water: Regular
Growth: Moderate

These two elegant North American natives make attractive features at edges of woodland gardens where larger trees can provide a backdrop and some shelter. Size is the chief difference between the two species. The silver bells

prosper in settings with azaleas and rhododendrons: give them good, organically enriched, acid soil and mulch to keep soil cool; then water regularly.

H. carolina, CAROLINA SILVER BELL, can become a 25- to 35-foot, arching tree with a spread perhaps as wide. Just as leaves emerge, clusters of ½-inch, bell-shaped white flowers appear, hanging along the length of branches. Then, after flowers fade, attractive four-winged pods form and remain on the tree into winter. Leaves are 4-inch ovals that yellow in autumn. By nature, Carolina silver bell is somewhat shrubby. Prune to one stem for a single-trunked tree or select several to develop a multitrunked specimen.

H. monticola, MOUNTAIN SILVER BELL, is nearly twice the size of its Carolina kin. It can reach 60 feet, bearing leaves to 6 inches long and 1-inch flower bells that resemble clusters of cherry blossoms. The form *H. m. rosea* offers barely pink blossoms that fade to white.

Jacaranda (see page 93)

KOELREUTERIA
Sapindaceae

Deciduous: Hardiness varies
Flowers: Yellow; summer
Exposure: Sun
Water: Moderate
Growth: Slow to moderate

Appearing on neat, graceful trees, large, upright clusters of small, yellow

Koelreuteria paniculata

summer flowers precede an equally showy crop of seed capsules that resemble Chinese paper lanterns. Root systems are deep and noninvasive.

K. bipinnata (K. integrifoliola), CHINESE FLAME TREE, is hardy to 20°F/–7°C. The 2-inch, papery seed capsules of orange, red, or salmon light up the tree with "flames" during late summer and autumn. Branch structure is upright and spreading, eventually to about 40 feet high; old trees may be flat topped. Individual leaves are 1 to 2 feet long, but each is pinnately divided into many 3-inch oval leaflets that turn yellow in late autumn. This species grows in a wide range of soils and needs only moderate watering.

K. paniculata, GOLDENRAIN TREE, is hardy to –20°F/–29°C. As if to compensate for its lack of autumn color, goldenrain's new spring foliage emerges salmon red. Leaves may reach 15 inches long but are pinnately divided into 3-inch oval leaflets, either toothed or lobed. The showiest period comes in early to midsummer, when the 15- to 25-foot tree billows with large blossom clusters. The lanternlike fruits that follow are red when young but mature to buff and brown shades and last well into autumn. Goldenrain tree is not particular about soil and will perform well even in hot, windy regions. Give young trees regular watering; established specimens tolerate considerable drought.

Halesia carolina

LABURNUM WATERERI 'VOSSII'
Goldenchain tree
Leguminosae

Deciduous: Hardy to –20°F/–29°C; best with some winter chill
Flowers: Yellow; spring
Exposure: Sun
Water: Regular
Growth: Moderate

For an accurate image of this tree, visualize a tree wisteria hung with brilliant yellow blossoms. Its midspring flowering occurs after leaves have emerged, but foliage in no way detracts from the spectacle: flowers may reach nearly 2 feet long. When trained to a single trunk, the outline will be vase shaped to about 25 feet high and half as wide; if you let several trunks develop, the vase will be broader. Leaves are bright green, resembling clover with their three leaflets; there is no autumn color change.

Give goldenchain tree reasonably good, well-drained soil and place it where it will be sheltered from strong winds. It performs best in the Northeast region and Pacific Coast states; trees will grow poorly or fail in the lower Midwest and lower South.

Despite its considerable grace and beauty, goldenchain has some debits that demand consideration. For one thing, all parts of the plant are poisonous. The breathtaking floral display is followed by brown, beanlike pods that remain into winter unless removed—and removal is wise, because a heavy seed crop drains the tree's strength. Finally, staking a tree is prudent, even for older specimens: the root systems don't always provide adequate anchorage.

Laburnum watereri 'Vossii'

LAGERSTROEMIA INDICA
Crape myrtle
Lythraceae

Deciduous: Hardy to 0°F/–18°C
Flowers: Purple, red, pink, lavender, white; summer
Exposure: Sun
Water: Moderate
Growth: Moderate

Here is one of the glories of summer, its showy to absolutely gaudy flowers demanding attention. Individual crinkle-petaled blossoms are only about 1½ inches across; the display comes from the dense, foot-long flower clusters carried at branch tips plus smaller clusters that form lower on stems. But flowers aren't crape myrtle's only asset. In autumn, the 1- to 2-inch oval leaves turn yellow, orange, or glowing red—the colors more pronounced when trees are kept on the dry side in late summer. At all times of year, and especially in winter, you can appreciate the beauty of the smooth gray bark that flakes off to reveal patches of pinkish inner bark. Trained to a single trunk, crape myrtle becomes a rather vase-shaped tree with a rounded top; multitrunked specimens will develop a broader canopy. In climates approaching its hardiness limit, growth will be slower and may be shrubby—particularly if plants are periodically damaged by freezes.

Nurseries in crape myrtle country offer selections in the full spectrum of available colors. Sometimes they will be labeled just by color, but more often you'll find named individuals. Among the latter, 'Peppermint Lace' is unique in having pink flower petals edged in white. Because mildew can be a problem in some regions, breeders have developed resistant specimens. The Indian Tribes group was the first of these; 'Catawba' (purple), 'Cherokee' (red), 'Potomac' (pink), 'Pawhatan' (lavender), and 'Seminole' (pink) are examples. Several other Indian names pertain to highly mildew-resistant hybrids between *L. indica* and a Japanese species. These include 'Choctaw' (bright pink), 'Muskogee' (lavender), 'Natchez' (white), 'Tonto' (purple), and 'Tuscarora' (warm pink).

Lagerstroemia indica

The "Petite" series—and plants sold as crape myrtlettes—are shrubs.

Crape myrtles aren't particular about soil, though where it is alkaline or high in salts you may need to treat plants periodically for chlorosis or marginal leafburn. The best watering practice is to give trees infrequent, deep watering. Best flower production comes where summer is warm to hot. With little to just moderate heat—especially combined with atmospheric moisture—mildew will plague all but the most resistant selections. To encourage greater flower production, cut back branches lightly during the dormant season.

LARIX
Larch
Pinaceae

Deciduous (conifer): Hardiness varies; needs winter chill
Flowers: None
Exposure: Sun, partial shade
Water: Regular
Growth: Moderate to fast

The larches belong to that select group of cone-bearing trees that lose their foliage in autumn. Soft needles grow in clusters on all but vigorous new shoots, where they appear singly. Cones resemble small, partially open roses and persist on the trees during winter, creating a polka-dot pattern among the bare branches. Larches have much the same pyramidal shape as the other needle-leafed evergreens, but their drooping branchlets give them a particularly graceful aspect.

These softly symmetrical trees are mostly high-altitude and/or high-

Larix laricina

latitude natives, growing well where summers are cool and winters cool to cold. They are not fussy about soil but do prefer regular moisture—even lawn watering. Woolly larch aphids may be a problem in the Northeast.

L. decidua, EUROPEAN LARCH, is hardy to –40°F/–40°C. Its fresh, grassy green foliage is the lightest of the larches. Moderate to fast growth builds a 30- to 60-foot tree; young specimens are pyramidal, but older ones develop wide-spreading branches. The selection 'Pendula' features branches that arch out and down, the branchlets hanging almost vertically.

L. kaempferi (**L. leptolepis**), JAPANESE LARCH, is hardy to –20°F/–29°C. Fast growth produces a bluish green, wide-spreading tree 60 or more feet high. The reddish young branches add a subtle touch of color in winter. This species also has a selection 'Pendula', with long, weeping branches. This is the one larch that will perform satisfactorily in milder regions of the Pacific and Atlantic states, though not in hot-and-arid or hot-and-humid areas.

L. laricina, TAMARACK OR AMERICAN LARCH, is hardy to –40°F/–40°C. Where it is native—in the northern states and throughout much of Canada—this open, feathery tree will grow well even in boggy soil. The inch-long needles are bright green. Maximum height will be 50 to 60 feet; the pyramidal outline consists of ascending upper branches, horizontal middle limbs, and lower branches that angle downward.

L. occidentalis, WESTERN LARCH, is hardy to –20°F/–29°C. This larch is native to the mountains of the Pacific Northwest and eastward into the Rockies. Within its native area, it is a satisfactory garden tree, reaching about 50 feet despite its much greater height in the wild. In outline this tree

forms a much narrower pyramid than the other larches, with an open habit and short, stiff, bright green needles.

Ligustrum lucidum
(*see page 64*)

LIQUIDAMBAR STYRACIFLUA
American sweet gum, Liquidambar
Hamamelidaceae

Deciduous: Hardy to –10°F/–23°C
Flowers: Insignificant
Exposure: Sun
Water: Regular
Growth: Moderate to fast

At first glance, you might mistake this tree for a maple: it has five-lobed leaves like those of many maples, which in autumn also turn brilliant shades of red, orange, or yellow. But quite unmaplelike are a few details. Young twigs and branches have prominent, almost winglike, corky ridges. And the seed vessels are 1½-inch hanging spheres covered with spikes, like tiny medieval maces. Trees are pyramidal to conical, to 60 feet tall, maintaining a fairly narrow outline with a tall, straight trunk for many years. Only in maturity do trees become more round-topped and fill out, the branches thickening and becoming more pronounced. American sweet gum is also a natural to plant in informal groves.

Autumn foliage color varies in seedling trees (the ones most frequently offered in nurseries), but named selections guarantee specific

autumnal shades. 'Burgundy' becomes deep purple-red, its leaves hanging on into winter. 'Festival', a nearly columnar tree, turns shades of yellow, pink, and orange. 'Palo Alto' exhibits flaming maple tints of orange and red. (All three selections are a bit less cold tolerant than the average seedling tree.) Other selections are 'Aurora' (yellow, orange, red, and purple) and 'Kia' (orange to red and purple). 'Moonbeam' has yellow-tinted leaves during the growing season; leaves of 'Worplesdon' have particularly long, narrow lobes. 'Rotundiloba' has rounded leaf lobes, and the tree produces no seeds.

Give American sweet gum good garden soil, from slightly acid to barely alkaline. In strongly alkaline soil, the inevitable chlorosis will be hard to correct. The most rapid growth comes with deep watering during dry periods: every 3 to 4 weeks in clay soils, about twice a month in sandy soils. Roots are fairly shallow, competing with other garden plants and able to lift or crack nearby pavement. Shallow watering—as for a lawn—exacerbates the tendency.

LIRIODENDRON TULIPIFERA
Tulip tree
Magnoliaceae

Deciduous: Hardy to –20°F/–29°C
Flowers: Green-and-orange; late spring
Exposure: Sun
Water: Regular
Growth: Moderate to fast

Liquidambar styraciflua

Liriodendron tulipifera

For the large garden, this magnolia relative will become a good shade-maker as well as conversation piece. Its leaves are unique. Variously described as lyre shaped, saddle shaped, and truncated, they're like blunt-tipped maple leaves missing the end lobe. The blossoms—appearing on trees 10 years or older—do resemble 2-inch green-and-orange tulips. But because they bloom among the leaves and above eye level, they're not really showy. A straight trunk carries a pyramid-shaped foliage canopy about half as wide as the tree's 60- to 90-foot height. From a bright yellow-green, the leaves turn buttery yellow in autumn, even in mild-winter regions. Nurseries may carry two slower-growing selections that are smaller than the species. 'Arnold' ('Fastigiata') has a rigidly columnar habit; 'Majestic Beauty' ('Aureo-marginatum') has yellow-edged leaves.

Tulip trees realize their potential in deep, rich, moist soils that are slightly acid to neutral. Give them plenty of water during dry periods. Like magnolias, their wide-spreading network of shallow, fleshy roots is easily damaged by digging and compaction.

MAGNOLIA
Magnolia
Magnoliaceae

Deciduous, evergreen: Hardiness varies
Flowers: White, pink, purple; spring, summer
Exposure: Sun, partial shade
Water: Regular
Growth: Slow to moderate

The delicate beauty of magnolia blossoms is perhaps the most elegant offering to spring that any flowering tree provides. Thick, waxy petals and a pleasant fragrance are typical in blossoms of most species. Seed structures that follow bloom are elongated and cylindrical, shaped something like cucumbers and studded with orange-red seeds when ripe.

The best soil for magnolias is fairly rich, well drained, and neutral to slightly acid; if appropriate, add generous amounts of organic matter when you plant (see page 25). You can grow

Magnolia soulangiana

most magnolias where soil is somewhat alkaline, but plants may develop chlorosis. Where salts are present in the soil, you can leach them from the root zone as long as drainage is good.

The shallow, fleshy roots are easily damaged by digging and by soil compaction from repeated foot traffic. Best locations for a magnolia are in a lawn (leaving a generous grass-free area around the trunk) or in a shrub border that won't be dug. At least in the early years, keep a cooling mulch over the root area. Stake any newly planted tree large enough to offer much wind resistance; otherwise, its movement in wind will tear the fleshy roots. Prune as little as possible, preferably just after flowers fade. In hot-summer regions, be wary of removing lower limbs of young trees: their trunks are susceptible to sunburn.

Specialty nurseries in the South and West may offer a tantalizing assortment of Asian species, their named selections, and hybrids. The following magnolias are more common in the general nursery trade.

Deciduous magnolias

The deciduous species fall into two groups: those that flower early on bare branches and those that flower later, when trees are in full leaf. Where late frosts are a possibility, the early-flowering species may experience flower damage, especially if they're grown in sheltered locations that encourage early bloom. Except for *M. soulangiana*, none of the deciduous kinds will succeed in the desert.

M. acuminata, CUCUMBER TREE, is hardy to −20°F/−29°C. In a departure from the general rule, showy blossoms aren't this magnolia's forte. The greenish yellow, 3-inch, tulip-shaped flowers get a bit lost in the full foliage of late spring. Handsome leaves are pointed ovals, 5 to 11 inches long and to 6 inches across, casting dense shade; in autumn they turn pale yellow. Growth is fast: mature trees reach 60 to 80 feet tall and about 30 feet wide, becoming round headed with age. The yellow cucumber tree, *M. a. cordata* (*M. cordata*), is hardy to −10°F/−23°C. For garden purposes, consider this a half-size (including the foliage) version of cucumber tree. Because its flowers are more yellow and appear just as leaves expand, they show up better.

M. denudata (*M. conspicua, M. heptapeta*), YULAN MAGNOLIA, is hardy to −10°F/−23°C. Its fragrant, creamy white, cup-shaped blossoms to 7 inches across decorate bare branches in early spring. This tree grows moderately to become a 40-foot specimen of rounded to irregular habit; flowering begins after about 7 years. Medium green, oval leaves, downy on their undersides, reach 7 inches long.

M. kobus, KOBUS MAGNOLIA, is hardy to −10°F/−23°C. This small, fairly upright tree reaches about 30 by 20 feet. Lightly fragrant, 4-inch white flowers precede the leaves. Its hybrid, 'Wada's Memory', is a choice, faster-growing tree with slightly larger flowers and coppery red new growth. It flowers as a young plant, whereas the basic species must be about 15 years old.

(Continued on next page)

M. macrophylla, BIGLEAF MAGNOLIA, is hardy to –10°F/–23°C. This native of the southeastern United States looks like a migrant from the tropics. The leaves can reach an amazing 1 to 3 feet in length and 1 foot across. Equally impressive are its blossoms: 12 inches (or more) across, creamy white, appearing as leaves mature in late spring or early summer. The tree grows slowly to an eventual 50 by 30 feet, flowering when 12 to 15 years old. For a 25-foot version with only slightly smaller blossoms, look for *M. m. ashei*; it starts to flower while still a youngster. Locate these trees where they'll be sheltered from wind that would tatter their magnificent leaves.

M. salicifolia, ANISE MAGNOLIA, is hardy to –10°F/–23°C. Graceful, slender, upright to pyramidal growth builds fairly slowly to an eventual 30 feet. Narrow-petaled white flowers to 4 inches across appear before the leaves do; the smooth, 3- to 6-inch, lance-shaped leaves smell of anise when crushed. Named selections include 'Kochanakee' and 'W. B. Clarke'—both of which have larger-than-usual flowers—and the heavily blooming 'Miss Jack'.

M. soulangiana, SAUCER MAGNOLIA, is hardy to –10°F/–23°C. Impressive, goblet-shaped blossoms to 6 inches across decorate saucer magnolia's bare branches in a lavish early spring burst of color. After flowering, the tree is clothed through spring and summer in somewhat coarse-surfaced, 4- to 6-inch obovate leaves that turn brown before dropping in autumn. Winter showcases the patterns formed by the gray trunk and branches.

This is a hybrid (between *M. liliiflora* and *M. denudata*), so you can choose from a range of flower colors from white through pink to purplish red; nurseries offer numerous excellent named selections that guarantee specific colors. Late frosts can damage buds and blossoms; if this is likely, plant a late-flowering selection such as 'Lennei' or 'Alexandrina'.

Raising a saucer magnolia requires patience and advance planning. For many years, it will function as a fairly open, multistemmed shrub as it gradually increases in size to an ultimate

Magnolia grandiflora

height and spread of about 25 feet. Locate it where you can use a shrub now, a tree later. This is the one deciduous magnolia that may succeed in desert gardens if special attention is paid soil, water, and shelter from sun and wind.

Evergreen magnolias

Two natives of the southern states are the magnolias that evoke images of moonlight, plantations, and Spanish moss. Both flower from summer into autumn.

M. grandiflora, SOUTHERN MAGNOLIA OR BULL BAY, is hardy to 0°F/–18°C (but read on for exceptions). Few trees can touch southern magnolia for year-round beauty. The great, white flowers with their heady fragrance have a long season, after which you are left with a statuesque tree covered in unusually handsome, lacquered-looking leaves. Each blossom, about 10 inches across, contains up to a dozen boat-shaped, waxy white petals; conelike 4-inch fruits may follow. Slow to moderate growth builds a statuesque tree to a possible 80 feet high and half as wide; the canopy casts dense shade from broadly oval, thick, and leathery leaves up to 8 inches long.

Most trees have some amount of attractive, rust-colored down on leaf undersides and young twigs; the amount varies on seed-raised plants. Seedling trees may take 10 or more years to flower; those with the most down on leaves and twigs are likely to

bloom sooner. Nurseries offer a number of named selections—grafted plants that will flower after only 2 to 4 years—most of which offer smaller size or greater hardiness than the average tree. Hardiest is 'Edith Bogue', which will take temperatures to –20°F/–29°C, followed by 'Pioneer' and the Canadian selection 'Victoria', both of which are hardy to –10°F/–23°C. 'Little Gem', 'San Marino', and 'St. Mary' are large shrubs unless trimmed and trained to become small trees. 'Majestic Beauty', 'Samuel Sommer' (a fairly fast grower), and 'Timeless Beauty' feature especially large leaves. 'Russet' is a narrow tree with narrow foliage.

Where hardiness is questionable, you may succeed with southern magnolia if you plant against a south-facing wall and grow it as an espalier. In the desert, give it shelter from wind and be sure to water regularly.

Southern magnolia's undeniable beauty comes at a price, however. Surface roots will lift and crack nearby pavement, and surface roots plus dense shade eventually defeat any lawn planted underneath. Maintenance is another consideration. Leaves with the texture and seemingly the durability of plastic drop throughout the year; and from late spring into autumn you have additional litter from fallen petals and seed "cones."

M. virginiana, SWEET BAY, is hardy to –10°F/–23°C. In all respects, this is smaller than its southern magnolia relative. Grayish green leaves with white undersides reach about 5 inches long, and its creamy white, globe-shaped, fragrant flowers are only about 3 inches across. Specimens tend to carry foliage and branches to the ground, behaving as giant shrubs unless pruned to tree form. The ultimate height is 50 feet with a 20-foot spread, forming a dense, often multitrunked specimen.

Another common name for this species is "swamp bay," reflecting its ability to grow in continually moist soils as well as in average, well-drained garden soil. Where frosts are light or absent, these trees will retain foliage throughout the year. But at the colder end of the hardiness range, they will lose some or all of their leaves in winter.

MALUS
(see chart on page 72)
Crabapple
Rosaceae

Deciduous: Hardiness varies; all need some winter chill
Flowers: White, pink, red; spring
Exposure: Sun
Water: Regular to moderate
Growth: Rates and sizes vary

The line that separates crabapples from apples is drawn according to size: apples are simply larger fruits (over 2 inches in diameter) on larger trees. The ornamental crabapples—those not raised for edible fruits—derive their chief landscape value from the masses of spring flowers that usually emerge before the leaves. Flowers may be single, semidouble, or double, from 1 to 2 inches across. The double-flowered kinds seldom produce fruits, but most others form small red, orange, or yellow fruits (tiny apples) that ripen from midsummer into autumn and (in some types) can be decorative later in the season, after leaves are shed. Birds are fond of the small-fruited types. Few crabapples have noteworthy autumn foliage color.

Because most crabapples are small- to medium-size trees (averaging about 25 feet high and wide), they serve well as lawn specimens, as foreground trees in mixed borders, as high screens planted closely in rows, and as row trees lining a drive. Their roots are sufficiently deep, and their shade dappled enough, to grow spring-flow-

Malus floribunda

Malus 'Dolgo'

ering bulbs and semishade summer plants beneath them.

Although crabapples prefer good, well-drained, deep soil, they'll grow in soils that range from acid to slightly alkaline and in rocky or gravelly soils; their tolerance of wet soil is exceeded only by that of pears. Trees adapt to a variety of climates, but they're not at their best in the low desert or in the humid lower South.

Crabapples may be bothered by aphids, Japanese beetles, spider mites, or tent caterpillars—but these pests are minor compared with the potential disease problems: apple scab, fireblight, cedar-apple rust, and powdery mildew. Apple scab attacks foliage and developing fruits: on leaves it shows up as brown or black spots, on fruits as corky spots. Severe infestations can defoliate a tree during summer. Fireblight (see page 38) causes

dieback that can disfigure or, if unchecked, eventually kill a tree. The rust stage of cedar-apple rust can affect leaves of American species and their hybrids (defoliating trees, in heavy attacks) if eastern red cedar (*Juniperus virginiana*) grows near enough for wind-borne spores to reach the crabapple trees. Powdery mildew isn't life threatening, but it is unattractive and somewhat debilitating.

Resistance to disease varies among the species and hybrids; unfortunately, many of the widely sold crabapples are susceptible to one or more. Among them are 'Aldenhamensis', 'Almey', 'Eleyi', 'Hopa', 'Kelsey', 'Oekonomierat Echtermeyer', 'Radiant', 'Red Silver', and 'Vanguard'. The crabapples described on the next page are disease resistant or disease tolerant, and most bear small fruits that attract birds but create minimal litter if they fall.

(Continued on next page)

Malus

Name	Growth	Characteristics
M. 'Adams' −30°F/−34°C	20 feet Moderate Rounded	Deepest pink (virtually red) flowers put on the first show; then leaves emerge red and mature to red-tinted green. Later, ⅝-inch red fruits complete the picture. This tree grows about as wide as its height.
M. atrosanguinea CARMINE CRABAPPLE −20°F/−29°C	18 feet Moderate Upright, irregular	The masses of 1-inch, deep pink to crimson blossoms are followed by red-blushed yellow fruits that age to brown (remaining into winter) but which are not especially ornamental. Leaves are dark green and fairly glossy. Growth is open, with upright branches that droop at the tips.
M. 'Beverly' −30°F/−34°C	20 feet Moderate Spreading	A good show of pink flowers is followed by bright red, ⅝-inch, long-lasting fruits. Light green leaves densely cover a round-headed tree that spreads as wide as high.
M. 'David' −30°F/−34°C	15 feet Moderate Rounded	Palest pink blossoms fade to white, giving an overall white effect. The dense, compact, small tree bears glossy, light green foliage; red ⅜-inch fruits persist after leaf drop.
M. 'Dolgo' −30°F/−34°C	40 feet Moderate Rounded	This is both the largest tree, with spread equal to height, and the only one that bears useful, edible fruits. White blossoms appear in early spring, later forming red fruits to 1¼ inches in diameter that ripen in August and are good for jelly making. Good crops may appear in alternate years. The tree is vigorous, rather open in growth, and may need some pruning of willowy limbs to establish a good framework. Dense foliage is resistant to scab.
M. 'Donald Wyman' −30°F/−34°C	25 feet Moderate Rounded	Pure white blossoms produce a showy crop of ⅜-inch red fruits that last well after leaves fall. Young trees grow fairly upright but become more rounded and spreading as they mature.
M. 'Dorothea' −20°F/−29°C	25 feet Moderate Rounded	Bright pink 2-inch blossoms are semidouble to double, yet still produce a good crop of ½-inch bright yellow fruits. The dense tree grows about equally high and wide.
M. floribunda JAPANESE FLOWERING CRABAPPLE −20°F/−29°C	20 feet Moderate Spreading	Rosy red buds open to pink flowers that fade to white, making each tree a multicolored spectacle; yellow to reddish ⅜-inch fruits ripen in late summer to autumn, are a favorite bird food. This tree grows broader than high and is generally dense, with irregularly angled branches.
M. 'Indian Summer' −30°F/−34°C	20 feet Moderate Rounded	A lavish display of dark rose blossoms is followed in late summer by a good show of red fruits to ¾ inch across. Branches grow in a spreading vase shape, producing a broadly rounded canopy.
M. 'Liset' −30°F/−34°C	15 feet Moderate Rounded, spreading	Here's a color-coordinated crabapple: rose pink blossoms produce maroon ½-inch fruits on a tree with purple foliage. Branch spread is about equal to tree height.
M. 'Ormiston Roy' −30°F/−34°C	20 feet Moderate Rounded, spreading	From pink buds come 1½-inch white blossoms that cover the broadly rounded network of branches. Small (⅜-inch) fruits are colored like 'Royal Ann' cherries: yellow blushed with pink to red.
M. 'Prairie Fire' −30°F/−34°C	20 feet Moderate Rounded, upright	Shades of red color all parts of this crabapple. Blossoms are a dark pinkish red; fruits that follow are red-purple. Leaves emerge red-purple, mature to reddish-tinted dark green, and turn bronzy red in autumn. Even the bark is dark red and glossy. The tree is taller than broad, with a vase-shaped structure.
M. 'Red Jewel' −30°F/−34°C	15 feet Slow Oval, upright	Modest size and slow growth make this an especially fine crabapple for small gardens. Flowers are white; small fruits are bright red and persist on branches through winter.
M. 'Snowdrift' −30°F/−34°C	20 to 25 feet Moderate to fast Rounded	Single white flowers open from red buds; ½-inch fruits are orange-red, remaining on branches into winter. This vigorous, dense tree is particularly symmetrical, needing little shaping.
M. 'White Angel' −30°F/−34°C	20 feet Moderate Rounded, spreading	Another pink-budded, white-flowered hybrid with ½-inch red fruits that hold their color well after ripening and last well on branches after leaf drop. Branch structure is broadly vase shaped, with a spread equal to the height.
M. zumi calocarpa −10°F/−23°C	25 feet Moderate Pyramidal, spreading	Its soft pink flowers that fade to white are lovely, but its small fruits are the special feature. Glossy and bright red, they ripen in late summer (contrasting with the still-green leaves) and remain until birds consume them or until the next spring. The typical tree is dense and reaches 15 feet across. On vigorous, nonfruiting branches, leaves are lobed.

Maytenus boaria

MAYTENUS BOARIA
Mayten tree
Celastraceae

Evergreen: Hardy to 15°F/–9°C
Flowers: Inconspicuous
Exposure: Sun
Water: Regular to moderate
Growth: Slow to moderate

Here is all the delicacy and charm of a weeping willow in a 30- to 60-foot evergreen tree, minus the many problems that limit a willow's usefulness. Long, drooping branchlets hang down from all branches to create a gracefully weeping canopy, clothed in narrow, 2-inch, bright green leaves. The selection 'Green Showers' is an especially good form, with dark green leaves slightly broader than usual.

Mayten tree will grow in a variety of soils but does need good drainage. If you water it deeply, it will develop a deep, fairly noninvasive root system; with shallow watering, you'll get a network of greedy surface roots that sucker profusely whenever disturbed by digging or mowing. Be sure to stake a young tree to develop a good trunk; remove side shoots, unless you want a multitrunked specimen. Established trees will tolerate some drought, but their appearance is much better with routine watering.

MELALEUCA
Melaleuca
Myrtaceae

Evergreen: Hardy to 20°F/–7°C
Flowers: White, lavender, pink, purple; season varies
Exposure: Sun
Water: Regular to moderate
Growth: Fast

Like the related *Callistemon* species—and for the same reason—these Australian trees are sometimes called "bottlebrushes." The small flowers have prominent long stamens, so that clustered flowers resemble long, circular brushes. Also like *Callistemon*, new growth emerges from the tops of flower clusters; after flowers fade, they form woody seed capsules directly attached to branches. Many melaleucas become rather gnarled with age, with thick bark that peels in spongy or papery layers. Most will perform well under the fairly trying conditions of heat, wind, salty ocean air, poor soil, and drought.

M. quinquenervia (M. leucadendra), CAJEPUT TREE, may grow as high as 40 feet, forming a relatively narrow canopy. Its trunk and major limbs are covered in light brown to nearly white bark that is thick and spongy, peeling in sheets. Young branches tend to droop, but the tree's overall habit is actually upright and rather open. Narrowly oval, stiff leaves are pale green and shiny, 2 to 4 inches long; young leaves are covered with silky hairs. Flowers in 2- to 3-inch spikes appear in summer and autumn; the usual color is creamy white but is occasionally pink or purple. It will grow well with little to regular watering.

M. styphelioides is another potentially 40-foot specimen. But compared with cajeput tree, it has more distinctly drooping branches and a finer texture; it's also more inclined to multiple trunks. Its bark, too, is thick and spongy, peeling in layers, but the color is light tan to charcoal. Narrow, prickly, light green leaves are less than an inch long. In summer and autumn, creamy white blossoms appear in 1- to 2-inch clusters. Best growth is in neutral to acid soil.

Melaleuca quinquenervia

METASEQUOIA GLYPTOSTROBOIDES
Dawn redwood
Taxodiaceae

Deciduous (conifer): Hardy to –15°F/–26°C
Flowers: None
Exposure: Sun
Water: Regular
Growth: Fast to moderate

Dawn redwood is one of the few needle-leafed, cone-bearing trees that entirely sheds its foliage every autumn. It's remarkable in another respect, too: it was identified and named from fossil remains rather than from a living specimen. Thought to have been extinct for thousands of years, living specimens were unexpectedly found growing in a few isolated locations in China during the 1940s. Like the maidenhair tree, *Ginkgo biloba*, dawn redwood is a relic from the dinosaur era.

The tree's general appearance suggests that of coast redwood, *Sequoia sempervirens*, except that its pyramid shape is decked out in soft, light green needles and its branchlets tend to turn

Metasequoia glyptostroboides

upward. In autumn, needles turn bronzy brown before falling; then you can appreciate the deeply fissured, red-brown trunks of older trees during winter's bare period. When spring returns, a haze of light green new needles envelops the tree. Young trees grow very fast in fairly mild regions, moderately fast in cold-winter climates, reaching about 90 feet (though trees haven't been grown long enough to determine a maximum height).

Best growth occurs in good, organically enriched, well-drained soil with regular water. This is a good tree for lawns, though in time its surface roots may interrupt the smooth flow of turf. Excessive dry heat will burn foliage (this is not a tree for arid regions), as will salty ocean winds.

MORUS ALBA
White mulberry
Moraceae

Deciduous: Hardy to –20°F/–29°C
Flowers: Insignificant
Exposure: Sun
Water: Regular to moderate
Growth: Fast

Few people now grow mulberries for their tasty fruits. For one thing, the birds usually get to them first; for another, the fruits stain pavement, clothing, and the fingers that pick them. Nowadays, it is the fruitless forms of *Morus alba* that are widely grown— for shade. This is an extremely fast-growing shade tree that performs well in a wide range of conditions, including hot summers and alkaline soils. And if given ample water in its early

years, an established tree will withstand considerable drought.

White mulberry's ultimate height is about 35 feet, the canopy spreading a bit wider. Leaves reach 6 inches long and 4 inches wide, sometimes forming simple ovals but often showing one or more lobes. In autumn, they turn a vivid, clear yellow before falling. Nurseries offer several named selections, including 'Fan-San', 'Fruitless', and 'Kingan'; 'Stribling' ('Mapleleaf') has reliably lobed leaves, and 'Chaparral' has weeping branches and deeply cut foliage.

Plant a fruitless mulberry where its wide-spreading surface roots won't interfere with other garden plants. During its first few years, securely stake a young tree; growth is so rapid that the entire head can snap off in strong winds. Limbs, especially on young trees, may grow so long that they droop with their own weight; head these branches back to upward-facing buds to balance the canopy.

NYSSA SYLVATICA
Sour gum, Tupelo, Pepperidge
Nyssaceae

Deciduous: Hardy to –20°F/–29°C
Flowers: Insignificant
Exposure: Sun
Water: Regular to moderate
Growth: Slow to moderate

Like sweet gum (*Liquidambar*) and some maples (*Acer*), this is a large tree with blazing autumn color even in mild-winter regions. Lustrous, dark green leaves are 2- to 5-inch-long ovals; they emerge rather late in spring and

turn a hot, coppery red before falling in autumn. Male and female flowers are on separate trees; if both sexes grow near one another, the females bear small, black fruits that birds relish. Young trees are pyramidal with characteristic short, horizontal branches. In the garden, specimens may reach 50 feet high with a branch spread to 25 feet. The crooked branches, irregular outlines, and dark, red-tinged bark offer a picturesque winter silhouette.

Sour gum is undemanding and will grow well even in poorly drained soil. Wild trees are frequently found growing in moist, neutral to acid soil, often near water. In the garden, the best and most rapid growth comes with ample water, though established specimens will tolerate some drought.

OLEA EUROPAEA
Olive
Oleaceae

Evergreen: Hardy to 15°F/–9°C; in western states only
Flowers: Inconspicuous
Exposure: Sun
Water: Moderate
Growth: Slow to moderate

Despite leathery leaves and a tough constitution, an olive's appearance is one of softness. Narrow, willowlike leaves are 1 to 3 inches long: gray-green with silvery undersides, often carried in billowy masses. Bark on younger trees is smooth and gray, but as trees age they assume a look of antiquity, developing gnarled and knobby dark brown trunks and main limbs. Ultimate size is 25 to 30 feet

Morus alba

Nyssa sylvatica

Olea europaea

with equal width; young trees put on height fairly quickly but are much slower to fill out.

Olive fruit is attractive: green, then ripening late in the year to purplish black. But ripe fruits stain whatever they fall on and, in quantity, can harm a lawn. If fruit is not your objective, plant one of the "fruitless" selections (some of which may nevertheless bear fruit, but at least in reduced amounts). 'Fruitless' is a standard-size tree that may produce some olives. 'Majestic Beauty' is a smaller, more open tree with lighter green foliage that bears no mature fruits. Olive pollen, released in vast quantities, causes an allergic reaction in many. But 'Swan Hill' has deformed flowers that produce little or no pollen and no fruits.

If you want olives for curing, there are several standard selections. 'Manzanillo' has large fruits on a tree that is a bit shorter and more spreading than the average. 'Mission' is a taller, more compact, more cold-tolerant tree than 'Manzanillo', producing small fruits with a high oil content. 'Sevillano' is the common commercial olive: large fruits with a low oil content.

Olives need only full sun and well-drained soil. Established trees will endure much heat and drought, yet olives also grow well in cool, moist coastal regions. Most rapid growth will occur when trees are planted in deep, rich soil and given regular water, but olives will grow well (if more slowly) in soils that are shallow, rocky, alkaline, or nutrient poor.

When you plant a young olive, decide whether you want a single-trunked tree (branching either high or low) or a specimen with several trunks. An olive tree will sucker profusely from its base, so your decision will determine how you deal with suckers: remove them completely or selectively. For a single trunk, pull off (don't cut) all suckers and shorten side branches on the trunk below the height at which you want permanent branches. For a low-branching tree, leave the strongest shoots along the trunk to become branches. For a multitrunked tree, select some of the most vigorous suckers, stake them at any angle at which you'd like them to grow, and remove all others as they appear.

Scale is the one pest that may need attention. Olive knot is a gall that may appear as knots or knobs on branches; unchecked, it may kill the stems. To control it, cut out infected stems, disinfecting shears (with alcohol or chlorine bleach) after each cut. Olives are susceptible to verticillium wilt; where this is a problem, look for trees grafted on resistant understock.

Palms (see page 76)

PICEA
Spruce
Pinaceae

Evergreen (conifer): Hardiness varies; all need winter chill
Flowers: None
Exposure: Sun
Water: Regular to moderate
Growth: Moderate to fast

Spruces and firs (*Abies*, page 42) are similar in general appearance—pyramidal and stiff needled, with branches arranged in precise tiers. But unlike firs, spruces have pendant cones, and their needles are attached to branches by small pegs that remain after needles drop.

Most spruces are tall timber trees that lose their lower branches fairly early in life as they head upward. As they age, their canopies thin out conspicuously, revealing a somewhat skeletal branch pattern. Most species grow rapidly and have no special soil needs. The spruces, like the firs, grow best in regions where summer is cool or mild, not hot and humid. Only *P. pungens* will adapt to the summer heat

Picea pungens **'Glauca'**

and dryness of the lower Midwest and the Southwest.

Check spruces for aphids in late winter; if they're present, take control measures then to avoid defoliation in spring. Other possible pests are pine needle scale, spider mites (in Rocky Mountain territory), and spruce budworm (in northern regions).

P. abies, NORWAY SPRUCE, is hardy to –40°F/–40°C. Fast early growth is a selling point, but great height and a ragged appearance are the ultimate price you pay for it. A youthful tree is an attractive, dense pyramid of stiff, dark green needles, but eventually it becomes a 100- to 150-foot patchy canopy of drooping branches supported by a mastlike trunk. Young group plantings make good windbreaks that will let other trees get a start in their shelter. This tolerates heat and humidity better than most spruces.

P. engelmannii, ENGELMANN SPRUCE, is hardy to –40°F/–40°C. Dense, slenderly pyramidal trees eventually exceed 100 feet in height and spread to about 30 feet, but slow to moderate growth prolongs their period of garden beauty. Blue-green to gray-green short needles make this species resemble some forms of *P. pungens*, but Engelmann spruce needles are softer to the touch and the tree is narrower.

P. glauca, WHITE SPRUCE, is hardy to –40°F/–40°C. Where other spruces grow easily, this one suffers by comparison. Its best fit is with the upper Midwest and adjacent southern Canada, where cold winters alternate with possibly hot and dry summers. At a moderate rate, white spruce grows 50 to 90 feet high and 15 feet wide—a silver-green cone with drooping twigs.

P. omorika, SERBIAN SPRUCE, is hardy to –20°F/–29°C. In this species, beauty is linked with adaptability: it grows in nearly any moist soil, tolerates a polluted urban atmosphere, and can handle the muggy summers of the mid-Atlantic regions. Serbian spruce forms a dense, narrow spire to 90 feet high and 25 feet wide, with drooping branches or branchlets upturned at the tips. For many years it will retain branches to the ground. Needles are shiny green with silvery undersides.

(Continued on page 77)

Unlike the other plants in this book, palms are not woody. Most have a single, unbranched trunk topped by a fountainlike cluster of leaves, though a few clumping types have multiple trunks rising from a common point. No growth buds form along trunks, and, except for the clump-forming kinds, they won't sprout from the base if the growing tip is killed or cut off.

Nearly all palm leaves (often called "fronds") consist of linear leaflets. In the feather palms, leaves have a long, central leafstalk with many parallel leaflets along either side. On fan palms, leaflets radiate from one point at the end of a leafstalk, like the ribs of a fan. Some palms shed their dead leaves, while others retain them dangling against the trunk for many years. Removal is a matter of choice; most feather palms look better with clean trunks. All palms described here retain their dead leaves unless noted.

Though young palms tolerate shade, plant them (early spring is the best time) where the foliage will ultimately reach full sun. Give plants fertile, reasonably well-drained soil and regular water. Dig a hole 2 feet wider and 8 inches deeper than the palm's root ball. Place a 2-inch layer of organic amendment at the hole's bottom, then top with a 6-inch layer of soil. Set the root ball on the soil layer, fill in the hole with a half-and-half mixture of soil and organic amendment (but not manure), and water well.

Most palms come from mild-winter regions, but cold tolerance depends on a plant's size and the duration of low temperature. Older palms may resist a frost that kills young plants of the same species.

ARCHONTOPHOENIX cunninghamiana, KING PALM. Feather palm; hardy to 28°F/–2°C. Stately trees reach 50 feet or more, with fronds to 10 feet long. Dead leaves shed naturally.

ARECASTRUM romanzoffianum, QUEEN PALM. Feather palm; hardy to

Archontophoenix cunninghamiana

20°F/–7°C (but may be damaged at 25°F/–4°C). This is an elegant, graceful 50-footer; fronds are 10 to 15 feet long, the lax leaflets drooping like ostrich-feather plumes.

BRAHEA (Erythea). Fan palms; hardy to about 18°F/–8° C. These species grow slowly. Mexican blue palm, *B. armata,* supports 6-foot silvery blue leaves atop a trunk to 40 feet; cream-white flowers come in great, drooping clusters. Plant tolerates heat, drought, and wind. Guadalupe palm, *B. edulis,* is similar save for light green leaves, less showy floral display, 30-foot trunk, and dead leaves that shed. It will grow in both beach and desert climates.

LIVISTONA. Fan palms; hardy to about 22°F/–6°C. Growth is slow; dead leaves are shed. Australian cabbage palm, *L. australis,* reaches 50 feet with dark green leaves 3 to 5 feet across. Chinese fountain palm, *L. chinensis,* grows to 30 feet; leaflets of its 3- to 6-foot leaves droop vertically in about the last one-third of their length.

PHOENIX, DATE PALM. Feather palms. Majestic *P. canariensis,* Canary Island date palm, and *P. dactylifera,* the commercial date palm, are too large and tall for average-size properties.

Clump-forming Senegal date palm, *P. reclinata,* is hardy to about 28°F/–2°C. Its curving trunks reach 20 to 35 feet, topped by arching fronds of medium green, sharp-tipped leaflets. Cliff date palm, *P. rupicola,* is hardy to 26°F/–3°C. Its slender trunk (to 25 feet) supports arching fronds that form a circular head. Silver date palm, *P. sylvestris,* is hardy to 22°F/–6°C. A slim, tapered trunk to 30 feet also features arching leaves, but of gray-green.

SABAL, PALMETTO. Fan palms; most are slow growing, hardy to about 20°F/–7°C. Broad fans average about 6 feet across; dead leaves usually remain attached for a few years and then drop. Hispaniolan palmetto, *S. blackburniana (S. domingensis),* can reach 80 feet or more, bearing 9-foot leaves; Oaxaca palmetto, *S. mexicana (S. texana),* can reach 50 feet. Faster growth, drought tolerance, and silvery gray leaves distinguish Sonoran palmetto, *S. urseana.* From the southern states, cabbage palm, *S. palmetto,* is hardy to about 10°F/–12°C. It reaches 80 feet in the wild; in gardens, closer to 20.

TRACHYCARPUS fortunei, WINDMILL PALM. Fan palm; hardy to 10°F/–12°C. Moderate to fast growth carries a rounded head of 3-foot-wide, dark green leaves to 30 feet. The dark brown trunk is more slender at ground level than at the top, in part because the fibrous remains of leaf bases remain attached and gradually add girth.

WASHINGTONIA. Fan palms. Common in California landscapes, they grow rapidly but become too tall for many suburban gardens. California fan palm, *W. filifera,* is hardy to 18°F/–8°C. Its stouter trunks reach about 60 feet with long-stalked, 3- to 6-foot leaves. Mexican fan palm, *W. robusta,* is hardy to 20°F/–7°C. Its skinny, usually slightly curved or bent trunk can reach 100 feet. Its head of foliage is more compact, the shorter leafstalks having a red streak on the undersides.

...Picea

P. pungens, Colorado spruce, is hardy to –40°F/–40°C. This is the tree you see most often used as a piece of lawn geometry. Colorado spruce forms a broadly pyramidal tree with rigidly horizontal branches—so stiff that it appears almost artificial. Even the sharp needles are rigidly unbending. Slow to moderate growth eventually produces a tree to 100 feet high and about 25 feet across. This is the only spruce that will succeed in the Southwest and lower Midwest.

Foliage color varies in seed-raised trees, from dark green through all shades of blue-green to icy blue. 'Glauca', the Colorado blue spruce, is a solid blue-gray. 'Koster' (Koster blue spruce) and 'Moerheimii' are even bluer, the latter being the more compact and symmetrical of the two. 'Fat Albert' is a broadly conical, slow-growing specimen with blue needles. 'Hoopsii' may be the bluest of all but needs some early training to become a perfect cone. 'Thomsen' is the palest of them all: an icy blue-white.

PINUS
(see chart on pages 78–79)
Pine
Pinaceae

Evergreen (conifer): Hardiness varies
Flowers: None
Exposure: Sun
Water: Varies
Growth: Varies

Among the needle-leafed, cone-bearing trees known as conifers, pines are the best known and most widely grown. Pines display a great diversity in tree size and shape, color and length of needles, size and form of cones, and overall aspect. Cone character and needles are the principal identifying features. All pines carry their needles in clusters distributed around the branches. In a few extreme cases, the cluster consists of a single needle, but most species have needles in groups of two, three, or five. The group type has some implications for culture, as we'll see.

Pines grow best in full sun and will thrive in just about any soil that is reasonably well drained. Too much

Pinus contorta

water will result in yellow needles (this shows up first in the older needles) and a generally unhealthy appearance. Most pines are fairly drought tolerant; exceptions are generally among the five-needle species. Rarely does a pine need fertilizer—in fact, fertilizer usually produces undesirable, rank growth.

A number of pests and diseases can afflict pines, but a healthy tree generally manages with little or no intervention. Trees most at risk are those weakened by drought and pollution. Aphids, spider mites, and scale are possible wherever pines are grown. Most five-needle species are susceptible to white pine blister rust, primarily in the Northeast and Northwest; currants and gooseberries (*Ribes* species) are host plants to one part of the fungus's life cycle. In the Northwest, distorted or dead new shoots on two- and three-needle pines indicate an infestation of European pine shoot moth larvae.

You can manipulate the growth of pines by following the guidelines on pages 32–33. The best time for shaping a tree is in spring, when needles start to emerge from the "candles" of new growth. Cutting back partway into those candles will promote bushiness and allow some overall increase in tree size; cutting out the candles entirely will limit size. Don't cut the tree's leading shoot, however, unless you want to limit its height.

Pistacia chinensis

PISTACIA CHINENSIS
Chinese pistache
Anacardiaceae

Deciduous: Hardy to –10°F/–23°C
Flowers: Inconspicuous
Exposure: Sun
Water: Moderate
Growth: Moderate

Anyone familiar with the deciduous sumacs (*Rhus*) might guess this tree's kinship. Not only is its foliage similar—foot-long, pinnate leaves composed of lance-shaped, 4-inch leaflets—but it colors the same luminous orange to red in autumn. In fact, this is the only tree adapted to desert conditions that promises a bright red foliage change. Trees are either male or female; if both grow in proximity, the female will bear clusters of small, red fruits that ripen to blue-black. Mature trees are usually broadly rounded and fairly dense, to 60 feet high and nearly as wide. Young specimens, though, generally go through an awkward phase with an asymmetrical limb structure; head back any especially wayward branches for best shape.

Chinese pistache accepts a wide range of soils, including alkaline. Trees will take regular lawn watering, but established specimens in deep soil can thrive without irrigation through a dry summer. Where verticillium wilt is present, regular watering increases a tree's vulnerability.

Pinus

Name	Growth	Characteristics
P. bungeana LACEBARK PINE –20°F/–29°C	To 75 feet Slow Upright, rounded	Needles grow in threes and are bright green to dark green, to 3 inches long. The bark is a special feature: smooth and dull gray, it flakes off in patches to expose another, smooth cream to mottled red-and-green layer. Unlike most other pines, this species regularly develops several trunks and can resemble a giant shrub. Brittle limbs can break under heavy snow loads.
P. canariensis CANARY ISLAND PINE 20°F/–7°C	60 to 80 feet Fast Pyramidal	Needles grow in threes and are blue-green to dark green, to 12 inches long. From an awkward, spindly youth with widely spaced branch tiers, this tree fills out to become a graceful, slim pyramid; mature trees are round headed but still slender. Thrives on infrequent watering but is not totally drought tolerant in Southern California.
P. cembra SWISS STONE PINE –30°F/–34°C	To 75 feet Very slow Pyramidal	Needles grow in fives and are dark green to blue-green, to 5 inches long. Short, spreading branches create a dense, narrow pyramid that becomes more open and rounded only after many years. Unlike most other five-needle pines, this species resists white pine blister rust.
P. contorta BEACH PINE, SHORE PINE 0°F/–18°C	20 to 35 feet Moderate to fast Pyramidal	Needles grow in twos and are dark green, to 2 inches long. Native to the Pacific Coast (from Northern California to Alaska), this dense pine thrives wherever there is a maritime influence on the climate. It grows with regular or little water and in good or poor soil, but it languishes in hot, dry regions.
P. contorta latifolia LODGEPOLE PINE –30°F/–34°C	To 80 feet Slow Pyramidal	Needles grow in twos and are yellowish green, to 3 inches long. This is the mountain form of beach pine (P. contorta) but differs in height, hardiness, density, and needle color. Slender trees are open and somewhat irregular, yet still attractive. See beach pine for soil and watering advice; This one's not suited to arid regions, either.
P. halepensis ALEPPO PINE 10°F/–12°C	30 to 60 feet Moderate to fast Irregular	Needles grow in twos and are light green, to 4 inches long. Aleppo pine's virtue is its ability to grow in poor soils under trying conditions: in desert heat, exposed to seashore winds, and with little or no water. Trees are fairly upright but often asymmetrical. Where growing conditions are more favorable, you can find more attractive pines to plant.
P. monticola WESTERN WHITE PINE –10°F/–23°C	To 60 feet Varies Pyramidal	Needles grow in fives and are blue-green, to 4 inches long. Although shorter and more slender, this species resembles Eastern white pine (P. strobus) and replaces it in regions where humidity and summer water are lacking. Young trees grow rapidly but slow down as they mature; youthful specimens are pyramidal and open, while older ones are broader with slightly drooping branches. The needles are soft textured.
P. muricata BISHOP PINE 10°F/–12°C	40 to 50 feet Fast Pyramidal to rounded	Needles grow in twos and are dark green, to 6 inches long. For coastal-influenced California, this is a better garden choice than the larger, pest-prone Monterey pine (P. radiata). Pyramidal young specimens progress to a rounded, dense shape and then to an eventual irregular silhouette.
P. nigra AUSTRIAN BLACK PINE –20°F/–29°C	40 to 60 feet Slow to moderate Pyramidal	Needles grow in twos and are dark green, to 6½ inches long. Symmetrical growth produces a stout, dense pyramid that in age becomes flat topped. Needles are very stiff. Use it as a specimen accent and as windbreak planting. This species is subject to diplodia tip blight in Eastern states.
P. palustris LONGLEAF PINE 10°F/–12°C	To 80 feet Fast Upright, oblong	Needles grow in threes and are dark green, to 9 inches long on mature trees. Very young specimens are grasslike fountains of 18-inch needles, remaining like that until a long taproot is established. Then fast growth produces a narrow tree with widely spaced branches. This species is the primary timber and naval stores tree of the South.
P. pinea ITALIAN STONE PINE 10°F/–12°C	40 to 80 feet Moderate Rounded, spreading	Needles grow in twos and are bright green to gray-green, to 8 inches long. This is one of the signature trees of Mediterranean landscapes. Young specimens are globular, but mature trees have heavy, spreading limbs supporting an umbrella-shaped canopy. Ultimate size rules it out for small gardens. Established trees endure heat and drought.
P. radiata MONTEREY PINE 15°F/–9°C	80 to 100 feet Fast Conical to rounded	Needles grow in threes and twos and are bright green, to 7 inches long. Fast growth (to 6 feet in a year) and beauty are its assets. Young trees are broadly conical; older specimens lack lower branches but support a rounded canopy. Monterey pine's many liabilities suggest caution: Roots are shallow, so trees may be blown over. Because it prefers a coastal-influenced climate, it's short-lived and not at its best where summers are hot and dry. Yet in its ideal regions, it's subject to water mold root rot and several serious pests (scale, mites, engraver beetles). Furthermore, its needles are damaged by smog.

Name	Growth	Characteristics
P. strobus EASTERN WHITE PINE −30°F/−34°C	100 feet or more Fast (once established) Pyramidal to irregular	Needles grow in fives and are blue-green, to 6 inches long. Young trees are symmetrical cones with horizontal branches; older trees are irregular in outline and broader, to 60 feet across. Named selections include 'Fastigiata' (narrowly upright while young) and 'Pendula' (with weeping branches). This is a handsome pine if given what it needs: regular water and shelter from strong winds. Subject to white pine blister rust, white pine weevil, and diplodia tip blight.
P. sylvestris SCOTCH PINE, SCOTS PINE −40°F/−40°C	70 to 100 feet Moderate Pyramidal to irregular	Needles grow in twos and are blue-green, to 3 inches long. Young trees are symmetrical pyramids; mature trees are picturesquely irregular, with widely spaced horizontal branches carrying plateaus of foliage. In cold regions, needles turn red-brown in winter, greening up again in spring. Endures wind but not dry heat.
P. thunbergiana JAPANESE BLACK PINE −20°F/−29°C	Varies Varies Conical to irregular	Needles grow in twos and are bright green, to 5 inches long. Growth is fast in cool and moist climates, slow in arid regions; height ranges, depending on conditions, from 20 to 100 feet. Young trees are broadly conical but asymmetrical. Older trees are irregular and spreading, often with leaning trunks. Thrives in direct seacoast locations.

PITTOSPORUM
Pittosporaceae

Evergreen: Hardy to 20°F/−7°C
Flowers: White, yellow, purple; season varies
Exposure: Sun, partial shade
Water: Regular to moderate
Growth: Fast (with one exception)

Gardeners in mild-winter areas of the West Coast and Southwest value the pittosporums for their good-looking foliage. All bear clusters of small, fragrant flowers followed by fairly conspicuous fruits the size of large peas. Growth is vigorous but never rank or straggly.

Most established pittosporums will tolerate some drought, but nearly all look better (and grow faster) with a regular moisture supply. Aphids and scale are potential pests. Ripe fruits (usually orange) split open to reveal sticky seeds; as they drop, they can be a nuisance on paved surfaces.

Pittosporum eugenioides

P. eugenioides is so frequently seen as a high hedge or screen plant that its tree potential goes unrealized. Unpruned, it becomes an upright specimen to 40 feet high by about 20 feet wide clothed in 2- to 4-inch-long, glossy, lance-shaped leaves with distinctly wavy edges. Leaf color varies from yellowish green to deep green, according to the plant's environment, but it's always a pleasing contrast to the tree's gray bark. Fragrant spring flowers are yellow.

P. rhombifolium, QUEENSLAND PITTOSPORUM, grows at a slow to moderate rate into a round-headed, 35-foot specimen. Its diamond-shaped, 4-inch leaves are deep green and glossy. They cover the tree well, but not so densely as to obscure the clusters of showy yellow to orange fruits decorating the limbs during autumn and winter. White blossoms appear in spring.

P. tenuifolium (P. nigricans) is, superficially, so similar to *P. eugenioides* that if you were to see the two separately you might think they were the same species. Their size, shape, and uses are indeed the same, but several details distinguish them from one another. This species has deeper green leaves—broader and shorter (to 1½ inches long)—with less wavy margins; its foliage cover is a bit denser. Twigs and leaf stems are also darker and the small flowers purple. Specialty nurseries offer selections with dark purple and variegated leaves. For coastal gardens, this is a better tree than *P. eugenioides*.

P. undulatum, VICTORIAN BOX, can be maintained as a hedge or screen, but its real beauty shines when you let it become a tree with one or more trunks—a truly handsome dome-shaped specimen to 40 feet high and wide. Growth is rapid to about half that size and then slows down. The dense canopy consists of lance-shaped, 4- to 6-inch, glossy, dark green leaves with wavy edges. Early spring brings clusters of highly fragrant, creamy white blossoms (it is sometimes incorrectly called "mock orange"), followed by fruits that ripen to yellowish orange in autumn. Roots are fairly shallow; on older trees, they dominate the soil beneath.

Platanus (see page 64)

PODOCARPUS
Podocarpaceae

Evergreen (conifer): Hardiness varies
Flowers: None
Exposure: Sun, partial shade
Water: Regular
Growth: Slow

Although slow growth keeps these plants shrubby for many years, their ultimate destiny is 50 to 60 feet of definite tree. Rather than cones, podocarpus trees produce fleshy fruits after many years. Sexes are on separate trees; female trees bear fruit only if a male pollenizer grows nearby. Both species are slender in habit, with good-looking, narrow leaves; aside from

Podocarpus gracilior

specimen use, you can plant them as hedges, high screens, and in groves.

Podocarpus trees grow well in most soils, though they may develop chlorosis where soil is alkaline or heavy and damp. In hot-summer regions, give trees some shade and shelter from wind; in the low desert, all-day shade is best.

P. gracilior (also sold as *P. elongatus*), FERN PINE, is hardy to 20°F/−7°C. The method of propagation determines this tree's growth habit. Grown from seed, young fern pines will sport narrow, 2- to 4-inch, glossy, dark green leaves somewhat sparsely set on the branches of a fairly upright plant. Some years later, when the tree has matured, it will produce soft grayish to bluish green leaves 1 to 2 inches long and more closely spaced on branches. However, plants grown from cuttings (or grafts) of a mature tree retain the small, closely set leaves but have very limber branches and are often reluctant to make strong vertical growth. These more willowy plants are usually sold as *P. elongatus*; the larger-leafed, more upright kinds are typically labeled *P. gracilior*.

Both *gracilior*- and *elongatus*-type plants will eventually become tall trees and should be staked until strong trunks develop. Even so, the *elongatus* specimens will persist for some time in drooping their feathery foliage mass.

P. macrophyllus, YEW PINE, is hardy to 0°F/−18°C. Compared with fern pine,

this species makes a stiffer-appearing, more definitely upright specimen with rather horizontal branches and only slightly drooping branchlets. Bright green leaves reach 4 inches long and ½ inch wide. Yew pine's greater tolerance of heat and drought makes it the better choice for arid regions.

Populus (*see page 64*)

PROSOPIS
Mesquite
Leguminosae

Deciduous: Hardy to 0°F/−18°C; in the Southwest only
Flowers: Yellow; spring, summer
Exposure: Sun
Water: Regular to little
Growth: Moderate to fast

Much of mesquite's success is due to its far-reaching roots that will travel great distances to tap into water. An established tree is highly drought tolerant, yet it will easily take regular lawn watering. Without water, a young tree will remain shrubby. Mes-

quites are unfazed by poor, rocky, or alkaline soil.

Because the species hybridize freely with one another, and because their appearances vary depending on culture, exact identification is sometimes a problem. But all mesquites have dark bark and cast airy shade as sun filters through their thicket of branches, spines, and tiny green leaflets. Height may reach 30 feet, the canopy wide-spreading. Small spikes of tiny, greenish yellow flowers (favored by bees) are followed by 2- to 6-inch, flat, bean-like seedpods.

Nurseries offer three species. Argentine mesquite (*P. alba*) is single-trunked, with nearly evergreen, blue-green leaves and spines that may be insignificant. Chilean mesquite (*P. chilensis*) represents two trees sold under the same name. The more common one is deciduous, with a dense canopy of deep green leaves; the true species is less dense and deciduous only in chilly winters. Honey or Texas mesquite (*P. glandulosa*) tends to be multitrunked, with bright green leaves and drooping branchlets.

Prosopis glandulosa

Prunus serrulata 'Tai Haku' (cherry)

Prunus cerasifera (plum)

Prunus serrula (cherry)

PRUNUS
(see chart below)
Flowering cherry, Nectarine, Peach, Plum
Rosaceae

Deciduous: Hardiness varies
Flowers: White, pink, red; spring
Exposure: Sun
Water: Regular to moderate
Growth: Varies

These related flowering fruit trees produce one of the most cherished spring blossom displays. Bare branches cover themselves with frothy flower clusters—delicate and ethereal in the flowering cherries to garish in some of the flowering peaches. During the rest of the year, some maintain a more subtle landscape ornamentation with decorative bark, leaf color, or distinctive form. Most produce no fruits—or at most so few that there is no litter to contend with.

Flowering cherries, peaches, and nectarines demand well-drained soil; flowering plums are much less particular but will fail if soil is waterlogged for prolonged periods. All are good small trees for a mixed garden, due to their uncompetitive root systems and moderate shade. Flowering cherries are true showcase trees, available in diverse growth habits. Flowering plums are valued chiefly for their purple-leafed selections. Flowering peaches put on a nearly overpowering floral display but are much less ornamental during the rest of the year; plant them where they'll be relatively inconspicuous after they flower

Flowering peaches (and nectarines) fare best given a heavy annual pruning during or immediately after bloom. This produces much new growth that will bear the next year's floral display. Prune flowering cherries and plums, on the other hand, only to establish the height of their canopies. Thereafter, only remove crossing or poorly placed branches.

Several pests and diseases are potential problems. Aphids, spider mites, caterpillars, and pear slugs (a fly larva) may appear on the foliage; peach leaf curl fungus afflicts peach and nectarine. Peach tree borers can make inroads at or just below ground level on trunks of peach, nectarine, and plum.

Prunus

Name	Growth	Characteristics
Cherry		
P. 'Accolade' −20°F/−29°C	20 to 25 feet Fast Spreading	A hybrid between *P. sargentii* and *P. subhirtella,* this cherry bears many-flowered, drooping clusters of semidouble pink blossoms in late winter to early spring. The vigorous, twiggy tree spreads as wide as its height.
P. campanulata TAIWAN FLOWERING CHERRY 10°F/−12°C	20 to 25 feet Moderate Upright	This is *the* flowering cherry for warm-winter regions. Single, bell-shaped blossoms hang in clusters of two to five, their shocking rosy red color a beacon in the late-winter or early-spring garden. Its habit is graceful, densely branched, and slender.
P. 'Okame' 0°F/−18°C	25 feet Moderate Upright, oval	A hybrid of *P. campanulata,* this is also early flowering, with single, deep pink blossoms on a broadly oval tree. Fine-textured foliage is dark green in summer, turning bright yellow, orange, and red in autumn.
P. sargentii SARGENT CHERRY −30°F/−34°C	40 to 50 feet Fast Upright, rounded	The largest of the flowering cherries, this has a spreading, vase-shaped structure and glossy, red-brown bark. In spring, branches are covered with small clusters of single, blush pink blossoms. New leaves emerge bronze and mature to green before turning orange-red in autumn. 'Columnaris' ('Rancho') is a narrowly upright selection.
P. serrula BIRCH BARK CHERRY −20°F/−29°C	30 feet Moderate Rounded	Compared with those of the other flowering cherries, these small, white blossoms are nonshowy; they're also partly obscured by emerging new foliage. Mature leaves are narrow and willowlike, but the bark is the most striking feature: glossy mahogany red with horizontal tan or brown stripes, like a red-barked birch.

(Continued on next page)

Name	Growth	Characteristics

P. serrulata
JAPANESE FLOWERING
CHERRY
–20°F/–29°C
 	
This is the basic species from which the many Japanese-named selections and hybrids have been derived. All are small- to medium-size trees, but their growth habits and blossoms vary. The leaves are all oval to lance shaped.
	Varies
	Moderate to fast
	Variable
		'Amanogawa' is a bolt upright, narrow tree to 25 feet, with semidouble, light pink blossoms and bronzy green new foliage.
		    'Beni Hoshi' ('Pink Star') grows rapidly; its arching, spreading branches form an umbrella-shaped canopy. Vivid pink, single flowers hang below the branches.
		    'Kwanzan' ('Kanzan', 'Sekiyama') branches stiffly upright to form an inverted cone 30 feet high and 20 feet wide. Double, deep rose pink flowers in hanging clusters appear with red new foliage. Tree tolerates heat and humidity well.
		    'Shirofugen' has a horizontal branch pattern, to 25 feet high and wide. Double, pink blossoms fade to white, start flowering later than all others. New leaves (appearing with flowers) are coppery red.
		    'Shirotae' ('Mt. Fuji') branches horizontally, reaching 20 feet high and spreading wider. Single to semidouble flowers open white from pink buds, fade to purplish pink.
		    'Shogetsu' ('Shimidsu Sakura') is the shortest tree, at 15 feet, but its arching, spreading branches make a wider-than-high specimen with a flattened canopy. Double, pale pink and white blossoms open late in the cherry blossom season.
		    'Tai Haku' has the largest flowers (2½ inches across): single and pure white, they appear with bronze new foliage. The tree is rounded, to 25 feet high and wide.
		    'Ukon' bears green-tinted pale yellow, semidouble blossoms just as the bronzy new leaves emerge. The tree is open and rather sparse, to 30 feet high and wide.

P. subhirtella HIGAN CHERRY –20°F/–29°C	Varies Moderate Variable	Nurseries offer several distinct selections of the basic species. 'Autumnalis' will produce single, white to pink-tinted flowers during warm autumn or winter weather as well as in early spring. Its canopy is rather open and flat topped, reaching 25 to 30 feet high and wide. 'Rosea' ('Whitcombii') is horizontally branched, 25 feet high and 30 feet across. It bears single, pink blossoms in early spring. Two weeping selections form umbrella-shaped specimens to 12 feet high and wide, with branches that may sweep the ground. 'Pendula' has single, pale pink flowers; 'Yae-shidare-higan' has double blossoms of a darker pink.
P. yedoensis YOSHINO FLOWERING CHERRY –20°F/–29°C	40 feet Fast Rounded	This tree can reach 30 feet across, its horizontal branches making a graceful, open pattern; at maturity, it's fairly flat topped. Early-blooming, almond-scented blossoms are single and white to pale pink. The selection 'Akebono' ('Daybreak') is a popular smaller tree (to 25 feet high and wide) with light pink flowers.

Peach & Nectarine

Name	Growth	Characteristics
P. persica FLOWERING PEACH –10°F/–23°C	15 to 20 feet Fast Rounded	A flowering peach (or nectarine) tree is just like its fruiting counterpart: broadly rounded, with narrow, curving (almost sickle-shaped) leaves. But it produces no fruits—or at least no edible fruits. Where early spring is followed by a hot summer, choose early-flowering selections. Among the earliest-blooming peaches are 'Early Double White', 'Early Double Pink', and 'Early Double Red' (a neon-bright, dark rosy red). Midseason-flowering 'Peppermint Stick' has flowers striped red and white, as well as entirely white and all-red blossoms. Late-flowering kinds include 'Helen Borchers' (large, clear pink), 'Icicle' (double white), and 'Late Double Red'. 'Weeping Double White', 'Weeping Double Pink', and 'Weeping Double Red' are smaller trees with distinctly weeping branches.
P. persica nectarina FLOWERING NECTARINE –10°F/–23°C	20 feet Fast Rounded	The one flowering nectarine, 'Alma Stultz', bears delicate, azalealike, 2½-inch blossoms of pink-tinted white with a sweet fragrance. After flowering, you may get a small crop of white-fleshed fruit.

Plum

Name	Growth	Characteristics
P. blireiana –20°F/–29°C	To 25 feet Fast Upright, rounded	Semidouble to double, 1-inch pink blossoms cover branches in late winter or early spring. Red-purple leaves follow flowers, mature to greenish bronze in summer, and turn rusty yellow in autumn. Branches are long and slender; they may need heading back for compactness. Trees are shallow rooted, hence subject to blowing over in summer storms when in full leaf.
P. cerasifera MYROBALAN PLUM, CHERRY PLUM –20°F/–29°C	Varies Fast Variable	Several purple-leafed selections are popular small trees. 'Krauter Vesuvius' has the darkest (black-purple) leaves on an upright tree to 18 feet high; light pink flowers produce few or no fruits. 'Newport' reaches 25 feet high, bearing purplish red leaves; single pink flowers produce a few small plums. 'Mt. St. Helens' is a sport of 'Newport', differing in faster growth, richer foliage color, and a more rounded profile, to 20 feet. 'Thundercloud' is a rounded, 20-foot specimen with dark copper leaves; pale pink to white flowers sometimes bear a crop of red plums. Three other purplish-leafed selections—'Allred' (20 feet), 'Atropurpurea' (25 to 30 feet), and 'Hollywood' (30 to 40 feet)—regularly bear fruit crops that create litter if not harvested.

Pseudotsuga menziesii

PSEUDOTSUGA MENZIESII
Douglas fir
Pinaceae

Evergreen (conifer): Hardy to –10°F/–23°C (with one exception); needs a bit of winter chill
Flowers: None
Exposure: Sun to shade
Water: Regular to little
Growth: Fast

Rapid growth, dense foliage, symmetrical form, and a soft grace that rivals that of the true hemlocks (*Tsuga*) put this magnificent western timber tree high on any list of choice ornamentals. In forests it grows from 70 to over 200 feet. Young specimens are cone shaped and foliaged to the ground; as trees age, they retain the conical profile, but it is elevated on increasingly rugged trunks. Main limbs vary from slightly upright to slightly drooping (sometimes upright toward the top and drooping toward the bottom). The soft, densely set needles are typically dark green and 1½ inches long, radiating in all directions from the branches. Apple green new growth conspicuously contrasts with mature foliage. Cones are oval and about 3 inches long, hanging from the branches; beneath each cone scale protrudes a three-pronged bract.

Douglas fir ranges from Alaska through Northern California, eastward into the Rocky Mountains, and southward in that chain into northern Mexico. Within that varied range, the tree is adapted to each region. In Alaska, coastal-influenced Northwest areas, and Northern California thrives the "typical" fast-growing, feathery, dark green form with slightly drooping branchlets. But the growth habit becomes increasingly more compact and stiff, the foliage more blue tinged, on trees found farther east toward the Rocky Mountains and farther south in inland California. The inland forms are also slower growing and more cold tolerant than the coastal forms.

The bluish-needled Rocky Mountain subspecies, *P. m. glauca*, is especially hardy, to –30°F/–34°C; it will grow in the colder parts of the Northeast, whereas the basic species grows only about as far north as Long Island Sound. If you live within Douglas fir's native range, try to find trees grown from seed collected in a climate similar to yours.

You can plant Douglas fir in almost any soil except one that is waterlogged. The most compact specimens develop in full sun, but trees grow well (with a more sparse and rangy habit) in partial to nearly full shade. Where summers are dry, even with regular water a tree will be denser, with shorter spaces between branches, than it would be where atmospheric moisture is high. Trees are quite wind tolerant; you can even plant them in a row and keep them trimmed as a high hedge.

PYRUS
Pear
Rosaceae

Deciduous, evergreen: Hardiness varies
Flowers: White; winter, spring
Exposure: Sun
Water: Regular to moderate
Growth: Moderate

The pears are highly attractive all year round. All have glossy, healthy-looking leaves that, on deciduous kinds, color up spectacularly in autumn. During the leafless period, the deciduous pears present a sturdy silhouette of dark limbs; they're smothered in flowers just before leaves emerge. In the evergreen species flowering is nearly as profuse, the handsome foliage forming a backdrop.

Pyrus calleryana 'Bradford'

Pears aren't fussy about soil, even growing well in heavy clay, but they don't do their best in shallow soil. Established trees need only moderate watering during the growing season. Fireblight is a potential problem, particularly on evergreen pear.

P. calleryana, CALLERY PEAR, is hardy to –20°F/–29°C and needs some winter chill. The basic species is a small, thorny, horizontally branching tree; leathery, glossy leaves are 1 to 3 inches long, dark green with scalloped edges. Following the early bloom (which can be nipped by late freezes in coldest areas) come small, round, inedible fruits that are prized by some birds.

Nurseries offer named selections that are great improvements on the species. These vary in size and growth habit, and most lack thorns. Autumn foliage color is blazing red to maroon, except as noted. 'Bradford' was the original selection, a horizontally branched, multileader specimen with an oval silhouette that can reach 50 feet high by 30 feet across. 'Aristocrat' differs in having upcurving branches and a broadly pyramidal outline. 'Redspire' forms a shorter, narrower pyramid and bears especially large blossom clusters. 'Capital' and 'Chanticleer' reach 35 to 40 feet high but only about 15 feet across, growing as narrow, nearly columnar pyramids. In the 30-foot range, 'Trinity' makes a rounded foliage canopy nearly as broad as it is tall; autumn color is orange to red. 'Whitehouse' is more narrowly oval with lighter green, less lustrous leaves.

P. kawakamii, EVERGREEN PEAR, is hardy to 10°F/–12°C. Except for its leaf appearance and white blossoms, this 30-foot tree is a notable departure from other pears. First, it is evergreen in the mildest parts of the Southwest and West, where bare winter branches sometimes look out of place. (Trees are partially deciduous as they approach their hardiness limit.) Second, it's a wayward plant that almost always needs training in its early years. The medium green leaves are highly glossy, broadly oval, and pointed, to 4 inches long. Clusters of small flowers may cover the tree in late winter to early spring, the timing dependent on the weather.

Branches are willowy and drooping. Without guidance, a young evergreen pear may form a sprawling shrub; only as it ages will it become treelike, usually with several trunks. For the most rapid progress toward becoming a tree, stake one or several main stems and shorten their side growth; keep these trunks staked until they are sturdy enough to support themselves. To build up framework limbs, shorten overlong, pendant branches to upward-facing growth buds or branches.

QUERCUS
(see chart on pages 85–86)
Oak
Fagaceae

Deciduous, evergreen: Hardiness varies
Flowers: Insignificant
Exposure: Sun
Water: Varies
Growth: Varies

Among the oaks are some of our most treasured large shade trees. But the oaks are a diverse lot, including small- and medium-size trees as well. Though many have the "typical" lobed leaves, a great number do not. Some of the deciduous species color well in autumn—to red, orange, or yellow—but

others simply turn brown. The one constant that links all oaks is acorns.

In general, oaks will grow in a variety of soil types, but a deep soil gives their root systems needed anchorage. All oaks will take regular to moderate watering if they are planted out as young specimens. In summer-rainfall regions, mature trees will also take moderate to routine garden watering. But in dry-summer western states, established native oaks are accustomed to a long dry period, from spring through summer into autumn. If these established trees are incorporated into gardens and watered during the normally dry months, they'll eventually succumb to root rot. Given congenial conditions, most oaks are long-lived specimens.

Caterpillars are the most serious pest potential. Most common in western states are oak moth larvae; in the East, watch for gypsy moth caterpillars. Heavy infestations of either can defoliate a tree, forcing it to replace the leaves later in the season. Unchecked, serious infestations two or more years in succession can weaken or even kill a tree. The following two oak diseases are inevitably fatal.

In the West, *Armillaria mellea*—oak root fungus, also known as honey fungus and shoestring root rot—spreads from oak to oak (and from oaks to

Quercus palustris

Quercus suber

many other plants) through infected roots. Black, shoestringlike threads appear in dead roots of infected trees; in late stages of infection, mushroom clumps appear at a tree's base. In the Midwest, an oak wilt fungus attacks some species, the first symptom being curling, blackening leaves. If an oak in your immediate area has succumbed to either oak root fungus or oak wilt fungus, you run some risk planting another. Above all, never plant a new oak near (or within the root zone of) a tree that has died.

You can speed the growth of some oaks by judicious pruning. Young trees of many species naturally produce much twiggy growth, and because the trees' energies are divided among many shoots, none develops rapidly. To encourage a more rapid gain in height, pinch off the tips of small branches that will not form the mature framework of the tree. However, leave on as much foliage as you can: it will contribute to the tree's growth.

Quercus

Name	Growth	Characteristics
Q. agrifolia CALIFORNIA LIVE OAK, COAST LIVE OAK 10°F/−12°C	70 feet Fast (given water) Rounded, spreading	Evergreen. The primary oak of California's coast range mountains, this has a mature, rugged beauty with a heavy trunk (often branching low) and angular limbs. You can train it to a single trunk, branching as high as you wish. Leaves are rather hollylike: dark green, slightly glossy, oval to elliptical, with toothed margins. Leaf size varies up to about 3 inches, as do shape and character (more or fewer marginal teeth, flat to cupped). Roots are close to the surface, fairly greedy; quantities of old leaves drop every spring.
Q. alba WHITE OAK −30°F/−34°C	60 to 90 feet Slow to moderate Rounded, spreading	Deciduous. The sturdy, gray-barked trunk supports a vaselike, spreading branch structure canopied in deeply lobed leaves. New spring leaves emerge rose pink, mature to bright green, becoming 4 to 9 inches long; in autumn, foliage turns to purplish red. Grows best in good (but not overly moist) soil, acid to neutral.
Q. bicolor SWAMP WHITE OAK −30°F/−34°C	60 to 70 feet Slow Upright	Deciduous. As the common name suggests, this oak is well adapted to moist soil—so long as it is not alkaline. Its habit is upright, with a branch spread no more than half the height; the scaly-barked trunk usually has numerous downward-pointing branches in the lower part of the canopy. Leaves are obovate to 6 inches, glossy dark green with pale undersides; their autumn color is tawny yellow to red.
Q. chrysolepis CANYON LIVE OAK 5°F/−15°C	20 to 60 feet Moderate Rounded	Evergreen. Nearly white, smooth bark supports a rounded to slightly spreading canopy of 1- to 3-inch oval leaves. Their upper surface is a glossy, medium green, their underside covered with pale yellowish down that disappears as the leaf matures; the margins may be toothed. This tree is widespread, from southern Oregon through California to Arizona.
Q. coccinea SCARLET OAK −20°F/−29°C	60 to 80 feet Moderate to fast Rounded	Deciduous. Its deep root system and open branching pattern make this a fine oak to grow other plants or lawn beneath. Shiny, bright green leaves are deeply lobed and toothed, to 6 inches long, coloring bright scarlet in crisp autumn weather. Needs acid to neutral soil.
Q. douglasii BLUE OAK −20°F/−29°C	To 50 feet Moderate Rounded, spreading	Deciduous. In its native California foothills, blue oak's decidedly blue-green foliage stands out against the prevailing golden brown hues of summer. Leaves are obovate, shallowly lobed, to 4 inches long; their autumn color is a mingling of yellow, orange, and pink. Successful where summer is dry, blue oak will tolerate regular garden conditions as well as drought.
Q. garryana OREGON WHITE OAK 0°F/−18°C	40 to 90 feet Slow to moderate Rounded, spreading	Deciduous. Checkered, scaly, grayish to white bark gives this oak its name. Glossy, dark green, leathery leaves are broadly elliptical, to 6 inches long with rounded lobes; their undersides are lighter or rust colored, and downy. A deep root system and moderate shade make this a good tree to garden beneath.
Q. ilex HOLLY OAK, HOLM OAK 0°F/−18°C	40 to 70 feet Moderate Rounded	Evergreen. Trees are especially dense and regular in outline; they branch to the ground for many years unless you remove lower limbs. Leaf surface is glossy and dark green, the underside yellowish to silvery. Leaves' size and shape are variable—to 3 inches long and 1 inch wide, with smooth or toothed edges. The tree takes moderate watering or lawn conditions and endures seacoast winds.
Q. kelloggii CALIFORNIA BLACK OAK 5°F/−15°C	30 to 80 feet Moderate Upright	Deciduous. Its dark, checkered bark makes this a black oak. Foliage is a special feature: the leaves are large—to 10 inches long, deeply lobed, with bristle-tipped points—and emerge soft pink, maturing to glossy, bright green, and finally turning brilliant yellow-orange in autumn. The upright branch pattern produces greater height than width.
Q. macrocarpa BUR OAK, MOSSY CUP OAK −40°F/−40°C	60 to 75 feet Moderate Upright	Deciduous. A thick, sturdy trunk supports many ascending branches that usually spread less than half the height; their twigs have conspicuous, corky ridges. Glossy green, irregularly lobed leaves to 12 inches long are the largest among oaks; autumn color is dull yellow. It grows best in good, deep, nonalkaline soil but will tolerate a great range of quality. This is a good oak for the Midwest.
Q. palustris PIN OAK −20°F/−29°C	50 to 80 feet Moderate to fast Pyramidal to rounded	Deciduous. The pyramidal outline of a young tree broadens at maturity with a dome-shaped, fairly open canopy. Main limbs angle upward, but many secondary branches sweep downward. Lower branches typically point downward and, if removed, will be mimicked by the lowest remaining branch tier. Glossy, dark green leaves are deeply cut into bristle-pointed lobes; autumn color is yellow to red and finally rusty brown. The leaves hang on well into or through winter. Pin oak needs acid to neutral soil, good drainage, and regular water.
Q. phellos WILLOW OAK −10°F/−23°C	50 to 90 feet Moderate to fast Pyramidal to rounded	Deciduous. Without the acorns, you'd hardly recognize this as an oak. Slender leaves to 5 inches long resemble willow leaves, offering the most delicate foliage pattern among the oaks; in autumn the leaves turn yellow. The growth habit and cultural needs are the same as for pin oak *(Q. palustris)*.

(Continued on next page)

Name	Growth	Characteristics
Q. rubra (Q. borealis) RED OAK −30°F/−34°C	To 90 feet Fast Rounded, spreading	Deciduous. Deep roots, high branching, and a fairly open canopy make this a good oak for a lawn or garden; only its size limits its usefulness. Young trees are pyramidal, maturing to broadly spreading, round-topped specimens. Broadly elliptical leaves, with three to seven pairs of pointed lobes, reach 8 inches long. New spring leaves and leafstalks are red; autumn color is dark red, ruddy brown, or orange. Red oak grows best in deep, fertile, moist, acid to neutral soil.
Q. shumardii SHUMARD RED OAK −10°F/−23°C	60 to 100 feet Fast Rounded	Deciduous. The general effect is much like that of scarlet oak *(Q. coccinea)*, and its landscape uses are similar. Glossy, dark green leaves are deeply lobed, to 6 inches long; they turn yellow to red in autumn. This oak needs acid to neutral soil but will thrive in soil that is poorly drained or subject to flooding. This is a better choice than scarlet oak for the lower South.
Q. suber CORK OAK 5°F/−15°C	70 to 100 feet Moderate Rounded	Evergreen. Commercial cork comes from the thick bark that covers the trunk and major limbs. Contrasting with the rugged, thick structure are small (to 3 inches long), oval, toothed leaves that are a glossy, dark green with gray undersides. Cork oak needs well-drained soil and may become chlorotic where soil is alkaline. Grows well in desert and other low-humidity regions; tolerates drought.
Q. virginiana SOUTHERN LIVE OAK 0°F/−18°C	60 feet Moderate Spreading	Evergreen. Here is the classic, massive southern oak, so often shown festooned with Spanish moss. Trees branch low and spread their heavy limbs nearly horizontally, to a width up to twice their height. Smooth-edged, oblong leaves to 5 inches long are glossy green with downy, whitish undersides. Trees prefer a deep, rich soil (but will grow in alkaline soil), ample water, and a hot-summer climate; will thrive in the low desert with water. 'Heritage' is a fast-growing selection.

RHUS
Sumac
Anacardiaceae

Deciduous, evergreen: Hardiness varies
Flowers: Insignificant
Exposure: Sun
Water: Moderate
Growth: Fast

Evergreen and deciduous sumacs are poles apart in appearance. What they share is a tough constitution, able to grow in poor soils or harsh environments. Male and female flowers are on separate trees.

R. lancea, AFRICAN SUMAC, is evergreen and hardy to 15°F/−9°C. Rather slow growth produces a 25-foot, open-branching tree with a spreading canopy distinguished by weeping branchlets. A graceful, lightweight appearance is enhanced by the leaves, each of which consists of three narrow, dark green leaflets to 5 inches long. Effective contrast is provided by the rough-textured, dark red bark. Female trees (if male trees are nearby) bear pea-size yellow or red, berrylike fruits that can be messy on pavement.

You can grow African sumac with multiple trunks (for an effect somewhat like olive) or train it to a single trunk. Established trees are drought tolerant but will also take the regular watering a lawn requires. They thrive in dry desert heat, though in the desert they're susceptible to Texas root rot.

R. typhina, STAGHORN SUMAC, and *R. glabra*, SMOOTH SUMAC, are deciduous and hardy to −40°F/−40°C and need some winter chill. Growing in poor soils and cleared land along roadways, these trees are often regarded as weedy shrub-trees in their native territories. It's true that their brittle wood breaks easily under winter snow and ice, and that shallow root systems sucker profusely when disturbed by cultivation (and anchor poorly in strong wind). But if you have the right sort of environment—a "wild"-garden, low-maintenance landscape, or perhaps a garden background or fringe area—you can use these sumacs to advantage.

Staghorn sumac grows 15 to 30 feet high, its new growth covered with fuzz that resembles the down on emerging deer antlers. Smooth sumac lacks downy new growth and makes a smaller tree: 20 feet at most. Otherwise, one description serves for both species. These are light-structured trees with comparatively few branches and essentially no twigs; their winter structure, in fact, is rather antlerlike.

Pinnately compound leaves contain up to 31 narrow leaflets to 5 inches long, deep green on upper surfaces and grayish white beneath. Their effect during the growing season is almost tropical, but they change to blazing orange or scarlet to herald autumn. Cone-shaped fruit structures on female trees are decorative during the dormant period. Growth may be single trunked, low branching, or a multi-trunked clump. These sumacs' ultimate size depends on the quality of soil and amount of water. Each species has a selection—'Laciniata'—that features finely divided leaflets, producing a lacier effect on trees a bit smaller than the basic species.

Rhus typhina 'Laciniata'

Robinia pseudoacacia 'Frisia'

ROBINIA
Locust
Leguminosae

Deciduous: Hardiness varies
Flowers: White, pink shades; spring
Exposure: Sun
Water: Moderate
Growth: Fast

Two locusts are commonly available, one native to eastern North America and the other a hybrid with several named selections. These locusts feature hanging clusters of sweet pea–like blossoms (almost as dramatic as wisteria, in the hybrids) that adorn the branches after leaves have formed. The pinnately compound leaves contain numerous small, rounded leaflets that turn yellow in autumn. Locusts tolerate dry heat, poor soil, and (when established) drought. Liabilities are brittle wood and shallow, aggressive roots that can sucker when disturbed.

R. ambigua is hardy to –20°F/–29°C. This hybrid of black locust offers showy to nearly gaudy pink blossoms on thornless trees. Three named selections are widely available. 'Decaisneana' is the largest—to 50 feet high by 20 feet wide—bearing 4- to 8-inch clusters of light pink flowers. 'Idahoensis' (Idaho locust) features 8-inch clusters of magenta-rose blossoms on a shapely tree to 40 feet. 'Purple Robe' is similar to Idaho locust but bears its darker, purplish pink flowers about 2 weeks earlier and over a longer period; new growth is reddish bronze.

R. pseudoacacia, BLACK LOCUST, is hardy to –30°F/–34°C. This lovely native tree is best planted west of the Rocky Mountains (that is, outside of its native area), where locust leaf miner is absent and attacks of locust borer are negligible. Where pest free, it needs no care to become a picturesque tree suitable for large or rural properties where lawn, at most, is its only companion. Trees reach 40 to 75 feet, with an open, rather sparse, frequently zigzagging branch pattern. Branches and deeply furrowed trunk bark are brownish black, making both a striking winter silhouette and a good contrast to the fresh green, feathery leaves. Paired thorns arm the branches. Fragrant white flowers come in dense clusters 4 to 8 inches long, followed by 4-inch brown, beanlike pods that remain on the tree through winter.

Selections offer variations on the basic theme. Most widely planted is 'Frisia'. Where summers are not hot and dry, it will develop into a graceful, 30-foot tree covered in chartreuse-yellow foliage; its new growth is orange, its thorns and new wood red. Thornless 'Fastigiata' ('Pyramidalis') is a narrow, columnar tree.

Salix (see page 65)

SASSAFRAS ALBIDUM
Sassafras
Lauraceae

Deciduous: Hardy to –20°F/–29°C; needs some winter chill
Flowers: Insignificant
Exposure: Sun
Water: Regular
Growth: Fast to slow

Sassafras albidum

Just one leaf from a sassafras won't conclusively identify the tree. Some leaves are simple, pointed ovals; others have a mittenlike lobe on one side. Still others have three lobes, which may be either shallow or very deep. Leaves reach 3 to 7 inches long and 2 to 4 inches wide. Autumn color varies from year to year; at its best, it's a glowing orange to red. Tiny greenish yellow flowers are far from showy, but the blossom clusters outline the bare branches in early spring. Male and female blossoms appear on separate trees; when both grow near one another, the female trees bear ½-inch dark blue berries on bright red stalks.

Sassafras isn't a storybook-perfect, symmetrical tree. Instead it's garden sculpture, irregular and picturesque. A heavy trunk supports rather short branches that frequently form nearly right angles with the trunk; from those limbs, smaller branches reach upward. Branching from the trunk tends to be randomly placed and fairly sparse, creating a rather open, patchwork canopy. Trees grow quickly to about 25 feet before slowing the pace—to an ultimate 50 or 60 feet high but just half to two-thirds as wide.

Best growth is in light to medium, well-drained, nonalkaline soil. Where summer is dry, trees need at least moderate watering. Roots will sucker profusely if disturbed during cultivation.

Schinus molle
(see page 65)

Schinus terebinthifolius
(see page 93)

SEQUOIA SEMPERVIRENS
Coast redwood
Taxodiaceae

Evergreen (conifer): Hardy to 0°F/−18°C
Flowers: None
Exposure: Sun, partial shade
Water: Regular to moderate
Growth: Fast

Here is the world's tallest tree: some individuals are over 300 feet high in the wilds of Northern California. But despite its ultimate natural height and rapid growth (3 to 5 feet a year, given ample water), a coast redwood isn't likely to overpower any but the smallest gardens in the owner's lifetime. Expect a maximum size of 70 to 90 feet, a branch spread of 15 to 30.

A typical coast redwood forms a symmetrical pyramid of soft-looking foliage. Narrow leaves are flat and pointed, up to an inch long. Medium green on the upper side but grayish beneath, they grow on either side of the twigs like the vane on a feather. After many years—or sooner, if you remove the lower branches—you'll see the straight-sided trunk, covered in red-brown, fibrous bark. The trunk is an indicator of health, in fact: nearly parallel sides show that the tree is

Sequoia sempervirens

growing well; a noticeable taper indicates less-than-ideal conditions.

Because most nursery trees are raised from seed, their actual aspect varies. Most will have branches that grow straight out from the trunk and curve up at the tips; from these main branches, the branchlets droop slightly. But coast redwood's natural variability has led to the selection of particularly distinct variants. 'Aptos Blue' has dense, blue-green leaves on branches that are nearly horizontal, with drooping branchlets. 'Los Altos' features a thick canopy of dark green needles on horizontal, arching branches. 'Santa Cruz' has slightly downward-angled branches and soft, light green foliage. Fine-textured 'Soquel' has slightly bluish green foliage on horizontal branches that turn up at their tips. The similar if not identical selections 'Filoli' and 'Woodside' are nearly as blue as Colorado blue spruce (*Picea pungens* 'Glauca') but need careful training to become shapely and symmetrical.

Coast redwoods are not particular about soil and will grow in full sun to light shade. They're at their best in an open location, planted either singly or in groves. If you plant one in or beside a lawn, the tree will certainly get the ample water it likes. Chlorosis, in alkaline soils, will show up most clearly on new growth in summer.

SEQUOIADENDRON GIGANTEUM
Giant sequoia, Big tree, Sierra redwood
Taxodiaceae

Evergreen (conifer): Hardy to −10°F/−23°C
Flowers: None
Exposure: Sun
Water: Moderate
Growth: Fast

If you've seen these trees in the wild—or even just in a photograph—and read statistics of the unsurpassed total bulk that makes them the largest trees in the world, it is hard to imagine considering one for the garden. Yet the young trees ("young" in terms of a 3,000-year life span) are neat, handsome trees for larger gardens.

Sequoiadendron giganteum

Foliage is gray-green, each leaf a pointed scale that overlaps the next one like a prickly cypress. Lower branches hang on for many years, forming a dense and increasingly large pyramid that can grow as much as 3 feet a year. Because both foliage and roots dominate the surrounding area, the giant sequoia is a tree to plant in solitary splendor: it's a perfect lawn ornament. Sometimes the lowest branches will root where they touch the ground, forming secondary "trees" that blend into the original.

Give giant sequoia good, deep, well-drained soil. Water deeply but not too often once it is established. If you decide to remove its lower branches, you'll reveal a fissured and craggy trunk of dark, red-brown bark. Although native to the semiarid mountains of central California, this magnificent tree will tolerate the humid-summer region from southern New England through mid-Atlantic states.

SOPHORA JAPONICA
Japanese pagoda tree, Chinese scholar tree
Leguminosae

Deciduous: Hardy to −20°F/−29°C
Flowers: Cream-white; summer
Exposure: Sun
Water: Moderate
Growth: Moderate

A mid- to late-summer blossoming period marks this tree as unusual among flowering types. Its yellowish white, sweet pea–shaped blooms are only half an inch across, but they amount to quite a show carried in

Sophora japonica

Sorbus aucuparia

branched, foot-long sprays at branch ends. To enjoy this spectacle, you need patience and the right climate: trees must be 5 years or older to bloom, and flowering is unreliable where summer is cool and damp.

Locustlike leaves consist of small, oval leaflets on opposite sides of a midvein; the effect is soft and fernlike. In autumn they drop without changing color and then disintegrate. Young trees may retain their green foliage during winter. Youthful wood is smooth and dark gray-green, but old bark develops a more rugged character. The selection 'Regent' is more upright, faster growing, and younger flowering (at about half the usual age).

Japanese pagoda trees aren't particular about soil or amount of water. Young trees tend to grow at a moderate rate to a rounded 20 or 30 feet, then slow down to reach an eventual 50 to 70 feet high and wide. Growth is faster in sandy loam soils with regular water, slower in more claylike soils. Fleshy seed pods impart a yellow stain to any surface they fall upon.

SORBUS
Mountain ash
Rosaceae

Deciduous: Hardiness varies; needs some winter chill
Flowers: White; spring
Exposure: Sun
Water: Regular to moderate
Growth: Moderate

Showy flowers and showier fruits account for part of the mountain ashes' popularity. Blossoms don't produce the smothering spectacle of most *Prunus* species, but rather are grouped in broad, flat clusters scattered over the foliage canopy. Later they develop into large hanging clusters of small, applelike fruits that color up in summer or early autumn. Red is the most usual fruit color, but orange, yellow, pink, and white occur in some species and named selections. Birds feed on the fruits, but usually not until after leaves have fallen. Autumn foliage generally colors orange to red.

All mountain ashes need good, well-drained soil and some supplemental watering during dry periods. Dislike of summer heat makes them poor candidates for planting in the lower Midwest, Southwest, and much of California. Like many other members of the rose family, they are very subject to fireblight. Other unwelcome guests are borers in trunks and branches and sawfly larvae on leaves.

S. alnifolia, KOREAN MOUNTAIN ASH, is hardy to 0°F/−18°C. Unlike other commonly planted mountain ashes, this species has simple leaves: broadly oval with toothed edges, shiny green, and up to 4 inches long. Young trees are fairly fast-growing pyramids that mature to become broadly oval specimens 40 feet high with lesser spread. Loose clusters of red fruits decorate branches well after the leaves yellow and fall.

S. aucuparia, EUROPEAN MOUNTAIN ASH, is hardy to −40°F/−40°C. This is the most familiar mountain ash, with its "typical" pinnately compound leaves, tawny yellow to red autumn color, and pendant clusters of pea-size, orange-red fruits. Moderate to rapid growth may carry the tree to 40 feet, the branches rising distinctly upward to form a dense oval or round canopy. The foliage is dull green with gray-green undersides; leaves contain nine to fifteen opposing leaflets, each a 1- to 2-inch oval toothed at the margin. 'Cardinal Royal' features larger red fruits that color soon after forming.

S. hupehensis 'Coral Cascade' is hardy to −20°F/−29°C. This red-fruited selection of a normally white-berried species is particularly resistant to fireblight. Trees reach about 35 feet, the upward-angled, purplish brown branches forming a compact oval. Leaves are bluish green; pinnately compound to 7 inches long, each contains 1- to 2-inch leaflets.

S. hybrida is hardy to −20°F/−29°C. Its red fruits are notably large: ½ to ⅝ inch across and borne in large, showy clusters. Upright trees reach 20 or 30 feet, clothed in distinctive foliage. Each leaf is pinnately divided into several pairs at its base but terminates in a lobed, oaklike leaflet. *S. thuringiaca* has similar foliage, on a slightly taller tree (to 40 feet) bearing smaller red fruits.

STEWARTIA
Stewartia
Theaceae

Deciduous: Hardy to −10°F/−23°C
Flowers: White; summer
Exposure: Partial shade
Water: Regular
Growth: Moderate to slow

These refined trees offer camellialike blossoms in summer, outstanding autumn foliage color, and handsome, multicolored bark. They grow best in good, organically enriched, neutral to acid soil in a sheltered, partly shaded garden location. They're good woodland-garden trees and handsome foreground specimens against a backdrop of larger, darker-foliaged trees. Success is limited to the West Coast, Southeast, and (with careful location) mid-Atlantic regions.

S. koreana, KOREAN STEWARTIA, forms a rather narrow, pyramidal tree 20 to 40 feet high, clothed in pointed oval leaves up to 4 inches long; autumn

Stewartia koreana

color is orange to red-orange. The 3-inch single flowers appear among the leaves; each is pure white with five wavy petals and yellow-orange stamens. Some botanists consider this a form of *S. pseudocamellia*.

S. monadelpha, TALL STEWARTIA, is actually the shortest of these three species in the garden, reaching about 25 feet with slender, upward-angled branches. Narrowly elliptical leaves turn brilliant red in autumn. Its blossoms are white with violet stamens, a bit less than 2 inches wide.

S. pseudocamellia, JAPANESE STEWARTIA, may reach 30 to 40 feet after many years. It's pyramidal in outline with oval, 1- to 3-inch leaves that put on a bronze to purple autumn show. The single white flowers with orange stamens reach 2½ inches across and are more cup shaped than those of Korean stewartia.

Styrax japonicus

STYRAX
Snowbell
Styracaceae

Deciduous: Hardiness varies
Flowers: White; late spring
Exposure: Sun, partial shade
Water: Regular
Growth: Slow to moderate

Here are two neat, well-behaved flowering trees of modest size that are fine choices for planting in patios, lawns, or in front of larger, darker-leafed trees. Both put on a spring show of white, bell-shaped flowers as well as an autumn foliage display. Deep, non-aggressive roots allow for easy under-canopy gardening. Give them good, nonalkaline soil and regular water during dry periods. Neither snowbell will succeed in the dry heat of the Southwest or lower Midwest.

S. japonicus, JAPANESE SNOWBELL, is hardy to –10°F/–23°C. A strongly horizontal branching pattern produces a spreading, rounded to flat-topped specimen to about 30 feet high. Leaves are dark green ovals to 3 inches long that turn yellow or red before autumn leaf drop. The five-petaled, lightly fragrant flowers are wide-open bells resembling small white stars. They're particularly conspicuous because the small flower clusters hang beneath the branches whereas the leaves angle upward from them. Because of the horizontal branch pattern, the effect is one of parallel tiers of green and white.

Tilia cordata

S. obassia, FRAGRANT SNOWBELL, is hardy to 0°F/–18°C. Although this tree may reach the same height as Japanese snowbell, it makes a narrow rather than a wide-spreading specimen with an overall coarser texture. The fragrant, 1-inch white bells appear in 6- to 8-inch drooping clusters at branch tips and may be partly obscured by foliage. Dark green leaves are oval to round and 3 to 8 inches long.

Tabebuia (see page 93)

TILIA
Linden
Tiliaceae

Deciduous: Hardiness varies; needs some winter chill
Flowers: Creamy white; summer
Exposure: Sun
Water: Regular
Growth: Moderate

Lindens are large, dense trees, usually taller than wide, characterized by a stately regularity that has made them favorite park and street trees. All have irregularly heart-shaped leaves and small, fragrant, creamy white flowers in drooping clusters that attract bees.

Best growth is in deep, rich soil with plenty of water. Where winter cold is slight, leaves will drop without significant color change; but in colder regions, autumn foliage is a good yellow. Aphids may be a problem.

T. cordata, LITTLE-LEAF LINDEN, is hardy to –30°F/–34°C. Its smaller leaves—1½ to 3 inches long and equally wide—give this species a finer texture than the other lindens. Foliage is dark green with lighter undersides, densely clothing a pyramidal tree about half as wide as it is high. In western states it may reach 50 feet, but in eastern North America it can soar to 90; this is not a successful tree in the plains states. Nurseries offer several named selections. 'June Bride' has smaller leaves than the basic species and bears a heavy flower crop. Other selections include 'Greenspire' (small leaves, dense canopy) and the symmetrical, regularly branched 'Olympic' and 'Shamrock'.

T. euchlora, CRIMEAN LINDEN, is hardy to –20°F/–29°C. This tree is a hybrid of little-leaf linden, differing from it in greater hardiness, larger leaves (2 to 4 inches long), and a slightly drooping branch carriage. Specimens reach 35 to 50 feet high with nearly equal spread and cast a more open shade than the little-leaf parent. Of all the lindens, this one is most tolerant of heat and drought. Its hybrid 'Redmond' is more narrowly pyramidal, with a denser foliage canopy.

T. tomentosa, SILVER LINDEN, is hardy to –10°F/–23°C. The "silver" in this linden's common name comes from the grayish white fuzz on the underside of each 3- to 5-inch leaf. Leaves flutter in the slightest breeze, revealing the silvery contrast with the dark green upper surfaces. Trees reach about 60 feet high in the West (taller in the East), with a spread of about half their height. Established trees will tolerate some drought.

TSUGA
Hemlock
Pinaceae

Evergreen (conifer): Hardiness varies; all need winter chill
Flowers: None
Exposure: Sun, partial shade
Water: Regular
Growth: Moderate to slow

Hemlocks are in the running for the title of Most Graceful Conifer. Characteristically they are fine textured, slightly pendulous, dense, and compact. Foliage consists of flattened needles, each less than an inch long.

Because all hemlocks need atmospheric moisture and summer rain-

Tsuga caroliniana

fall, their usefulness is limited to eastern North America, the Pacific Northwest, and along the Northern California coastline. Trees are rather shallow rooted and need regular moisture in a nonalkaline soil. Plant all hemlocks where they'll be sheltered from strong winds. Spider mites, scale, and hemlock woolly adelgids (an aphid) are their most serious pests.

T. canadensis, CANADA OR EASTERN HEMLOCK, is hardy to –30°F/–34°C. This species makes such an excellent hedge plant that the sight of a 60- to 90-foot, broadly pyramidal, untrimmed specimen may come as a surprise. It frequently grows with two or more main trunks but maintains a pyramidal outline with fairly horizontal branches and drooping outer branchlets. Dark green needles are banded white on their undersides and arranged mostly in opposite rows on the twigs. Nurseries sometimes offer named selections that differ in being smaller and having varied shapes or leaf colors.

T. caroliniana, CAROLINA HEMLOCK, is hardy to –20°F/–29°C. Its overall appearance suggests a somewhat slimmer, shorter, fluffier version of Canada hemlock (about 40 feet high by 20 feet wide). At close range, though, you'll notice that its longer needles are disposed all around the twigs instead of in opposite rows. It's more tolerant of polluted air and an urban atmosphere than is the Canada hemlock, but it's less well adapted to the hot lowlands of the Carolinas and Georgia.

T. heterophylla, WESTERN HEMLOCK, successful only on the West Coast, is hardy to –20°F/–29°C. Except for its foliage color, this tree appears from a distance to be a deodar cedar (*Cedrus deodara*, page 49). It's a fast-growing pyramid (to 200 feet in the wild), each of its horizontally spreading branches festooned with drooping branchlets. Even the leader's tip bends over, just as a deodar's does. The feathery foliage is soft and plentiful; color ranges from dark green to yellowish green, each needle banded white on its underside. Like Canada hemlock, this also makes an elegant clipped hedge.

Ulmus (see page 65)

Zelkova serrata

ZELKOVA SERRATA
Sawleaf zelkova, Japanese zelkova
Ulmaceae

Deciduous: Hardy to –10°F/–23°C; needs some winter chill
Flowers: Insignificant
Exposure: Sun
Water: Moderate
Growth: Moderate to fast

This close relative of the elms (*Ulmus*, see page 65) has similar foliage and is now used as a substitute for the ill-fated American elm. Leaves are tooth-edged ovals to 5 inches long; autumn color varies from yellow through orange-red to dark red or reddish brown. A mature sawleaf zelkova may be as wide as its 60-foot height, with a distinctive, bulky structure. The trunk is short and thick; from it spring many branches originating at nearly the same point. The silhouette ranges from urn-shaped to quite spreading.

Nurseries offer several named selections that approach the vase shape of American elm. 'Halka' is both the fastest growing and the best elm mimic. 'Green Vase' has a narrower vase shape than 'Village Green'.

Sawleaf zelkova grows in a range of soils (including alkaline) and diverse climates (for example, both hot-and-humid and hot-and-dry). Water trees deeply to encourage deep rooting; established trees are fairly drought tolerant. You may need to train and prune young trees to establish a good framework. Foliage may be visited by Japanese beetles and by elm leaf beetles if local elms have died.

Mild-Winter Trees

The mild-winter, virtually frost-free regions offer the year-round warmth necessary for success with several subtropical trees. These six are favorites for flowers or foliage.

BAUHINIA. ORCHID TREE. *Leguminosae.* Semievergreen and deciduous; hardy to about 25°F/−4°C. Lightweight limb structure, small stature, and a season of showy flowers recommend orchid trees for patio and small-garden planting in the mildest parts of Arizona, Southern California, and Florida. Blossoms resemble cattleya orchids and come in appropriate colors. Each leaf has two lobes, as though a single, roundish leaf were cleft down the middle.

Orchid trees are not particular about soil so long as it is reasonably well drained. What they do need is warmth; they're not at their best in mild yet cool, foggy regions. Plant in sun, water moderately.

B. blakeana, the Hong Kong orchid tree, forms an umbrella-shaped canopy to about 20 feet high. During the autumn and winter flowering season, some of the gray-green leaves drop—the better to show off the 5- to 6-inch, fragrant blossoms in rose to orchid to cranberry shades.

B. variegata (often sold as *B. purpurea*) is naturally a multitrunked large shrub. Trained to a single trunk, it forms a dome-shaped canopy 20 to 35 feet high. When flowering begins in January all the light green leaves drop, leaving the tree covered with light pink to orchid purple 3-inch blossoms; for a white-flowered version, look for *B. v.* 'Candida'. Flowering ceases around April, usually leaving a great crop of beanlike, flattened seedpods.

ERYTHRINA. CORAL TREE. *Leguminosae.* Deciduous, partly deciduous; most are hardy to about 25°F/−4°C. Like many other deciduous trees from tropical and subtropical regions, most coral trees shed their leaves in winter or spring. With or without leaves, their strong, sculptural branch patterns show up clearly. Most have thorny branches, at the ends of which come spikes of brilliantly colored blossoms. Flat, beanlike seedpods following bloom contain poisonous seeds. Leaves of all species consist of three oval leaflets.

All coral trees need well-drained soil and deep watering at regular but infrequent intervals during dry periods. Plant in full sun. The following are among the most widely grown by nurseries in Southern California, Arizona, and Florida.

E. caffra (E. constantiana), Kaffirboom coral tree, grows 25 to 40 feet high, but its branches spread 40 to 60, with conspicuous surface roots beneath the canopy. Leaves drop in January, followed by large clusters of tubular, orange-red flowers that drip honey. After 4 to 6 weeks of bloom, new light green leaves emerge. Dense foliage gives good shade; wicked thorns on young wood disappear as the wood matures.

E. coralloides, naked coral tree, is so called because its 8- to 10-inch leaves turn yellow and drop in autumn, revealing the twisted, irregular branch pattern decked out in black thorns. Fiery red flowers in pineconelike clusters adorn branch tips in early to midspring; then leaves reappear to give summer shade. Overall size may be 30 feet high and wide.

E. crista-galli, cockspur coral tree, has a multitrunked growth habit 15 or 20 feet high and wide. Leaves reach 6 inches long, drop in winter, and reappear in spring before flowers emerge. The blossoms come in large, loose spikes at the branch tips—each flower is a birdlike sweet pea shape in colors from warm pink to wine red, depending on the tree. You may get as many as three flowering bursts from spring to autumn. For best appearance, cut off old flower stems after each bloom cycle.

E. humeana, Natal coral tree, flaunts bright orange flowers shining like candles above the dark green foliage. They appear in elongated clusters at branch tips nearly continuously from late summer through autumn. Trees reach about 30 feet; the selection 'Raja' is a bit smaller.

E. lysistemon (sometimes sold as *E. princeps*) may become 40 feet tall and 60 feet across, with a heavy, angular branch structure. Its profile is broadly oval to nearly flat topped. Black thorns are a decorative feature. Light orange to shrimp pink flowers appear sporadically from October to May—a few even scattered through the summer months. Roots are particularly sensitive to overmoist soil.

E. sykesii features spikes of showy red flowers on bare trees from January into March. This species produces no seed-pods following bloom. Its spreading foliage canopy may reach 30 feet high and wide.

FICUS. FIG. *Moraceae.* Evergreen; hardiness varies. These figs are handsome foliage plants with smooth, glossy leaves on trees of regular outline. Many species can become vast, spreading trees; those presented here are the sizes most suited to home gardens.

F. benjamina, weeping Chinese banyan, is hardy to 30°F/−1°C. This is doubtless the most graceful fig, but because it is so tender most people know it only as a house plant. Outdoors it may reach 30 feet tall and become broadly spreading; branches are arching to drooping, carrying elegantly tapered bright green, oval leaves that are leathery and glossy. There is a selection with cream-variegated foliage, as well as 'Exotica', which features wavy-edged leaves with long, twisted tips. Foliage tolerates salt air and ocean winds; weeping Chinese banyan also makes an elegant hedge.

F. microcarpa (F. retusa), INDIAN LAUREL FIG, is hardy to 20°F/−7°C. This species, and its form *F. m. nitida*, are justly popular urban street and garden trees in favored climates. The basic species grows at a moderate rate to 25 or 30 feet high with long, drooping branches that, untrimmed, may weep nearly to the ground. The dense foliage cover consists of blunt-tipped, 2- to 4-inch glossy oval leaves; new growth, produced throughout the year, is pale pink to light chartreuse. The graceful foliage canopy is supported by a slender, gray-barked, smooth trunk. In contrast, *F. m. nitida* has upright branches that make a more formal rounded head.

In California, both Indian laurel figs are troubled by a thrips that disfigures and destroys foliage: it curls leaves, protecting the insects that stipple the foliage and cause leaf drop. Systemic insecticides offer some control; *F. m.* 'Green Gem', with thicker leaves, is virtually thrips-free.

F. rubiginosa, rustyleaf fig, is hardy to 20°F/–7°C. The dense, broad canopy of this fig may reach 50 feet high and wide, supported by single or multiple trunks. The dark green, 5-inch oval leaves usually have rust-colored fuzz on their undersurfaces; *F. r. australis* has somewhat less fuzzy leaves. Trees thrive in seacoast conditions as well as where summer is hot. Selections 'El Toro' and 'Irvine' have particularly dark-colored foliage; 'Florida' has leaves of a lighter green. There is a cream-and-green variegated form, 'Variegata', which is usually offered as a house plant.

JACARANDA mimosifolia. Jacaranda. *Bignoniaceae.* Deciduous; hardy to 20°F/–7°C. Spectacular jacaranda marches to its own drumbeat. Usually it's an open, rather irregularly shaped tree as much as 40 feet high and 30 feet wide, supported by a single trunk. But it may also have several trunks or even be shrubby—particularly after a young tree is frozen to ground level. Leaves usually drop in late winter, leaving

branches bare until flowering ceases. But new leaves may sprout again right after leaf drop. Although blossoms usually appear in mid- to late spring, they may start earlier or open at any time through the summer.

Flowers are lavender blue (there is a white form) and tubular, to 2 inches long; they appear in 8-inch clusters that cover the tree in a copious haze of Edwardian hue. Attractive seedpods that follow the flowers are nearly circular, flattened, and woody. Individual leaves are large, but each is so finely divided into leaflets that the effect is fernlike.

A jacaranda needs heat to produce flowers. Though not really fussy about soil, it grows best in a sandy soil with deep but infrequent watering. Too little water stunts growth; too much encourages rank, weak stems. Young trees may freeze to the soil level at 25°F/–4°C but grow back as multistemmed shrubs; established trees will survive lower temperatures with little or no damage.

SCHINUS terebinthifolius. Brazilian pepper tree. *Anacardiaceae.* Evergreen; hardy to 25°F/–4°C. Brazilian pepper is an easy-to-grow, dense, umbrella-shaped tree to about 30 feet high and spreading as wide. Nurseries usually offer it trained to a single trunk, but multitrunked specimens—which reach the same dimensions—are attractive and sometimes look more balanced against the broad foliage canopy. Pinnately compound leaves consist of 7-inch-long oval leaflets, glossy and dark green. Prominent clusters of bright red berries ripen in time for the December and January holiday season. Trees raised from seed vary in quality of foliage and fruits. Winter is a good time to select trees at nurseries, for the largest, showiest berries and best foliage.

Trees prosper in a wide range of soils, from sandy to quite heavy. Stake young trees while they develop a

Jacaranda mimosifolia

sturdy trunk or trunks. Root systems tend to be shallow; water deeply but infrequently to discourage surface rooting. To lessen the chance of limb damage during storms, shorten long, lanky limbs and thin the canopy in late summer to let winds pass through easily. Roots are susceptible to verticillium wilt fungi.

TABEBUIA chrysotricha. Golden trumpet tree. *Bignoniaceae.* Deciduous; hardy to 25°F/–4°C. Related to *Jacaranda*, this flamboyant South American native shares its preflowering leaf drop and year-round occasional blossoming. The 3- to 4-inch, trumpet-shaped, midspring flowers are golden yellow—sometimes with maroon-striped throats—and come in increasingly dense clusters as trees mature. In bloom, trumpet tree's effect is something like a gigantic deciduous azalea. Palmate leaves consist of five lance-shaped leaflets to 4 inches long; leaf undersides and young twigs are covered with a beige fuzz. Trees reach 25 to 30 feet, somewhat irregular in outline but generally rounded and spreading. Flowers are most profuse in warm areas.

Golden trumpet tree isn't particular about soil, but it does best in good soil with regular watering and fertilizing. Established trees are drought tolerant.

Choosing Your Shrubs

AN ILLUSTRATED ENCYCLOPEDIA

*A*long with trees, the shrubs you select for your garden will give it that special character and form that make it pleasant to look at as well as comfortable to be in. From boxwood maze to rose bower to rhododendron dell, shrubs display their beauties in delightfully varied ways. In the encyclopedia descriptions that follow, you'll find shrubs of all kinds. Tall or short, dense or open, with or without flowers—each one is the perfect choice for a garden somewhere. With these plant profiles and the guidelines presented in the first chapter, you're certain to compile a selection of shrubs just right for your landscape.

Common lilac, Syringa vulgaris, is cherished for its spring show of memorably fragrant flowers.

Daphne odora 'Marginata'

Abelia grandiflora

Using Our Encyclopedia

The descriptions that follow are organized in an easy-reference format. Each entry begins with the plant's botanical name, followed by its common name and the plant family to which it belongs. Some entries contain references to a number of species and hybrids, so the entry is headed simply by the plant genus name — **Berberis***, for example. Other entries cover just one plant, so they appear listed by genus name followed by the species—such as* **Calluna vulgaris***.*

Following the plant and family names, five points of information serve as a quick selection guide: whether the shrub is evergreen or deciduous and its hardiness to cold; the color and season of its flowers; its preferred sun or shade exposure; its moisture needs, expressed in watering frequency; and its growth rate.

Finally, the text offers descriptive profiles of the shrub or shrubs: verbal portraits of shape and structure, foliage, and flowers (see the glossary on page 142 for illustrations of descriptive terms). Potential weak points, liabilities, or cautions are mentioned along with the assets. Cultural information includes soil preference, climate restrictions if they apply, any special pest or disease cautions, and advice on any pruning that may be needed on a regular or recurrent schedule.

ABELIA GRANDIFLORA
Glossy abelia
Caprifoliaceae

Evergreen: Hardy to 0°F/–18°C
Flowers: White, pink; late spring, summer, autumn
Exposure: Sun, partial shade
Water: Regular
Growth: Moderate to fast

What these shrubs lack in showiness they make up for in overall grace and quiet beauty. Main branches spring from the ground in arching fountains, well clothed in glossy oval leaves to 1½ inches long. New growth is bronzy, and even mature leaves usually have a reddish tinge; in autumn, leaves may take on bronze to purple tints that last through the winter. Numerous clusters of small tubular to bell-shaped flowers appear at branch tips; when flowers drop, they leave behind copper to purplish sepals.

Unpruned plants reach about 8 feet high and 5 to 8 feet wide, bearing white to pink-tinted blossoms. The selection 'Sherwoodii' is a compact plant, just 3 to 4 feet high and a bit wider. 'Edward Goucher' is also a smaller plant — 3 to 5 feet high — bearing smaller leaves and orange-throated, lavender-pink flowers. 'Francis Mason' is a bit shorter than the preceding two, its pink blossoms appearing against a backdrop of yellow-variegated to yellow leaves.

Plants may lose some or all leaves when temperatures drop to 15°F/–9°C; at 0°F/–18°C the stems will freeze, but new growth usually resumes from the roots in spring. To control size or rejuvenate plants, thin and selectively head them back. Shearing only turns them into graceless lumps.

ARBUTUS UNEDO
Strawberry tree
Ericaceae

Evergreen: Hardy to 5°F/–15°C
Flowers: White; autumn
Exposure: Sun, partial shade
Water: Varies
Growth: Slow to moderate

All of this shrub's details add up to a handsome plant year-round. Dark green, semiglossy, ovate leaves to 3 inches are borne in whorls around branches, making a dense foliage cover; young stems (and leaf petioles) are rhubarb red. Small, urn-shaped, white flowers in drooping clusters open in autumn and early winter, precisely when fruits ripen from last year's flower crop. They mimic strawberries in their yellow to red shades and technically are edible, but each is spherical, to ¾ inch in diameter, and of bland flavor. As plants age, older stems develop shaggy, decorative red-brown bark.

Without restrictive pruning, strawberry tree will indeed fulfill its name, usually sporting several trunks and a picturesquely gnarled branch pattern. But it is easily maintained as a shrub for specimen, screen, or unclipped hedge planting; with occasional judicious pruning, you can restrict plants to an 8- to 12-foot height. Two named selections are permanently shrubby. 'Compacta' seldom exceeds 10 feet. 'Elfin King' grows to about half that size, bearing flowers and fruits throughout the year.

Given reasonably well-drained soil, strawberry tree is remarkably adaptable, thriving in a range of climates from seashore to desert, with little to regular watering.

Arbutus unedo 'Elfin King'

Aucuba japonica 'Crotonifolia'

Arctostaphylos (see page 140)

AUCUBA JAPONICA
Japanese aucuba
Cornaceae

Evergreen: Hardy to 0°F/−18°C
Flowers: Insignificant
Exposure: Shade, partial shade
Water: Regular to moderate
Growth: Slow

In shaded gardens (from light to deep shade), Japanese aucuba is a near-foolproof shrub offering solid bulk and unassertive bits of color in return for minimal care. Glossy, leathery, oval leaves with toothed margins reach 8 inches long, densely covering a broad-as-tall plant (to 10 feet). Small maroon flowers in late winter are inconspicuous, but female plants will bear clusters of showy ¾-inch red berries (sometimes partly hidden among the leaves) from autumn through winter if a male plant is nearby for pollination.

The basic species is a solid dark green, but nurseries usually offer named selections (usually female plants) with variegated leaves. These range from yellow-edged or yellow-centered to the widely sold 'Variegata', which looks as though its foliage were heavily spattered with yellow paint. There are also white-variegated selections as well as some—such as 'Crotonifolia', a male plant—with both yellow and white markings. Among the purely green-leafed types are two distinctive female plants. 'Longifolia' ('Salicifolia') has narrow, willowlike leaves, whereas 'Nana' has the standard oval foliage on a small plant to about 3 feet high.

Japanese aucuba grows in a broad range of soils (though it does better if sandy and heavy soils are amended), even competing well with tree roots. Established plants get by on moderate to little watering. Spider mites and mealybugs are potential pests.

Azalea (see page 133)

BERBERIS
Barberry
Berberidaceae

Deciduous, evergreen: Hardiness varies
Flowers: Yellow, orange; spring
Exposure: Sun, partial shade
Water: Regular to moderate
Growth: Moderate

Stems armed with needlelike spines put barberries in the front rank of barrier hedge plants. But their overall attractiveness—including bright flowers and colorful berries—combined with their tough constitution elevates these plants beyond the purely utilitarian. Most are fine textured, the oval to obovate leaves (spiny-edged, in some species) usually under 2 inches long; deciduous kinds provide yellow to red autumn color. The cup-shaped, six-part flowers are small but often plentiful enough to be a real spectacle. Small oval berries come later (generally red, dark blue, and black) and are decorative during autumn and winter.

Adaptability, a barberry virtue, is most pronounced among the deciduous kinds. Give them rich soil and a benign climate, or poor (even alkaline) soil in a hot and dry region. They'll take either extreme and all gra-

Berberis darwinii

dations between. Thin out and head back plants as needed (wear gloves!) to remove twiggy and dead stems and to encourage strong renewal growth.

Barberry availability varies by region; a few species are forbidden in grain-growing areas because they are hosts for black rust in wheat. This sampling includes the most popular kinds.

B. darwinii, Darwin barberry, is evergreen; it's hardy to 10°F/−12°C and is among the largest and showiest of all species. Fountainlike growth can reach 10 feet high and 7 feet wide, the arching stems covered in inch-long, hollylike, dark green leaves. When in bloom, its yellow-orange flowers practically hide the foliage; dark blue berries follow. It will spread by underground runners to form a thicket.

B. mentorensis is hardy to −20°F/−29°C, but it's evergreen to around 0°F/−18°C and semi- to totally deciduous at lower readings. Dense, compact plants reach 7 feet high, clothed in inch-long, slightly spiny, dark green leaves that turn bright red in autumn where winters are cold. Small yellow flowers produce dull red berries. This may be the best barberry for withstanding midwestern summer heat.

B. stenophylla, rosemary barberry, is evergreen and hardy to 0°F/−18°C. It's a hybrid between two other species; several selections have been named from the cross. The basic characteristics are very narrow, spine-tipped leaves to an inch long, arching stems to 8 feet high, and masses of yellow blossoms. Most selections offer lower, more compact growth. 'Corallina Compacta' is an orange-flowered shrublet no taller than 2 feet. Yellow-flowered *B. irwinii* is sometimes included here; its fountainlike growth reaches just 1½ feet high.

B. thunbergii, Japanese barberry, is deciduous; it's hardy to −20°F/−29°C. Including its named selections, this is probably the most widely grown species. Unfettered plants reach 4 to 6 feet high and wide, the arching stems covered with nearly round leaves to 1½ inches long. In the basic species the foliage is deep green during the growing season, turning to a mixture of yellow, orange, and red in autumn.

(Continued on next page)

Red berries hang from stems like translucent beads, persisting into winter after leaf drop.

Named selections differ from the basic pattern in leaf color and plant habit. 'Atropurpurea', the red-leaf Japanese barberry, is outfitted in bronzy to purplish red leaves when grown in full sun, bronze to purple-infused green in shade. 'Rose Glow' features variegated leaves: pinkish white and bronzed red new growth darkens to deep rose and bronze. 'Crimson Pygmy' (also sold as 'Atropurpurea Nana'), hardy to –10°F/ –23°C, makes a bright, bronzed red mound to about 2 feet high; 'Kobold' has the same size and habit, with bright green leaves. At about the same size, 'Aurea' offers bright yellow foliage.

Brunfelsia pauciflora
(see page 126)

BUDDLEIA
Butterfly bush
Loganiaceae

Deciduous: Hardy to –20°F/–29°C
Flowers: Purple, pink, lavender, white; spring, summer
Exposure: Sun
Water: Regular to moderate
Growth: Fast

As its common name implies, *Buddleia*'s floral display attracts an additional show of colorful butterflies. Plants are fairly open, with narrow leaves; the small flowers are showy by virtue of their profusion in clusters. Butterfly bushes will grow in a wide

Buddleia alternifolia

range of well-drained soils (including somewhat alkaline soil) and will survive with casual attention and little water.

B. alternifolia, FOUNTAIN BUTTERFLY BUSH, is a rather billowy plant of slender, arching branches that attains at least 10 feet high and wide. Narrow leaves to 4 inches long are dark green with gray, hairy undersides; clusters of lavender blossoms form along the branches to create long streamers of color in spring. Flowers appear on the previous year's growth, so prune to shape and renew only after flowers have faded. Remove oldest stems each year to encourage strong new growth for the next year's blossoms.

B. davidii, COMMON BUTTERFLY BUSH, is a summer garden standby. Vigorous, slightly arching stems terminate in long, foxtail-like clusters of small, orange-centered flowers. Coarse-textured, lance-shaped leaves, which may reach 12 inches, are dark green on their surfaces but white and felted underneath. Nurseries offer named selections in addition to the common lavender sort. These range from dark through light purple, wine red, violet-blue, and rosy lavender to white.

Cut back plants heavily in late winter to early spring to keep them tidy and to promote strong new growth for good flowering. Plants may freeze to the ground in coldest part of their hardiness range, regrow each year from the roots.

BUXUS
Boxwood
Buxaceae

Evergreen: Hardiness varies
Flowers: Insignificant
Exposure: Sun to shade
Water: Regular
Growth: Slow

What would formal gardens be without boxwood? These are the neat, small-leafed plants that hedge shears easily transform into geometrically precise ribbons of green to separate pathways from planting beds—and just as easily into fanciful bits of topiary sculpture. Gardeners who only know these artificial shapes may be

Buxus sempervirens

surprised by how attractive these plants are if left to grow their own billowy, buxom way.

In general, boxwoods do best with average to good soil and regular watering, though they will survive—climate permitting—with less careful tending. Your soil's pH and your region's amount of summer humidity will determine which boxwood you plant. Scale and spider mites are potential pests.

B. microphylla japonica, JAPANESE BOXWOOD, is hardy to 0°F/–18°C. This is the best boxwood for dry-summer regions and where soil may be alkaline. Round-tipped, oval leaves reach no more than an inch long, bright green during summer but distinctly bronzed during winter in many areas. Unpruned, it may reach 4 to 6 feet, but you can keep it clipped to under a foot. Several selections are available. 'Richardii' is a potentially taller, faster-growing plant with larger, darker leaves. 'Winter Gem' will withstand temperatures down to about –15°F/ –26°C. 'Green Beauty' is also hardier, to –10°F/–23°C; its leaves remain green throughout winter.

B. microphylla koreana, KOREAN BOXWOOD, is hardy to –18°F/–28°C. This true Korean boxwood is a smaller (to about 2 feet), slower-growing plant than Japanese boxwood, with no more than ½-inch-long leaves. Another plant is also sold as Korean boxwood in California and labeled "*B. harlandii.*" Neither true Korean boxwood nor *B. harlandii,* it's still a good plant, with bright green, oval leaves, for hot-and-dry summer regions. It's hardy to 0°F/–18°C.

B. sempervirens, COMMON BOXWOOD, is hardy to –10°F/–23°C. This is the classic boxwood of European formal gardens and historic Williamsburg plantings. Very old, untrimmed plants may reach 15 to 20 feet high and wide, a solid mass of shiny, dark green, oval leaves to 1¼ inches long. Plants need cool to moderate summer temperatures and neutral to acid soil. Numerous selections exist, differing in habit, growth rate, foliage size, or color (including yellow- and white-variegated leaves). The most common—and an excellent choice for formal hedging—is the slow-growing 'Suffruticosa', whose leaves are less than an inch long. Untrimmed, it may make a 4- to 6-foot billowing globe, but only after many years. For colder regions, look for 'Inglis' and 'Vardar Valley'; both are hardy to –20°F/–29°C.

Calliandra (see page 126)

CALLISTEMON
Bottlebrush
Myrtaceae

Evergreen: Hardy to 20°F/–7°C
Flowers: Red, cream; spring, summer, some throughout the year
Exposure: Sun
Water: Regular, but tolerates drought
Growth: Fast

Here are the scaled-down counterparts of the tree-size bottlebrushes described on page 48. These, too, have narrow leaves and cylindrical or round flower clusters of prominent stamens, but the

Callistemon citrinus

plants, with one possible exception, remain under 10 feet tall. They perform best in well-drained soil with regular watering but will endure some drought; chlorosis is possible in alkaline soils.

C. citrinus, LEMON BOTTLEBRUSH, has produced some entirely shrubby variants that otherwise form the same bright green, lance-shaped leaves from copper-colored new growth; flowers appear in bursts throughout the year. 'Compacta' may reach 4 to 6 feet high and wide, its red flower spikes a bit shorter than the usual 6 inches. 'Jeffersii' is an upright plant to 6 feet, more rigid than the species and bearing red-purple flowers that fade to lavender. A similar, slightly taller plant with rose pink flowers is sold simply as C. 'Rosea'.

C. linearis, NARROW-LEAFED BOTTLE-BRUSH, is an upright shrub usually 6 to 8 feet high (but occasionally to 15 feet), with linear leaves to 5 inches. Red, 5-inch flower spikes appear during summer. Another red-flowered bottlebrush is sold as C. cupressifolius, though its true identity is uncertain. It makes a rounded, spreading plant to about 6 feet high and wide, with drooping branchlets and pink new growth that matures to gray-green.

CALLUNA VULGARIS
Heather, Scotch heather
Ericaceae

Evergreen: Hardy to –30°F/–34°C
Flowers: Purple, lavender, pink, white; summer, autumn
Exposure: Sun
Water: Regular
Growth: Slow to moderate

Small details separate heather from the heaths (*Erica*, page 109); from the standpoint of appearance and culture, they might as well be one individual with countless variations. In the wild, heather is a mounding, spreading, billowy plant roughly 2 to 3 feet tall bearing tiny (almost scalelike) leaves and one-sided spikes of small bell-shaped flowers in purplish pink.

Fortunately for gardeners, the species is highly variable, accounting for hundreds of named selections. Spe-

Calluna vulgaris

cialists—and even retail nurseries in good heather-growing regions—offer heathers that range from rock-garden tuffets to ground covers to stiffly upright plants. Flowers come in many shades of pink, lavender, purple, and white; a few even have double blossoms. Foliage offers a variety of shades of green as well as chartreuse and yellow, gray, and rusty red; leaves of many selections will change color during the colder months. Heather enthusiasts can easily compose "tapestry plantings" that mix foliage and flower colors and plant habits; these compositions can be even more varied by incorporating *Erica* species, which can extend the blooming period throughout the year.

Climate is the major factor in success with heather. Wherever weather is congenial, soil and water deficiencies can be corrected to suit these plants.

What they need is coolness and atmospheric moisture—an "English climate" readily found in the Pacific Northwest, along the Northern California coast, and in parts of New England. They have also succeeded in other, warmer areas of the Northeast and East. Heat is their nemesis, either dry or extremely humid. Heathers thrive in full sun; they'll grow in partial shade (especially in marginally warm climates), but plants will be leggier, with less bloom. Give them a fast-draining, acid soil—preferably sandy with peat or other organic matter added to retain moisture; they're not at all drought tolerant. Where plants are watered frequently, give them light applications of acid fertilizer to replace leached nutrients. Late winter to early spring is the best time for an annual application; follow this, if necessary, with a second application in late spring to early summer.

For neat appearance and to encourage compactness, you should shear off faded blooms right after flowering. For those that flower in autumn, delay this until early spring. You can also promote compact growth by clipping off about half the previous year's growth in early spring.

CAMELLIA
Camellia
Theaceae

Evergreen: Hardiness varies
Flowers: Red, pink, white; autumn, winter, early spring
Exposure: Partial shade, shade
Water: Regular to moderate
Growth: Slow to fast

If you were determined to design a perfect shrub, the product might be much like a camellia. Wherever they can be grown, these plants are esteemed for beauty of foliage as well as flower, appreciated for their relative ease of culture, and depended on for providing color at a time when little else is flowering.

Typical camellia foliage is dark green and glossy, each leaf a pointed oval; most kinds make dense plants that manage to appear both robust and formal. Among the popular japonica, reticulata, and hybrid types, individual blossoms can be impressive in size and meticulously geometric in form, the display at once spectacular and refined. The sasanqua and hiemalis types offer a mass display rather than individual floral perfection.

Even though you may see venerable old camellia plants thriving under all the "wrong" conditions, you should meet all their requirements when you set them out. Camellias thrive and bloom best when they're protected from drying winds and strong sunlight, though some individuals are more sun tolerant than others. For best growth and most attractive blossoms, locate plants where light is good but sunlight is moderated: under tall trees or lath, or on the north side of a building. Plant camellias in well-drained soil enriched with organic matter, being sure to keep the juncture of roots and trunk just a bit above soil grade. Mulch the soil beneath them to maintain coolness.

Vigorous, established plants are amazingly drought tolerant, but if you want plants to look as good as possible and bear quality flowers, water often enough to keep soil moist (not waterlogged) and cool. Where water is high in salts, it is better to grow camellias in raised beds or containers so that you can flush accumulated salts from the root zone with heavy watering. Fertilize established plants with a commercial acid fertilizer at the start of flowering (when plants are dormant), and then again just before new growth begins after (or at the end of) the bloom period. Where soil or water is alkaline, you may need to treat plants for chlorosis (see page 39).

Browned petal edges (especially in pastel and white flowers) may result from sun- or windburn. But if the brown rapidly runs into the flowers' centers, camellia petal blight is most likely the culprit. This is a fungus organism that infects flowers via soil-borne spores. Sanitation is your best defense: remove all sources for spores that would produce the next year's infection. Rake up all fallen flowers and petals, pick all infected flowers off plants, then put them in a trash bag for disposal. Remove any mulch from beneath the plants and see that it is disposed of far from the garden; then replace it with a thick new mulch. This may prevent germination of any remaining spores during this or the next bloom season.

It may take several years of cleanup before you gain control of petal blight. And as the disease knows no property boundaries, encourage your neighbors to attend to their camellias, too.

C. japonica is hardy to about 10°F/ −12°C, though some will survive temperatures closer to 0°F/−18°C. Selections of this species comprise the majority of the camellias familiar to most gardeners. Flowers come in all the camellia forms, from the simple row of petals in single blossoms to completely double flowers; colors include purest

Camellia 'Donation'

white, all shades of pink from blush to deepest rose, light to dark red, and combinations of those colors in different patterns. In size, flowers range from 2-inch-diameter miniatures to whopping 7-inchers.

The species is naturally a large shrub or small tree, but the selections vary in size, plant habit, and rate of growth. Old plants may attain 20 feet or more in height, but for garden purposes a workable size is 6 to 12 feet. They possess the best-looking leaves: large, glossy, and plentiful. Among the countless named selections, you can find ones that start flowering in late autumn and others that finish in late spring—an overall bloom period of nearly 6 months.

C. reticulata is hardy to 10°F/−12°C. In selections of this species you'll find the largest, most breathtakingly beautiful flowers—to 9 inches across, with silken petals. The typical blossom is semidouble with prominent stamens, but you can find named sorts that offer fully double, rose form, or peony-like flowers. Colors range from red through medium pink, including white-variegated kinds; recently introduced selections extend the range to light pink and even white.

These plants are more open and treelike than the japonica camellias, and their foliage is less glossy and plentiful. But a number of reticulata hybrids—chiefly from crosses with japonica selections—come close to fusing the magnificent reticulata flowers with the attractive japonica plants.

C. sasanqua and *C. hiemalis* are hardy to 5°F/–15°C. Named selections of these two similar camellias are usually listed simply as "sasanquas." As a group, they have dark green, glossy leaves that are smaller and narrower than those of the japonicas. Plant habit varies from upright and bushy to limber and nearly vinelike. The flowers introduce the camellia season, starting along with autumn's chrysanthemums and finishing before the japonicas come on strong.

Individual flowers are neither as large nor as long lasting as japonica blossoms, but their abundance compensates. Colors and flower forms are as for the japonicas. Some sasanquas are attractive as individual specimen plants, but their greater value is probably for mass planting: some make excellent hedges, and the limber-stemmed kinds can be used as ground covers.

Hybrid camellias. Generally these will be hardy to about 10°F/–12°C, though some have been developed for greater cold tolerance. Included here are crosses between two or more species, a great many of them having a *C. japonica* selection as one parent. Among the most widely distributed hybrids are those from japonicas crossed with the Chinese species *C. saluenensis.* The results—classed as *C. williamsii*— are free-flowering, adapt-

able, graceful plants such as pink-flowered 'Donation' and 'J. C. Williams'. Specialty camellia growers carry other appealing hybrids that derive from japonicas, reticulatas, sasanquas, and other, lesser-known species.

CARYOPTERIS CLANDONENSIS
Bluebeard, Blue spiraea
Verbenaceae

Deciduous: Hardy to –20°F/–29°C; best with some winter chill
Flowers: Blue; summer, early autumn
Exposure: Sun
Water: Moderate
Growth: Fast

These undemanding shrubs offer a haze of cooling blue during the hottest part of the year. Rounded plants send up many stems outfitted in jagged-edged lanceolate leaves varying from sage green to clear green, depending on the individual plant. Plants reach 2 to 2½ feet high and wide by the end of the growing season. Flowering starts from early to late summer and lasts for many weeks, as stems elongate and produce new blossom clusters along their length. Individual flowers are small, with prominent stamens; their color varies from clear light blue to fairly deep, intense blue shades.

In addition to seed-raised plants, nurseries offer named selections that vary chiefly in their shade of blue blossoms but also in their degree of foliage grayness and plant size.

Plants grow well in average to fairly poor soil, and they tolerate considerable drought. But in well-drained soil, they can take moderate to regular watering and look the better for it. Unpruned or just lightly cut back, plants may become ragged-looking after a few years. The standard practice is to prune stems to within about 6 inches of the ground each spring; this ensures plenty of new stems for flower production and keeps plants neat.

Ceanothus (see page 140)

Cercis occidentalis (see page 141)

CHAENOMELES
Flowering quince
Rosaceae

Deciduous: Hardy to –30°F/–34°C; needs some winter chill
Flowers: Red, orange, pink, white; late winter, early spring
Exposure: Sun
Water: Regular to moderate
Growth: Moderate

Flowering quinces announce that spring is on the way: in mild-winter regions, they may burst into flower in January. Blossoms are 1½ to 2½ inches across, single to semidouble or double, in colors that range from soft to strident. Some individuals even bear a sparse crop of small quinces. Bloom time is their sole moment of beauty; during the rest of the year, flowering quince plants make a neutral landscape statement of glossy green, oval leaves that may turn rusty yellow in autumn. In humid regions, lower leaves may drop in summer.

Nearly all flowering quinces offered in nurseries are named hybrids derived from *C. speciosa* and one or more other species. As a result, plant habit and size vary considerably. A typical mature plant has many angular branches, forming a fairly dense, interlaced shrub. Tall individuals grow to 6 feet or more and are usually fairly upright in habit; low-growing ones reach 2 to 3 feet and are often spreading. Most have needlelike spines on their branches.

Among tall-growing plants, these are widely available: 'Coral Sea' (coral pink), 'Enchantress' (soft pink),

Chaenomeles hybrid

Caryopteris clandonensis

'Hollandia' (red), 'Nivalis' (white), and 'Toyo Nishiki' (a mixture of pink, white, red, and variegated blossoms). Low growers include 'Cameo' (double soft, warm pink), 'Jet Trail' (white), 'Minerva' (cherry red), 'Orange Delight' (orange), 'Pink Lady' (rose pink), and 'Stanford Red' and 'Texas Scarlet' (both tomato red).

Once established, flowering quinces are equipped to endure hardship; old plants can subsist on rainfall alone in other-than-arid climates. They'll grow without difficulty in sandy to claylike soils, but if soil is alkaline they may become chlorotic. For best performance, though, give them moderate water and at least average soil.

CHOISYA TERNATA
Mexican orange
Rutaceae

Evergreen: Hardy to 15°F/–9°C
Flowers: White; spring, summer
Exposure: Sun, light shade
Water: Moderate
Growth: Fast

Where soil conditions suit it, Mexican orange becomes an elegantly handsome plant bearing quantities of delightfully fragrant, orange blossom–like flowers. Bloom begins in early spring, continuing for a month or more; then flowers appear sporadically through summer. Plants are rounded, 6 to 8 feet high and wide. The leaves are palmately compound, each having three 3-inch, oval leaflets; their bright, slightly yellowish green color and high gloss give the shrub a "lively" appearance.

Choisya ternata

Where summer is cool, plant Mexican orange in full sun; elsewhere, give it plenty of light but light shade (too much shade produces straggly plants with few flowers). Plants need a soil that is neutral to acid. Where soil is alkaline, and where water has a high salt content, plant and care for Mexican orange as directed for rhododendrons (page 132). Good drainage is also a must: roots will rot in heavy soil or when plants are overwatered. Watch for spider mites and other sucking insects. Head back stems to encourage compactness at any time during the growing season.

CISTUS
Rockrose
Cistaceae

Evergreen: Hardy to 15°F/–9°C
Flowers: Magenta, pink, white; spring, summer
Exposure: Sun
Water: Moderate to little
Growth: Fast

In their favored dry-summer climate, rockroses are truly carefree shrubs. With no pruning, no fertilizer, and little water, they'll knock themselves out producing flowers for a month or more—mostly in mid- and late spring, though a few have a later period that extends well into summer.

Blossoms are circular in outline, the petals having a silken surface and often looking a bit crumpled. Their five petals and clump of central stamens make them look much like single roses. Each blossom lasts just a day, but a seemingly inexhaustible supply of buds maintains a continuous display. Aromatic leaves are ovate to elliptical, somewhat rough textured, often wavy edged, and—in some kinds—slightly sticky. As is typical of many Mediterranean plants, the foliage of most rockroses is of a grayish or dull color.

Rockroses will grow in climates as diverse as seacoast and desert. Give them well-drained soil (from acid to slightly alkaline) and moderate water until they're established. In cool- and mild-summer regions, plants can get through summer with no supplemental water; where summer is hot, water occasionally. To increase bushiness or

Cistus purpureus

restrain growth, cut back plants lightly (but never into bare, leafless wood) or pinch off new growth.

Tall-growing species and hybrids mature in the 3- to 6-foot range. *C. incanus* (*C. villosus*) grows 3 to 5 feet high and wide with 3-inch, downy-surfaced leaves. The purplish pink, 2½-inch flowers bloom into summer. *C. ladanifer* (*C. ladanifer maculatus*), crimson-spot rockrose, reaches the same size but features 4-inch, dark green leaves. Late-spring to summer flowers are 3 inches across, each petal white with a dark red spot at its base. Orchid rockrose, *C. purpureus,* has 3-inch, red-spotted, reddish purple flowers on a 4-by-4-foot plant with 2-inch green leaves.

White rockrose, *C. hybridus* (*C. corbariensis),* will grow 2 to 5 feet and spread about as wide, straddling the line between tall- and low-growing kinds. Gray-green, 2-inch leaves are a backdrop for yellow-centered, 1½-inch white blossoms.

Among the shorter sorts, *C. skanbergii* grows about 1½ feet high, featuring narrow, gray-green leaves and 1-inch delicate pink flowers. With a distinctly wide-spreading habit, 2-foot *C. salviifolius* is often used as a ground cover; flowers are 1½ inches across, white petaled with yellow basal spots. *C. pulverulentus* 'Sunset' (usually sold simply as *C.* 'Sunset') features 1½-inch flowers of an assertive magenta hue backed by sage green leaves on a 2-foot, spreading plant. *C.* 'Doris Hibberson' flowers into summer on a gray-green–leafed, 3-foot plant; its 3-inch flowers are clear pink. At 4 inches across, the blossoms of *C. palhinhae* are the largest: pure white, on a 2-foot dark green–foliaged plant. Specialty nurseries may offer its taller hybrid offspring, 'Blanche' (pure white) and 'Paladin' (white with red petal spots).

Cornus stolonifera 'Flaviramea'

CORNUS
Dogwood
Cornaceae

Deciduous: Hardiness varies; all need some winter chill
Flowers: White, yellow; season varies
Exposure: Sun, partial shade
Water: Regular
Growth: Moderate to fast

In contrast to the tree-size dogwoods (pages 53–56), only one of these shrub species is grown for its flowers; the other three give a brilliant autumn foliage show and then decorate the winter scene with highly colored stems.

All four shrubby dogwoods grow best in a good soil given regular watering. The three colored-stem species will even grow in damp soil beside a stream or pond; *C. mas* will tolerate moderately alkaline soil. Types with colored stems need frequent pruning to produce new growth, which is the most colorful. You can cut all stems nearly to the ground late in winter for an entirely new crop of stems, or you can selectively thin out all growth that's several years old and then head back remaining stems as needed to control height.

C. alba, TATARIAN DOGWOOD, is hardy to –50°F/–46°C. Blood red stems fire up the winter scene on a spreading plant to 10 feet high that eventually forms a thicket of stems. Fragrant, small, cream-white flowers in flattened clusters appear in spring; small, bluish white fruits form later. Deep green, ovate leaves to 5 inches long turn rich red in autumn. The selection 'Sibirica', Siberian dogwood, makes a smaller plant—to 7 feet high and 5 feet wide—and features stems of coral red. 'Argen-

teomarginata' ('Elegantissima') has bright red stems with white-margined, grayish green leaves; plant it in shade to avoid leafburn.

C. mas, CORNELIAN CHERRY, is hardy to –20°F/–29°C. Late-winter to early-spring bare branches play host to clustered masses of small, soft yellow blossoms. Later, shiny green, oval leaves to 4 inches long cover the fairly upright, twiggy shrub while the cherry-size edible fruits form. In autumn the fruits ripen to red; leaves turn yellow or purplish red. Cornelian cherry can remain shrubby to 10 feet or more, or you can train it with one or several trunks into a 15- to 20-foot tree.

C. sanguinea, BLOODTWIG DOGWOOD, is hardy to –30°F/–34°C. Compared with the similar *C. alba*, this dogwood is taller (to 12 feet) and more distinctly upright, its stems a darker and duller purplish red to red. Tiny, greenish white flowers in flattened clusters produce black fruits by late summer; autumn foliage is a glowing dark red.

C. stolonifera (C. sericea), REDTWIG OR RED-OSIER DOGWOOD, is hardy to –50°F/–46°C. This is the largest and most rampant of the red-stemmed dogwoods. One plant will spread into a thicket of stems to 15 feet high, the underground stems and tip-rooting branches continually extending a clump's coverage unless you curb growth by digging and pruning. White to palest blue fruits follow small clusters of creamy white flowers. Autumn

foliage is bright red, dropping to fully reveal brilliant red stems. Several selections vary the theme. 'Silver and Gold' has variegated leaves. 'Flaviramea', the yellowtwig dogwood, is described by its common name. 'Kelseyi' ('Nana') grows to just about 1½ feet high. *C. s. baileyi* grows just 6 to 8 feet high. *C. s. coloradensis*, the Colorado redtwig, has stems of a less intense red on a 5- to 6-foot plant; selection 'Cheyenne' has brighter stems.

CORYLOPSIS
Winter hazel
Hamamelidaceae

Deciduous: Hardy to –10°F/–23°C
Flowers: Yellow; late winter, early spring
Exposure: Sun, partial shade
Water: Regular
Growth: Slow

The soft yellow flowers of winter hazel won't turn heads, as the blatant blossoming of *Forsythia* will, but these quietly lovely plants are no less welcome in that leafless period just before spring bursts on the scene. Their sweetly scented flowers are bell shaped, hanging from branches in short, chainlike clusters. Pink-tinted new growth emerges after flowers fade and matures to bright green, nearly round leaves with toothed margins. Plants may eventually become 10 feet high and wide, their open structure revealing an attractive branch pattern.

(Continued on next page)

Corylopsis pauciflora

Buttercup winter hazel, *C. pauciflora*, has ¾-inch, clear soft yellow flowers in small clusters, followed by leaves to 3 inches long. Spike winter hazel, *C. spicata*, offers larger clusters of smaller, pale yellow flowers; foliage matures to 4 inches long.

Give winter hazels good, organically enriched, nonalkaline soil. Partial shade—as at woodland edges or beneath high-branching trees—is good anywhere; in cool-summer regions, they will also take full sun.

CORYLUS
Filbert, Hazelnut
Betulaceae

Deciduous: Hardy to –20°F/–29°C
Flowers: Greenish yellow; winter, early spring
Exposure: Sun, light shade
Water: Regular
Growth: Slow

Although the nut-producing filbert plants are also attractive garden shrubs, several variant forms are planted purely for ornamental value. Each shrub bears separate female and male flowers. The female blossoms are small and held close to the stems, but the tiny male flowers appear in pendant catkins that make a conspicuous show on bare branches during winter. Leaves are nearly round, with toothed margins.

European filbert, *C. avellana*, has produced several distinct variants. Most widely planted is 'Contorta', popularly known as "Harry Lauder's walking stick." All stems—from major limbs to smallest twigs—are twisted, curved, even spiraled, each plant becoming a free-form sculpture

up to 10 feet high and wide. Leaves reach 2 to 2½ inches long, turning yellow in autumn. 'Fusco-rubra' ('Atropurpurea') may reach 15 feet high, its 4-inch leaves a rich reddish purple. 'Aurea' has soft yellow foliage on a smaller, less vigorous plant.

Giant filbert, *C. maxima*, makes a suckering shrub 12 to 15 feet high; it can be trained as a small tree. The selection 'Purpurea' features leaves to 6 inches long in dark purple—a darker shade than *C. avellana* 'Fusco-rubra'. Even the male catkins are heavily purple-tinted. Color fades to green in hot climates; leafburn is a problem where summers are hot and dry.

Filberts grow best in good neutral to acid soil, with regular water. Thin out plants as needed to open structure; remove all understock suckers on grafted plants and any unwanted suckers on own-root specimens.

COTINUS COGGYGRIA
Smoke tree
Anacardiaceae

Deciduous: Hardy to –20°F/–29°C
Flowers: Greenish lavender; summer
Exposure: Sun
Water: Moderate to little
Growth: Moderate

When you see this plant in summer, you'll understand the common name. As the large, airy clusters of tiny, greenish flowers fade, sterile flowers send out elongated stalks covered with purplish hairs; this transforms the clusters into what appear to be puffs of smoke.

The basic species has rounded, bluish green leaves to 3 inches long, but

Cotoneaster horizontalis

selections with purple foliage are more widely planted. 'Purpureus' begins the season with purple leaves, which gradually fade to green by midsummer. 'Royal Purple' and 'Velvet Cloak', however, both retain their purple foliage until autumn. All smoke trees give an autumn foliage show of tawny gold, orange, or bright red.

Typically, smoke tree is a billowing shrub to 15 feet high and possibly as wide, producing several main trunks from the ground. But you can train it to a single trunk, by means of which it may eventually grow to 25 feet. Be sure to give smoke tree well-drained soil and infrequent watering; too much moisture induces root rot. This is a plant that actually thrives in poor soil and drought.

COTONEASTER
Cotoneaster
Rosaceae

Deciduous, evergreen: Hardiness varies
Flowers: White, pink; spring
Exposure: Sun
Water: Moderate
Growth: Fast

Among the many *Cotoneaster* species and hybrids you'll find prostrate ground cover types to shrub trees that may reach 15 to 20 feet high, often with arching stems or erect major stems with arching branches. Individual details differ, but a general blueprint applies to all. Small, clustered flowers—each shaped like a wild rose blossom—produce a notable show of pea- to cranberry-size fruits that redden in autumn and may last through

(Continued on page 106)

Corylus avellana '**Contorta**'

Cotinus coggygria

Needle-leafed Evergreens

Instead of offering a seasonal flower show, the needle-leafed evergreens present a uniform appearance year-round: neat, orderly, and fine-textured.

JUNIPERUS. JUNIPER. *Cupressaceae.* Hardiness varies. Juniper is the ubiquitous evergreen. Nurseries sell a bewildering number of named selections that include ground-hugging mats, spires and cones, and midsize shrubs ranging from nearly round to arching, broadly spreading, vase-shaped, and even irregularly free-form. Foliage may be small prickly needles (juvenile foliage), tiny overlapping scales (mature foliage), or both on one plant.

Shrubby junipers are selected forms of the following species: *J. chinensis* (hardy to −30°F/−34°C), *J. communis* (hardy to −40°F/−40°C), *J. sabina* (hardy to −30°F/−34°C), *J. scopulorum* (hardy to −20°F/−29°C), *J. squamata* (hardy to −20°F/−29°C), and *J. virginiana* (hardy to −40°F/−40°C). Visit a well-stocked local nursery to discover the assortment of junipers suited to your area.

Junipers will grow in sun in virtually any (other than poorly drained and waterlogged) soil, either acid or alkaline. They also accept hot climates, cool climates, wind, and drought. Potential pest problems include aphids, spider mites, and scale; browning, dying branch tips indicate twig borer. Juniper blight (a fungus disease) kills branch tips and then progresses to the entire branch; control it with a copper spray in midsummer.

PINUS mugo mugo. MUGHO PINE. *Pinaceae.* Hardy to −40°F/−40°C. Mugho pine makes a small, billowy shrub. Branches tend to be spreading, with upturned tips, forming a mounded plant clothed in paired needles to 2 inches long. A plant's width usually exceeds its height, but size is variable; specimens eventually top out at 4 to 8 feet. Plants with shorter needles are likely to be slower grow-ing, denser, and ultimately smaller. Like its tree-size kin (*Pinus*, see page 77), mugho pine needs no special soil or fussy care.

PLATYCLADUS orientalis (Thuja orientalis). ORIENTAL ARBORVITAE. *Cupressaceae.* Hardy to −10°F/−23°C. Foliage is carried in flattened sprays, held vertically, forming a conical to pyramidal plant. Juvenile leaves are tiny and needlelike, but mature leaves are minute, overlapping scales.

Nurseries offer shrubby selections that mature at heights from 3 to about 10 feet, depending on the individual. Several selections offer yellow or yellow-tinted foliage. Oriental arborvitae takes the place of American arborvitae (*Thuja occidentalis*) in warmer climates of the South, lower Midwest, and Southwest. It grows best in good soil with regular watering.

TAXUS. YEW. *Taxaceae.* Hardiness varies. Yews, a classic topiary plant, are excellent as hedges, screens, and specimens. Growth habits include upright, spreading, and variations between the two. Short, flattened, dark green needles densely cover the branches. Female trees bear cup-shaped, usually red fruits; their seeds (as well as yew foliage) are poisonous if eaten.

Yews will grow in a variety of well-drained soils as long as the pH is neither strongly acid nor highly alkaline. They'll accept regular watering; established plants are somewhat drought tolerant. Reflected summer heat can burn foliage; in cold-winter regions, protect plants in winter from wind and bright sunlight.

English yew, *T. baccata*, is hardy to −10°F/−23°C. Shrubby selections include 'Stricta' (Irish yew), a broad, flat-topped column, and the more strictly upright 'Erecta'. 'Repandens' has nearly horizontal branches spreading to 6 feet but rising only 2 feet high. Short-needled 'Adpressa' reaches 5 feet high and wide.

Pinus mugo mugo

Japanese yew, *T. cuspidata*, is hardy to −20°F/−29°C. Its selection 'Capitata' makes a dense pyramid, eventually to 25 feet high. 'Nana' spreads widely but stays 3 to 4 feet high; 'Densiformis' is about as tall but spreads to only twice its height.

T. media is the hybrid between English and Japanese yews. 'Hicksii' makes a bulky column, 'Hatfieldii' a broad-based pyramid—both to about 20 feet high. 'Brownii' is conical to rounded, to about 8 feet high.

THUJA. ARBORVITAE. *Cupressaceae.* Hardiness varies. The arborvitaes are symmetrical plants with scalelike, soft leaves, usually carried in flat sprays. Give plants good, well-drained soil and regular watering. They need humidity and suffer in regions where summer is hot and dry.

American arborvitae, *T. occidentalis*, is hardy to −40°F/−40°C. Its many named selections run to globes, cylinders, and columns. 'Rheingold', a rounded, spreading plant 4 to 6 feet high, has pinkish gold summer foliage that turns bronzed gold in winter.

Western red cedar, *T. plicata*, is hardy to −10°F/−23°C. Most of its shrubby selections carry their foliage sprays less stiffly than American arborvitae. Widely sold columnar and conical selections include those with contrasting yellow new growth.

winter. Leaves are oval to roundish, usually medium to dark green on the upper surface and pale gray or white beneath; in deciduous kinds, the autumn foliage offers shades of yellow, orange, or red.

These are truly easy-care plants. They'll grow in virtually any soil and, once established, require no more than moderate watering. Prune to remove old wood or badly placed branches. Choose the right size of individual for its intended location; heading back to fit a too-small space spoils these plants' natural grace. Fireblight (see page 38) is a potential disease problem.

Among the taller plants—those that top 6 feet—deciduous C. multiflorus is hardy to –20°F/–29°C. Stems are upright and arching, from 6 to 10 feet high and spreading wider; white spring flowers are showier than in most other kinds. Evergreen C. salicifolius, willowleaf cotoneaster, is hardy to –10°F/–23°C; its upright, arching stems form a fountainlike shrub that may reach 15 feet high and wide.

Three other species are hardy to about 0°F/–18°C. C. henryanus makes an arching, spreading plant 8 to 12 feet high, producing a heavy crop of red fruits; its narrow leaves partially shed during the cold months. Evergreen C. lacteus (C. parneyi), Parney cotoneaster, is an especially fine foliage plant whose arching stems form a rounded shrub to about 8 feet high and wide. The largest cotoneasters are the evergreen C. watereri group of hybrids. Upright to arching stems reach 15 to 20 feet high, eventually spreading about as wide. 'John Waterer' and 'Cornubia' are most frequently sold.

Among the 6-foot-and-under kinds, three deciduous species are hardy to –20°F/–29°C. C. divaricatus, spreading cotoneaster, is a rather stiff plant to 6 feet, the branches slightly arching and angled outward from the plant's center; its autumn fruit crop is particularly showy. Cranberry cotoneaster, C. apiculatus, features tiny, rounded leaves and notably large fruits. Its main stems are widely spreading, its stiffly upright branches to 4 feet high forming an undulating mound that can function as a high ground cover. Rock cotoneaster, C. horizontalis, is a similar

but slightly shorter plant with glossy leaves (just briefly deciduous) and small, shiny fruits. Hardy to 0°F/–18°C, fountainlike C. 'Hybridus Pendulus' grows to 6 feet, with a greater spread; in chillier parts of its range it may lose some of its leaves over winter.

CYTISUS
Broom
Leguminosae

Deciduous, evergreen: Hardiness varies
Flowers: Red, orange, pink, yellow, cream, white, bicolor combinations; spring, early summer
Exposure: Sun
Water: Moderate
Growth: Fast

From plants that are essentially all stems come lavish displays of sweet pea–shaped flowers in a range of colors and in shades from bright to soft. Tiny oval leaves may fall by summertime, but the multitude of green to gray-green stems successfully disguises actual leaflessness.

Brooms are among the easiest shrubs to grow. Aside from good drainage, their soil demands are nil (though alkaline soil can induce chlorosis) and their water needs minimal. Pruning is optional: after flowering, you can head back to reduce size or to remove beanlike pods that may follow the blossoms. Plants are short-lived in hot, humid regions.

C. praecox, WARMINSTER BROOM, is hardy to –20°F/–29°C. From a haystacklike plant to 5 feet high, a froth of pale yellow blossoms appears in midspring. Selected forms include bright yellow 'Allgold', pink 'Hollandia', and lavender-and-yellow 'Zeelandii'.

C. scoparius, SCOTCH BROOM, is hardy to –10°F/–23°C. This is the species with the well-deserved reputation as a roadside and pasture weed in both eastern and western states. Its brilliant yellow flowers form quantities of seed that colonize waste areas and crowd out native vegetation.

Selected named forms, though, are good garden plants with little or no

Cytisus praecox

tendency to self-seeding. Their plants are generally upright and 5 to 8 feet high, the grayish green stems becoming partially leafless after the late-spring to early-summer bloom period. Pale yellow 'Moonlight'—formerly classed with C. praecox—may be the most widely sold selection. Other colors include red, pink, white, and bicolor combinations.

DAPHNE
Daphne
Thymelaeaceae

Deciduous, evergreen: Hardiness varies
Flowers: Pink, white; winter, spring
Exposure: Sun, partial shade
Water: Moderate
Growth: Slow to moderate

Daphnes are an exacting lot. To succeed with them you must provide well-drained soil, moisture (but ample soil air as well), cool soil (a mulch provides this, as does a noncompetitive ground cover), and shelter from wind and extreme sun. For your care you'll be rewarded with lovely blossoms and, in several species, memorable fragrance. Each blossom is essentially fun-

Daphne genkwa

nel shaped but has four lobes that give the appearance of separate petals. All plant parts are poisonous if ingested.

D. burkwoodii is hardy to –30°F/ –34°C; though evergreen, it's semideciduous in the coldest regions. The compact, fairly upright but rounded plants to 4 feet tall feature narrow leaves radiating around the stems. But in late-spring blossom time, the leaves are nearly obscured by the countless small flowers that make of each stem a floral drumstick. In the most common form, fragrant white flowers fade to pink. 'Somerset' is a slightly larger plant offering pink blossoms. 'Carol Mackie' has light pink flowers, but its special feature is a yellow band around each leaf margin.

D. genkwa, LILAC DAPHNE, is deciduous; it's hardy to –10°F/–23°C. Although its flowers are unscented, their profusion compensates. Bare branches become flowering wands in midspring, each blossom a delicate bluish lavender. After the display, 2-inch oval leaves clothe a graceful plant 3 to 4 feet high and wide.

D. mezereum, FEBRUARY DAPHNE, is deciduous; it's hardy to –30°F/–34°C. This upright, 4-foot shrub is worth planting for the fragrance of the rosy purple flowers that appear along branches for several weeks in late winter or early spring. Bright red, oval berries follow bloom. A white-flowered form, 'Alba', bears yellow berries on a slightly taller, more compact bush. Leaves are thin textured and ovate, to 3 inches. To offset the stiff, somewhat angular appearance of February daphne, group several plants together.

D. odora, WINTER DAPHNE, is evergreen; it's hardy to 5°F/–15°C. When all conditions are suitable, winter daphne may seem trouble free, even indestructible. But it is the most temperamental species of these four, insisting on strict attention to the cultural demands listed earlier. The reward: intense, pervasive fragrance from waxlike flowers on a shrub of elegant polish.

Plants typically reach a rounded, spreading 4 feet, though specimens twice that height are possible under the best conditions. Truly handsome leaves to 3 inches long are like narrow ovals of polished green leather. Blossoms come in clusters during late winter. The typical flower is a pink-throated white with rosy red petal backs, but a form with pure white flowers is sometimes seen. Most widely planted is 'Marginata', whose leaves are edged with yellow.

Plant winter daphne where it will receive at least 3 hours of shade each day. To avoid water mold root rot (the chief cause of failure), roots need well-aerated soil. Dig the planting hole twice as wide as the root ball and 1½ times its depth; refill with a mixture of one part soil, one part sand, and two parts ground bark. When planting, see that the top of the root ball remains higher than the soil surface. During dry periods, water as infrequently as you can—just enough to keep the plant from wilting.

DEUTZIA
Deutzia
Saxifragaceae

Deciduous: Hardy to –20°F/–29°C
Flowers: Pink, white; spring
Exposure: Sun, partial shade
Water: Regular
Growth: Moderate

The deutzias can be forgiven their lack of autumn color and even their undramatic summer appearance: their delicate floral display makes up for it all. Masses of funnelform but starlike blossoms cover the leafy branches during the latter part of spring, contributing lavish yet refined masses of color to the springtime extravaganza along with that other old-fashioned favor-

Deutzia crenata

ite, lilac (*Syringa*). After flowering, you have a basic shrub covered with lance-shaped to oval leaves of an ordinary green.

Plant deutzias in average soil and give them routine garden care. Prune or thin after flowers have faded; this encourages new growth that will bear the next year's blossoms. On the low-growing and medium-height kinds, remove a few of the oldest stems about every other year. The vigorous, tall-growing sorts should be cut back fairly heavily each year; remove stems that have flowered.

Among the low- and medium-height kinds, *D. rosea* offers pink-and-white flowers on a plant 3 to 4 feet high. *D. gracilis* may reach 6 feet, but the stems arch gracefully, especially when festooned with snowy white blossoms. Its selection 'Nikko' grows just 1 to 2 feet high but can spread to 5 feet across. Flowers of delicate pink decorate the 4- to 6-foot stems of *D. elegantissima*; its selection 'Rosealind' forms an upright and arching mound 4 to 5 feet high, covering itself with fragrant, deep rose pink flowers.

Among the tall-growing species, *D. scabra* is the best known. Upright stems may reach 10 feet tall, clothed in dull green leaves after the spring display of white or blush flowers in upright clusters. Nurseries sometimes offer named selections, including 'Pride of Rochester', whose double flowers are flushed purple on the outside of the petals. *D. crenata* is similar except for its pure white flowers; unlike other species, its foliage makes an autumn statement in dark purplish red.

DODONAEA VISCOSA
Hop bush, Hopseed bush
Sapindaceae

Evergreen: Hardy to 15°F/–9°C; in the West only
Flowers: Inconspicuous
Exposure: Sun, light shade
Water: Regular to little
Growth: Fast

Rugged, undemanding hop bush grows equally well in seacoast and desert gardens, in well-watered landscapes and water-thrifty plantings. The plant is rather billowy, to 15 feet high

Dodonaea viscosa

Elaeagnus pungens 'Maculata'

Enkianthus campanulatus 'Red Bells'

and wide, but the upright branching habit and narrow, willowlike, 4-inch leaves emphasize its vertical lines. With little water, it may remain under 10 feet; with water and training, you can grow it as a small tree.

In the basic species, leaves are green. 'Purpurea', the purple hop bush, has strongly bronze-tinted leaves that darken in winter. 'Saratoga' offers rich purple leaves throughout the year. These purple-leafed forms need full sun to retain their color. Although the flowers are inconspicuous, the cream- to pink-winged fruits may put on a subtle show in late summer.

ELAEAGNUS
Elaeagnus
Elaeagnaceae

Deciduous, evergreen: Hardiness varies
Flowers: Inconspicuous; spring, autumn
Exposure: Sun
Water: Moderate
Growth: Fast

These shrubs' deserved reputation for being "tough" shouldn't imply any lack of beauty. Floral display isn't their strong point (though the small flowers are fragrant), but the broadly oval, silver-tinted leaves are distinctly attractive. In deciduous species, leaves are typically silvery gray. Leaves of evergreen kinds are covered by silver (or brown) dots that reflect sunlight, giving them a sparkling sheen. Small, olivelike, generally red fruits are a subtly decorative feature; most are edible as well. And branches of most species

are armed with enough spines to make these plants good barrier hedges.

Adaptable elaeagnus thrive in a variety of climates. You'll find them near seacoasts, in the desert, in semiarid regions (such as the prairie states)—where wind and heat are limiting factors—as well as in temperate zones. Soil type and quality are not an issue. Moderate watering will establish and maintain these plants; mature specimens tolerate some drought.

Deciduous, spring-blooming kinds are the most cold tolerant. Silverberry, *E. commutata*, is hardy to –50°F/–46°C. An upright shrub, it may reach 10 to 14 feet under ideal conditions. Red-brown, spineless branches become coated with silvery scales that match its leaves, silvered gray on both surfaces. The dry, mealy fruits, also silver coated, are a favorite bird food. *E. multiflora*, cherry elaeagnus, is hardy to –20°F/–29°C. A 6- to 9-foot rounded shrub, it features dark green leaves strongly silvered on their undersides, lightly so on their surfaces. Bird-tempting fruits are orange-red.

Evergreen species are hardy to about 0°F/–18°C and produce fragrant flowers in autumn. The evergreen silverberry, *E. pungens*, has wavy-edged, grayish olive leaves that (like the spiny branches) are covered with tiny, rusty brown dots. Spring fruits, from autumn flowers, are red with a silver coating. This rounded shrub attains 8 to 15 feet high and wide. 'Fruitlandii' is a superior form, with larger leaves of a more silvery sheen. Most widely planted are three selections with variegated foliage. Gold-centered leaves of 'Maculata' are irregularly edged in

green. 'Marginata' has silvery white leaf margins; 'Variegata' has leaves edged in cream to light yellow.

Upright *E. ebbingei* (*E. macrophylla* 'Ebbingei') grows to about 12 feet, with spineless branches. Its 2- to 4-inch leaves are totally silver when young, dark green with silvery undersides at maturity. The selection 'Gilt Edge' has yellow-margined foliage. Red fruits ripen in summer.

ENKIANTHUS
Enkianthus
Ericaceae

Deciduous: Hardiness varies
Flowers: Yellow, red, white; spring
Exposure: Sun, partial shade
Water: Regular
Growth: Slow

Compared with their flashy rhododendron relatives, these shrubs offer a more subtle, intricate beauty. After oval leaves have emerged in spring, countless small, bell-shaped flowers appear, suspended from threadlike flower stalks beneath the whorled or clustered leaves at branch tips. Plants are upright, with horizontal lateral branching that displays leaves and flowers in tiered layers. Autumn foliage is spectacular.

Like most members of the heath family (*Ericaceae*), the enkianthus species need very well drained, moist, slightly acid soil. Amend soil liberally with organic matter, set root ball higher than the surrounding soil when planting, and mulch well. Plants will take sun where summer is cool; otherwise, give them light or partial shade.

E. campanulatus, REDVEIN ENKIANTHUS, is hardy to –20°F/–29°C. Flowers are ½-inch bells of greenish yellow veined in red, hanging below 3-inch, bluish green leaves. *E. c. palibinii* has solidly red blossoms, with dark veins against a lighter red background. 'Albiflorus' has white flowers. In time, these shrubs may reach 20 feet. 'Red Bells' has red flowers on a 3-foot plant. Autumn foliage color runs from bright yellow through orange to red.

E. cernuus is hardy to –10°F/–23°C. White bells decorate a shorter, bushier plant (to about 10 feet) with smaller leaves. The basic species is less frequently sold than its dark red–flowered form *E. c. rubens* (*E. c.* 'Matsudai'). Both have vivid red autumn foliage.

E. perulatus is hardy to –10°F/–23°C. This is both the shortest (to 8 feet high) and the smallest-flowered species, but its earlier flowering makes a display of white blossoms before new foliage emerges. The broadly oval, 2-inch leaves are brilliant scarlet in autumn.

ERICA
Heath
Ericaceae

Evergreen: Hardiness varies
Flowers: Purple, red, pink, lavender, white; all seasons
Exposure: Sun
Water: Regular
Growth: Slow to moderate

Though they differ in small details, the heaths and heather (*Calluna,* see page 99) are so similar in appearance, use, and culture that horticulturally they seem as one. All have tiny (sometimes needlelike) leaves, small flowers that are urn shaped or bell shaped (tubular in some South African *Erica* species), and a need for excellently drained but moist soil. An important difference is that some heaths are less finicky than heather about atmospheric coolness, being capable of turning in good performances in Mediterranean as well as English climates. And with careful selection, you can have heaths flowering throughout the year.

Heaths need a light, organically enriched soil, and all but a few species need acid soil, as well. Water fre-

Erica carnea

quently enough to keep soil moist but never saturated. If plants begin to look paler than normal, give them a light application of an acid fertilizer in early spring. After flowers fade, shear or cut off spikes of spent flowers. You can shape plants of the larger-growing kinds by cutting back to branches or to a leaf; if you cut back into leafless wood, new growth may not sprout.

The *Erica* species are both geographically widespread and diverse in appearance. Most of the lower-growing, spreading (and hardiest) kinds hail from the British Isles, northern Europe, and the Alps. Those from Portugal, Spain, southern France, and northern Africa are likely to be bushier shrubs, tolerating more heat and dryness but less cold. The South African species are the most cold sensitive.

Northern European heaths. In plant habit and size, these species resemble *Calluna* (heather) selections. *E. carnea* and its named selections (sometimes sold as *E. herbacea*), hardy to –20°F/–29°C, are widely sold; plants are spreading with upright branches, to about 1½ feet in the tallest kinds. Flowers come from midwinter into spring; colors include white, pink shades, and both light and dark red.

Two other species—both hardy to about 0°F/–18°C—make spreading plants with growth mounding to about a foot. *E. ciliaris,* Dorset heath, has rosy red summer flowers and light green leaves; named selections offer white and red blossoms and darker foliage. *E. cinerea,* twisted heath, spreads its purple summer blossoms over tiny, dark green leaves; named selections

include plants with red flowers and with both compact and bushy habits.

E. tetralix, cross-leafed heath, is also hardy to 0°F/–18°C. Upright, foot-tall plants have rosy pink flowers from summer into autumn; new growth is yellow, orange, or red, maturing to dark green. Named selections offer white or pink flowers and grayish foliage. *E. vagans,* Cornish heath, is hardy to –10°F/–23°C. These bushy plants may grow to 2 feet or more, producing purplish pink flowers in summer; selections include those with white and nearly red blossoms.

Mediterranean heaths. These plants are all sizable, one even capable of becoming a small tree. The most cold-tolerant is *E. erigena* (*E. mediterranea*), Biscay heath, which is hardy to 0°F/–18°C. Growth is upright and fairly open, from 5 to 10 feet. Deep green foliage is a backdrop for lilac-pink flowers from midwinter to midspring; 'W. T. Rackliff' has white blossoms with contrasting brown anthers. This species will grow well in neutral soil.

Two species are hardy to about 10°F/–12°C. *E. australis,* southern heath, is an upright plant to 10 feet with spirelike branches that make a spiky outline. Rose red flowers bloom from early to late spring; 'Mr. Robert' is a white-flowered selection. *E. lusitanica,* Spanish heath, grows to 12 feet as an upright, feathery shrub with light green leaves and palest pink flowers from midwinter to spring.

E. arborea, tree heath, is hardy to about 5°F/–15°C. This is a dense, bulky shrub or multitrunked shrub tree capable of reaching 20 feet after many years. Fragrant white blossoms come in late winter through midspring.

South African heaths. These species include growth habits from low and spreading to sizably shrubby. All are hardy to about 15°F/–9°C, limiting their use chiefly to California.

E. canaliculata (often sold as *E. melanthera*) makes a 6-foot, rounded and spreading plant with a somewhat spiky outline. Pink to rosy purple flowers come in autumn and winter; leaves are dark green with white undersides. Its selection 'Boscaweniana' features nearly white flowers on a potentially larger shrub to shrub tree.

(Continued on next page)

E. mammosa grows stiffly upright to about 3 feet, its bright green foliage setting off pink flowers that arrive in early spring and then repeat in bursts through summer into autumn. Named selections include some with flowers in warm pink tones. *E. persoluta* also grows stiffly upright but to about 2 feet; pink or white flowers appear in winter and early spring.

Tubular blossoms, like little firecrackers, set two species apart from those just described. *E. doliiformis* is a foot-tall plant with needlelike leaves and clusters of rosy red flowers from early summer into autumn. *E. hyemalis* grows upright and spiky to 3 feet, its inch-long blossoms appearing in winter. Colors include white, pink, coral, and orange. The hybrid 'Felix Faure' (sometimes sold simply as "French heather") also has tubular flowers: lilac-pink with white tips, flowering in winter on compact, foot-tall plants.

Hybrid heaths. The cross of *E. carnea* with *E. erigena* produced a group of plants designated *E. darleyensis*; these are hardy to about –20°F/–29°C. Plants are full and bushy, growing 1 to 2 feet high depending on the individual. They grow well in neutral soil and tolerate more heat and dryness than most others. 'Darley Dale' has light rose purple flowers from midautumn to midspring; 'George Rendall' bears darker purple flowers at the same time of year. Taller-growing 'Silberschmelze' ('Molten Silver') sports white flowers in winter and spring.

Hybrids of *E. ciliaris* and *E. tetralix* are called *E. watsonii*. 'Dawn' is a widely sold selection: a good, foot-high ground cover plant with golden new growth in spring and deep pink blossoms from late spring into autumn.

ESCALLONIA
Escallonia
Saxifragaceae

Evergreen: Hardy to 15°F/–9°C; West Coast only
Flowers: Red, pink, white; season varies
Exposure: Sun, partial shade
Water: Regular
Growth: Fast

Escallonia langleyensis 'Apple Blossom'

With their neat, glossy leaves and dense growth, escallonias rank high among choices for hedges, screens, and barriers. But their good overall appearance and prolonged flowering recommend them for specimen planting as well. They range in height from 3-foot shrubs to 15- to 20-foot shrub trees. Nurseries offer quite a few species and named hybrids, all of which feature small, trumpet-shaped, five-petaled blossoms clustered at the ends of new growth. Principal flowering times are late spring, summer, and early autumn.

Escallonias are premier seacoast plants, where they will grow in full sun and exposed to ocean winds. In hot-summer territory, give them partial shade. They'll grow well in averagely fertile soil, from slightly alkaline to somewhat acid; established plants (particularly in coastal climates) are somewhat drought tolerant.

Three species encompass the tallest-growing plants. White escallonia, *E. bifida* (*E. montevidensis*), is a broad 10-foot shrub that can be trained as a small, multitrunked tree to about 25 feet. Dark, 4-inch leaves back large clusters of white flowers in late summer and autumn. (Note: There is some mislabeling in the nursery trade. Plants of this name with small flower clusters and resinous-smelling leaves are the strictly shrubby *E. illinita*.) Pink escallonia, *E. laevis* (*E. organensis*), reaches 12 to 15 feet high with bronzy green leaves; pink to white blooms come in early summer. In exposed seacoast sites and where summer is especially hot, expect burned leaves. *E. rubra* is an upright plant reaching 6 to

15 feet high, bearing small clusters of red flowers over a long period.

Midsize plants include a number of hybrid selections. *E. exoniensis* 'Frades' (*E.* 'Fradesii') makes a dense shrub to 6 feet with small leaves and a virtually year-round production of rose pink flowers. *E. langleyensis* 'Apple Blossom' features palest pink blossoms from late spring into autumn on a dense but sprawling 5-foot plant. *E. l.* 'Pride of Donard' grows 5 to 6 feet high and spreads wider, producing rosy pink flowers nearly all year; *E. l.* 'Donard Brilliance' is similar, but with deep rose red blossoms. *E. l.* 'Gwendolyn Anley' (sometimes listed as a selection of *E. virgata*) offers flesh pink flowers on a 4- to 6-foot plant that is partly deciduous; this selection and its parent *E. virgata* are the hardiest escallonias. *E.* 'Jubilee', an *E. laevis* hybrid, is a dense 6-footer with rose pink blossoms that can appear throughout the year.

Several low-growing escallonias reach about 3 feet tall. These include *E.* 'Compakta' (rosy red), *E. rubra* 'C. F. Ball' (crimson red), and *E. r.* 'William Watson' (ruddy cerise, on a plant to 4 feet). Shortest of all is *E.* 'Newport Dwarf', a spreading plant to 2½ feet high with nearly red blossoms.

EUONYMUS
Euonymus
Celastraceae

Deciduous, evergreen: Hardiness varies
Flowers: Insignificant
Exposure: Sun, light shade
Water: Moderate
Growth: Moderate

The deciduous and evergreen euonymus species are two distinct plants, recognizable as related only if you compare their characteristic squarish "hatbox" fruits. The deciduous species are noted particularly for their neon-bright autumn foliage color; the evergreens include some of the most cold-tolerant broad-leafed plants.

The deciduous species are best planted in full sun; the evergreen kinds will also take light or partial shade. None is particular about soil, and, once plants are established, they'll need just

Euonymus alata

moderate watering. Scale can bother any of the species.

E. alata, WINGED EUONYMUS, is deciduous, hardy to –30°F/–34°C. Two characteristics immediately identify this species. Its branch pattern is distinctly horizontal, forming a fairly flat-topped shrub to 10 feet high by 15 feet wide; and young stems exhibit flat, corky, winglike ridges. Its fruit is smaller and less profuse than that of European spindle tree, but autumn color is a blinding red. The selection 'Compacta' is a bit smaller (with smaller corky "wings" on stems), forming a dense, rounded mound.

E. europaea, EUROPEAN SPINDLE TREE, is deciduous, hardy to –30°F/–34°C. This is potentially the tallest species—up to 20 feet—and may be trained into a widely spreading small tree with green stems in an angular branching pattern. The 3-inch, oval leaves change in autumn to a bright rosy pink, coincident with the ripening of pink to red fruits that split open to reveal orange seeds. Its selection 'Aldenhamensis' bears heavier crops of larger fruits. Native North American *E. atropurpurea*, burning bush or Wahoo, is similar except for its definite red autumn foliage color.

E. fortunei (sometimes erroneously labeled *E. radicans*) is evergreen, hardy to –20°F/–29°C. Like ivy, this vining plant produces shrubby mature growth with flowers and fruits; plants propagated from mature growth remain shrubby. The neat, attractive plants have leathery, lustrous, oval leaves 1 to 2 inches long. 'Carrierei' makes a spreading shrub 4 to 6 feet high with dark, glossy leaves; showy orange fruits may appear in autumn. 'Silver Queen' differs only in having white-margined leaves. Other widely sold green-leafed selections—all with upright growth—include 'Emerald Charm' (to about 6 feet), 'Emerald

Pride' (to about 4 feet), and 'Sarcoxie' (to 4 feet and slightly less cold tolerant). 'Golden Prince' (4 to 5 feet) has yellow-tipped new growth that matures to solid dark green.

The numerous variegated-leaf selections of *E. fortunei* include 'Emerald Gaiety' (white leaf margins) and 'Emerald 'n' Gold' (yellow leaf margins), both of which reach 4 to 5 feet tall. Low, compact plants to about 1½ feet are 'Canadale Gold' (light green leaves with yellow margins) and 'Sparkle 'n' Gold' (deep green leaves with yellow margins).

E. japonica, EVERGREEN EUONYMUS, is hardy to –5°F/–21°C. Solid, bulky plants with dense foliage thrive in good or poor soil, with regular or moderate watering, in heat as well as in seashore coolness. The leathery, glossy leaves and intermediate height—to 10 feet tall by 6 feet wide—recommend them as hedge and barrier plantings. Although the basic species offers dark green leaves, the many variegated-leaf selections are more widely planted. Your choices include green leaves edged in yellow or white and leaves with bold, yellow, central blotches.

Several other selections stand out as distinctive. 'Grandifolia' has dark green leaves larger than the normal 2½-inch ovals. 'Microphylla' (*E. j. pulchella*) is called "boxleaf euonymus" because of its relatively tiny foliage. Its plants are dense, to 2 feet high and 1 foot wide; 'Microphylla Variegata' has cream-margined leaves.

Unfortunately, *E. japonica* is the most pest-plagued euonymus. Powdery mildew can be a problem everywhere but the Pacific Northwest. Scale and thrips are common, as are spider mites where summer is hot.

E. kiautschovica (E. patens) is evergreen, hardy to –10°F/–23°C. In contrast with the other evergreen species, this has thinner-textured, light green leaves (partly deciduous in coldest regions) and tiny, greenish cream flowers profuse enough in late summer to put on a subtle show. Bloom is followed by conspicuous red-seeded pink to reddish fruits. Plants reach about 8 feet high, spreading as wide or wider, with some low branches trailing on the ground and rooting. Two selec-

tions are commendable hedge plants. 'DuPont' has dark green leaves on a 4- to 6-foot plant; 'Manhattan' is an upright grower with dark, glossy foliage.

EXOCHORDA
Pearl bush
Rosaceae

Deciduous: Hardy to –20°F/–29°C
Flowers: White; midspring
Exposure: Sun
Water: Regular to moderate
Growth: Moderate

Elongated clusters of nearly round white flower buds suggest strings of pearls—hence the common name. These buds open to five-petaled single flowers that blanket the plants, even though the 2-inch ovate leaves emerge at the same time. The foliage and arching growth suggest the related *Spiraea*, but with considerably larger individual flowers.

Most commonly sold is the hybrid *E. macrantha* 'The Bride', which carries its 1½- to 2-inch flowers on a mounded plant to 4 feet. Common pearl bush, *E. racemosa (E. grandiflora)*, forms a much larger and more upright plant—to 15 feet high and wide—bearing 1¼-inch blossoms.

Pearl bushes are not particular plants, given sun and soil that is well drained and reasonably fertile. Blossoms come on stems formed in the previous year; prune to shape or to thin out old, twiggy stems after flowering has finished.

Exochorda macrantha 'The Bride'

Fatsia japonica

FATSIA JAPONICA
Japanese aralia
Araliaceae

Evergreen: Hardy to 5°F/–15°C
Flowers: White; autumn, winter
Exposure: Sun to shade
Water: Regular to moderate
Growth: Moderate

Dreaming of bold, tropical-looking foliage on a fairly hardy plant? This choice has little competition. Great, palmately lobed leaves to 16 inches across are bright to dark green, with a highly polished surface. Each leaf is attached to the end of a long leafstalk that springs directly from a canelike stem; leaves tend to overlap like shingles. Stems rise directly from the ground, branching very little (or not at all) as they grow upward 5 to 8 feet.

Large, branching flower sprays consist of many ball-shaped clusters of tiny white blossoms; these are followed by small, black, berrylike fruits whose seeds may later self-sow. 'Variegata', with leaves margined in cream to yellow, is slightly less vigorous than the green-leafed species. 'Moseri' is naturally low growing and compact.

You can emphasize the naturally vertical, leggy look by selectively removing new stems as they sprout from the base. Or, to create a bushier, more rounded plant, cut back stems to any height; this forces branches to grow from beneath the cut. Any gangly, overgrown specimen can be rejuvenated by severely heading it back in early spring.

Japanese aralia grows in a range of soils from light to heavy, as long as soil doesn't remain saturated. Chlorosis may occur if the soil is alkaline. Where summer is cool, you can plant it in full sun (but not where heat will be reflected from walls or pavement) as well as in shade. In hot-summer regions give it partial to full shade. Scale is a potential pest, and slugs and snails can deface the leaves.

FORSYTHIA
Forsythia
Oleaceae

Deciduous: Hardy to –20°F/–29°C
Flowers: Yellow; late winter, early spring
Exposure: Sun
Water: Regular to moderate
Growth: Fast

In golden fanfare, blatant forsythia trumpets "spring is here." Leafless, lifeless-appearing stems suddenly burst forth in narrow-petaled blossoms that light up the wintry landscape in sprays of yellow flame. After their moment of glory, they put on broadly oval, rich green leaves; most lack any special autumn foliage color.

The most widely sold forsythias are selections of *F. intermedia* (itself a hybrid of two species) and offspring of *F. intermedia* selections crossed back to one of the parents. These are a varied group in height, spread, and general habit, but all have particularly fine flowers in abundance.

The basic growth habit is upright stems with arching lateral branches. 'Beatrix Farrand', upright to about 10 feet, is among the tallest: vivid yellow, 2-inch flowers are touched with orange. 'Spectabilis' is nearly as tall, bearing similar-size blossoms in a solid deep yellow. Stiffly upright to 7 feet, 'Lynwood' (often sold as 'Lynwood Gold') offers tawny yellow flowers, whereas 'Spring Glory' in the same height range varies the theme with 2-inch pale yellow flowers. 'Karl Sax' is similar to 'Beatrix Farrand' but with clear, unshaded yellow blooms on a shorter plant (6 to 8 feet) whose stems arch more gracefully. 'Meadow Lark', a somewhat arching plant 6 to 9 feet high, bears 1-inch bright yellow blossoms; its flower buds are reputedly hardy to –35°F/–37°C, and the plant itself will survive even lower temperatures.

Forsythia

Forsythias are content with average soil and demand no special attention. Flowers come on stems formed the previous year, so delay any pruning until after bloom. On established plants, you may want to remove a third of the oldest stems yearly; this encourages replacement stems that produce more and better blossoms. Thinning is the best pruning approach; shearing and heading back will destroy or compromise the shrub's natural grace.

Fremontodendron
(see page 141)

GARDENIA JASMINOIDES
Gardenia
Rubiaceae

Evergreen: Hardy to 20°F/–7°C
Flowers: White; spring, summer, autumn
Exposure: Sun, partial shade
Water: Regular
Growth: Moderate

Gardenias are synonymous with fragrance—a penetrating, heady scent that is worth the extra care these plants need. But they offer more than just olfactory delight. Plants are densely clothed in highly polished, medium to dark green oval leaves to 4 inches; double white flowers combine the appearance of camellias with the texture of magnolias. Gardenias make handsome landscape subjects but are also excellent in containers, where their cultural needs can be easily satisfied.

Several named selections give you choices in flower and plant size. 'Mystery', the most widely grown, is a somewhat rangy plant (unless pinched and pruned), 6 to 8 feet high with 4- to

Gardenia jasminoides 'Mystery'

5-inch, double blossoms in spring and summer. 'August Beauty' is a somewhat smaller, more compact plant that can produce 'Mystery'-size flowers from midspring into early autumn. Flowers of 'Golden Magic' have more petals than the others', opening white but aging to a deep tawny yellow; plants reach 4 to 6 feet high and wide.

Three selections offer smaller flowers (about 1½ inches across) in greater quantity than the large-flowered kinds. 'Veitchii' makes a compact, 3- to 5-foot plant that is less fussy than most gardenias; it blooms from spring into autumn. 'Veitchii Improved' bears heavier crops of slightly larger flowers on a bush to 5 feet. 'Kimura Shikazaki' ('Four Seasons') is a slightly less fragrant version of 'Veitchii' on a 2- to 3-foot plant.

To succeed with gardenias, you need to give them warmth for the best growth and flower production. Where summer is cool, plant in full sun; reflected heat from walls or pavement will boost heat in such climes. In hot-summer regions, give plants light or filtered shade—or morning sun but light shade thereafter. Rhododendron and azalea conditions suit gardenias, too: well-drained, organically enriched, acid to neutral soil that is always moist but well aerated. Set the root ball high so that moisture won't collect at the plant's base.

Give gardenias monthly fertilizer applications during the growing season; where soil or water tends to be alkaline, use an acid-reaction fertilizer. Unless your water has a high salt content (which can cause leafburn), sprinkle foliage in the mornings when plants are not in flower. Aphids, scale, and mealybugs are potential pests.

GREVILLEA
Grevillea
Proteaceae

Evergreen: Hardy to 15°F/–9°C
Flowers: Pink, red, orange, yellow; spring, autumn, winter
Exposure: Sun
Water: Moderate
Growth: Moderate

These Australian plants are entirely suited to Mediterranean-climate California plus intermediate- and low-desert parts of California and Arizona. Most have narrow, linear leaves, giving the shrubs a fine-textured (even filmy) appearance. Each flower is a narrowly tubular structure with a prominently extended stamen; clustered together, they make a conspicuous show and attract hummingbirds.

Grevilleas need well-drained, neutral to acid soil but aren't fussy about quality or fertility. During dry months, give plants no more than moderate watering; overwatering can be fatal.

Several hybrid grevilleas are widely grown. 'Noellii' has inch-long, nearly needlelike, glossy leaves and clustered red-and-cream flowers over nearly 2 months in spring. Plants reach 4 feet high and a bit wider. 'Canberra' also has inch-long, needlelike leaves but on a fairly open shrub to 8 feet high by 12 feet across. Clustered, dark red flowers are profuse in late spring but appear sporadically throughout the year. Orange-red 'Constance' is similar but even more wide spreading.

G. juniperina (G. sulphurea) features pale yellow, clustered blossoms in late spring. Plants may reach 6 feet with an equal spread, the stems clothed in needlelike leaves ½ to 1 inch long.

G. rosmarinifolia, ROSEMARY GREVILLEA, has narrow, rosemarylike leaves: dark green with silver undersides. Clustered red-and-cream (occasionally pink-and-white) blossoms come

Grevillea rosmarinifolia

mainly in autumn and winter. Dense plants reach 6 feet high and nearly as wide; a "dwarf selection" is identical but is only 3 by 4 feet.

HAMAMELIS
Witch hazel
Hamamelidaceae

Deciduous: Hardiness varies
Flowers: Yellow, orange, red; autumn, winter
Exposure: Sun, light shade
Water: Regular
Growth: Moderate

These shrubs prove that winter can be colorful even in chilly-winter climates. Falling somewhere between subtle and spectacular, their display could be called "cheering" on a clammy winter day. Plants are medium-size to large, and sometimes even treelike; they're generally of spreading habit, with angular or zigzag branching. Each flower is made up of numerous narrow, crumpled petals, whose effect is like a small bunch of shredded coconut; most types are fragrant. Leaves are generally rounded to obovate and rather filbertlike; they put on a fine autumn color display.

Give witch hazels a fairly good neutral to acid soil enriched with organic matter. Prune only to guide growth, remove poorly placed branches (and suckers, on grafted plants), or pilfer a few stems for winter bouquets.

H. intermedia comprises a group of hybrids between the Chinese and Japanese witch hazels; they are hardy to –20°F/–29°C. In general these are large shrubs, to around 15 feet in height. Of these hybrids, 'Arnold Promise' makes

Hamamelis intermedia 'Diane'

a large, vase-shaped plant bearing bright yellow blossoms in midwinter after the display of orange-red autumn foliage. 'Diane' has ruddy gold autumn foliage and red winter flowers on a large, spreading plant. 'Feuerzauber' (usually cataloged as 'Firecharm' or 'Magic Fire') features coppery red blossoms on an upright shrub.

'Jelena' (also listed as 'Copper Beauty') makes a large, spreading plant that colors yellow and orange in autumn; red-tinted yellow flowers register as orange in the landscape. 'Ruby Glow' offers coppery red flowers and rusty gold autumn color on an upright-growing shrub.

H. japonica, JAPANESE WITCH HAZEL, is hardy to –20°F/–29°C. Compared with its Chinese counterpart, this species has smaller flowers on a shorter plant; some forms add red bases to their yellow petals. Its chief distinction is its bright red autumn foliage, making it nearly unique among these plants.

H. mollis, CHINESE WITCH HAZEL, is hardy to –10°F/–23°C. Sweetly fragrant, bright yellow blossoms decorate its bare limbs in midwinter. This can become a widely spreading 12-foot shrub or, with guidance, a small tree perhaps twice that height. Dark green, broadly oval leaves to 6 inches are rough surfaced but gray-woolly beneath; they turn a luminous yellow in autumn. 'Brevipetala' is faster growing and more upright than the species, its flowers a bit smaller but tinged with red for an orange effect. 'Pallida' is a heavy producer of large, light yellow blossoms.

Two North American species are hardy to about –20°F/–29°C. H. vernalis is often the first shrub to flower in the new year. Its small yellow flowers make up in fragrance for what they lack in size; some individuals have red-based or red-tinted petals. The habit is upright to 10 feet, spreading about as wide; in autumn, leaves turn yellow. H. virginiana is the earliest or latest witch hazel to flower, depending on your point of view: its display of yellow flowers shares the spotlight with the vivid yellow autumn foliage. This plant is fairly dense in sun, wispier in partial shade—about 15 by 15 feet.

Hebe **'Autumn Glory'**

HEBE
Hebe
Scrophulariaceae

Evergreen: Hardy to 20°F/–7°C, except as noted; West Coast only
Flowers: Purple, lavender, rose, white; primarily summer
Exposure: Sun
Water: Regular
Growth: Fast

Where summer temperatures are cool to moderate, these shrubby relatives of perennial *Veronica* bloom over a long season on plants that always appear neat. Tiny flowers with prominent stamens are grouped in rounded to foxtail-like spikes at branch tips, decorating the surface of dense, glossy-leafed plants. Individual leaves are narrow, oval to lance shaped, in opposite pairs: every other pair is rotated, so leaves appear to radiate from the stems.

All hebes must have well-drained soil with regular moisture; these are fine plants for seacoast gardens and coastal climates. Plant in sun where summer is cool, in partial shade elsewhere. To keep plants compact, head back flowering stems by half after blooms have finished; you can rejuvenate old, rangy plants by thinning out oldest stems and then severely heading back remaining newer growth.

The most heat- and cold-tolerant of the readily available hebes is H. 'Autumn Glory', hardy to 15°F/–9°C. Short spikes of violet flowers come in late summer and autumn on a rounded plant about 2 feet in diameter.

Many other species and named hybrids are found in the nursery trade.

H. andersonii (actually a hybrid) reaches 5 to 6 feet high and wide; summer flower spikes are white lower down, violet toward the tips. Showy hebe, H. speciosa, reaches about 5 feet high and at least as wide; summer flowers are red-purple. Selected forms are available with red-tinted and variegated leaves. H. elliptica (H. decussata) may reach 6 feet, with lighter green leaves than other species and bluish lavender summer flowers. Boxleaf hebe, H. buxifolia, has appropriately tiny leaves on a shrub to 5 feet that can be clipped as a formal hedge; rounded clusters of white flowers come in summer. Shortest of these species is H. glaucophylla, a spreading, 2-foot mound of ½-inch blue-green leaves and white summer flowers in dense clusters; good drainage is essential to avoid root rot.

The named hybrids all are roughly 3-foot plants with different bloom times and flower colors: 'Carnea' (rosy red, late summer); 'Coed' (pinkish purple, late spring and summer); 'Desilor' (deep blue-purple, spring to autumn); 'Lake', sometimes sold as 'Veronica Lake' (lavender-pink, summer); 'Patty's Purple' (purple, summer); and 'Reevesii', sometimes sold as 'Evansii' (red-purple, summer).

Heteromeles arbutifolia
(see page 141)

HIBISCUS SYRIACUS
Rose of Sharon, Shrub althaea
Malvaceae

Deciduous: Hardy to –20°F/–29°C
Flowers: Lavender, purple, red, pink, white; summer
Exposure: Sun
Water: Regular to moderate
Growth: Fast

Resembling a bush full of hollyhock flowers, rose of Sharon enlivens the landscape from mid- or late summer until frost. It boasts blossoms 2½ to 4 inches across that may be single, semidouble, or double, depending on the selection; some flowers have a conspicuously contrasting red to purple throat. Plants reach about 12 feet high —narrowly upright when young, more wide spreading once established. You

Hibiscus syriacus

can even train a plant to a single trunk for a short tree. The coarsely toothed, oval or lobed leaves form a dense foliage cover. These plants leaf out later in spring than do most other deciduous shrubs, and they drop their foliage in autumn without coloring. Most single-flowered kinds form unattractive seed capsules that, if left to ripen, produce copious volunteer seedling plants. The triploid hybrids 'Aphrodite' (pink), 'Diana' (pure white), and 'Minerva' (lavender) are seedless.

These are easy-culture plants, needing just average, well-drained soil. Unpruned individuals produce masses of small flowers, but you can head back plants heavily before leaf-out to get larger blossoms. The hardiness listed is for established specimens. Where winter temperatures drop to 10°F/−12°C or lower, give young plants at least a protective winter mulch for the first few years.

HYDRANGEA
Hydrangea
Saxifragaceae

Deciduous: Hardiness varies
Flowers: Blue, red, pink, white; summer
Exposure: Sun, partial shade
Water: Regular
Growth: Fast

Hydrangeas, which have been called everything from voluptuous to coarse and common, are conspicuous shrubs, with showy (usually large) flower heads and large leaves on plants that are often sizable and bulky. They pro-

duce two kinds of flowers: their fertile flowers are tiny and starlike, but the sterile blossoms, with their petal-like sepals, produce the major display. The showiest kinds (many of the *H. macrophylla* selections, for example) have only sterile flowers in their blossom clusters. The type called "lace cap" has both flower types in each cluster: sterile flowers ringing the fertile ones.

All hydrangeas flower in summer, some into early autumn. The sterile flowers remain attractive for many weeks, then fade to dull pink or green while retaining their shape.

Hydrangeas' prime cultural requirements are good, well-drained soil and regular water to support the great expanse of foliage. In cool-summer regions, you can grow them in full sun. But the hotter the summer temperatures, the more plants will need high shade or filtered sunlight during the hottest hours. All benefit from annual pruning, the severity of which depends on the effect you want. Heavy heading back, plus thinning out old stems, guarantees the largest flower clusters; moderate pruning gives you more clusters of a smaller size. Pruning time varies according to species.

H. arborescens is hardy to −30°F/ −34°C. In the basic species, most flowers in a cluster are fertile; the few sterile ones are not plentiful enough for a full "lace cap" effect. It is the selected forms that make this a valuable flowering shrub. 'Grandiflora', often called "hills-of-snow," has 6-inch, snowball-like clusters of sterile white flowers on a plant to about 4 feet high and wide, densely clothed in gray-green oval leaves to 8 inches long. 'Annabelle' is a similar-size shrub, but the heads of its flowers can reach a foot across. In

Hydrangea quercifolia

both selections, flowers fade to green. Prune while they're leafless, in late winter or early spring.

H. macrophylla, BIGLEAF HYDRANGEA, is hardy to −10°F/−23°C. Here is the best-known hydrangea, widely planted for its truly impressive flower heads (easily a foot across) on a rounded shrub of large, glossy leaves. A great number of named selections exist—both lace cap types and those with all-sterile flowers (sometimes known as "hortensias")—though plants in the general retail nursery trade may be labeled only by color.

Typical plants reach 4 to 8 feet (and occasionally higher); French hybrids, the highly colored ones sold in florist shops, make smaller plants, in the 3- to 4-foot range. 'Domotoi' is an instantly recognizable selection: its all-sterile flowers are double. Another distinctive individual is the lace cap 'Tricolor' (often sold as 'Variegata'), its dark green leaves variegated in light gray-green and white.

Flower colors include white as well as light pink to crimson and from light blue to intense blue-purple. If you wish, you can manipulate color by soil treatment if you start well ahead of bloom time. Acid soil induces blue to purple colors; neutral to alkaline soil encourages pink to red. Apply aluminum sulfate to develop or enhance blueness, lime or superphosphate to maintain or intensify red tones.

Bigleaf hydrangeas flower on the stems formed just after the previous year's blossoms fade. Thus, the best time to prune for flower production (and perhaps to limit plant size) is in summer. As flowers fade, new growth will start lower on the stems; cut stems back to the strongest pair of new shoots or to a pair of buds that will send out stems where you want new growth to be. Then in winter you can remove old, unproductive limbs to the ground.

H. paniculata 'Grandiflora', PEEGEE HYDRANGEA, is hardy to −30°F/−34°C. With just a bit of coaxing, you can make this shrub a single- or multi-trunked tree perhaps 25 feet high. As a shrub, though, it reaches a rounded 10 to 15 feet, its branches arching from the weight of the blossom clusters. The basic species, with many fertile flowers to a cluster, is far less showy than the selection 'Grandiflora', whose mostly sterile flowers form 12- to 15-inch-long clusters resembling spikes of white lilac. Flowering starts in summer, the old blossoms aging to purplish pink. Oval, 5-inch leaves become bronzy in autumn. Prune in spring before leaf-out.

H. quercifolia, OAKLEAF HYDRANGEA, is hardy to –10°F/–23°C. Its foliage alone justifies planting this species. Not only are the 8-inch leaves deeply lobed like those of many oaks, but the autumn color is a very oaklike bronzy red. Each plant spreads slowly to form a multistemmed, upright clump to about 6 feet high. Mature stems feature cinnamon-colored, flaking bark. Elongated clusters (to 10 inches) of fertile and sterile white flowers come in late spring and early summer, turning pinkish purple as they fade. The selection 'Snow Queen' contains virtually all sterile flowers.

Stems may freeze to the ground where temperatures drop below 0°F/–18°C, forcing the plant to grow new stems each year. Because flowers are formed on old wood, this means no blossoms. In milder areas, cut back flowering stems halfway just after flowers have started to fade, as recommended for *H. macrophylla*. Thin out old and superfluous stems in winter.

HYPERICUM
St. Johnswort
Hypericaceae

Evergreen: Hardiness varies
Flowers: Yellow; summer
Exposure: Sun, partial shade
Water: Regular to moderate
Growth: Moderate

At first glance you might mistake a *Hypericum* flower for a single rose. The five-petaled blossoms are indeed roselike, but the simple, oval to lance-shaped leaves in opposite pairs are not. These are shrubby, upright to arching plants in the 2- to 6-foot range.

The various St. Johnsworts are not particular about soil; regular water produces a better appearance, but plants will tolerate some drought. All do best where there is some atmo-

Hypericum 'Hidcote'

spheric moisture. In hot-summer regions, give plants partial shade. Late frosts can kill developing flower buds.

H. beanii (H. patulum henryi) is hardy to 0°F/–18°C. Brilliant yellow 2-inch flowers decorate this gracefully arching plant from midsummer into autumn. 'Gold Cup' is a selection with slightly larger blossoms.

H. frondosum is hardy to –10°F/–23°C. This native of the southern United States will thrive in sun or shade and is notably drought tolerant. Growth reaches 3 to 4 feet high and wide, the bright yellow, 1½-inch flowers appearing at branch tips during summer. Its blue-green leaves are partly deciduous in coldest regions.

H. 'Hidcote' **(H. patulum** 'Hidcote') is hardy to 0°F/–18°C. From a bushy, rounded plant comes a profusion of 3-inch, eggyolk yellow flowers throughout summer. In colder regions, plants may lose some of their leaves over winter and freeze back enough to keep the total height as low as 2 feet.

H. kouytchense is hardy to 0°F/–18°C. Under this name belong the plants sold as *H.* 'Sungold'. Growth is rounded and twiggy, to 2 feet high with a greater spread. The plants are covered with 2- to 3-inch golden blossoms during the height of summer. Their foliage is partly deciduous at the cold end of their range.

H. 'Rowallane' is hardy to 10°F/–12°C. This hybrid has splendid 3-inch flowers on the tallest but wispiest plant. Upright growth, to a possible 6 feet, is graceful but open or sparse. Flowers bloom in late summer and autumn.

ILEX
Holly
Aquifoliaceae

Evergreen (except as noted): Hardiness varies; most need some winter chill
Flowers: Insignificant
Exposure: Sun, partial shade
Water: Regular
Growth: Moderate

Hollies are shrubby plants by nature, but they can surprise you. After many years, several of the species will end up at tree height but with branches carried to the ground—giant shrubs, in effect, unless you remove their limbs to expose the trunk. But hollies are a variable lot. Most tree-size species are also available in genuinely shrubby selections; and among the entire body of hollies you have quite a choice of foliage characters—even some that lose their leaves in winter.

Holly plants are either male or female; the colorful berries come only on female plants. A few female hollies will bear fruits without pollination, but in most cases you need both male and female plants growing nearby to get berries. The simplest solution is to plant a male of the same species as the fruiting females; if you use a different species, berries will form only if both species flower at the same time. One male plant will pollinate up to 10 nearby females. Some growers offer female plants with a male branch grafted onto them; this ensures pollen for berry set on that plant.

Although hollies will grow in sun or shade, best berry production and most compact growth occur in sun. For best performance, plant in well-drained, good garden soil that is slightly acid. High summer temperatures and drying winds rule out all but a few hollies in the Southwest and lower Midwest. Potential pests in any region are scale and mealybug; in the Northwest, leaf miner and holly bud moth also inflict damage.

I. altaclarensis 'Wilsonii', WILSON HOLLY, is hardy to 0°F/–18°C. This exceptional hybrid will perform well in frost-free areas and will even succeed in the Southwest and lower Midwest if given protection from wind and intense summer sun. Leathery, rich green, oval leaves reach 5 inches long, the margins adorned with evenly spaced spines. A heavy crop of bright red berries comes regularly without a pollenizer. Growth is shrubby to about 10 feet, but you can train it as a tree to about twice that height. It is not particular about soil, and established plants tolerate some drought.

I. aquifolium, ENGLISH HOLLY, is hardy to 0°F/−18°C. This is the "typical" holly, with spiny-edged, glossy leaves and clusters of brilliant red berries. Slow growth eventually produces a 40- to 60-foot tree with a 25- to 30-foot spread, but for many years it functions as an increasingly sizable, pyramidal shrub. It performs best where there is atmospheric moisture during the growing season; in hot, dry areas, shelter it from wind and intense sun.

This species has spawned a vast array of selections that differ in leaf color, shape, and amount of spines. Among those with variegated foliage, you'll find ones with leaves margined in cream or silver and others having cream or silver centers but green edges. A few selections—such as 'Fertilis' and 'San Gabriel'—produce berries without pollination. Shrubby male selections include 'Ferox' (small, with wickedly spiny leaves), 'Gold Coast' (yellow-edged leaves), and 'Little Bull' (small leaves). Visit a well-stocked nursery to see the range of choices.

I. aquipernyi is hardy to 0°F/−18°C. This group of hybrids takes its name from its parents, *I. aquifolium* and *I. pernyi.* Two selections, 'Brilliant' and 'San Jose', make dense cones to 10 feet (taller after many years) of 4-inch, sparsely spined leaves. Large berry crops come without pollination.

I. cornuta, CHINESE HOLLY, is hardy to 0°F/−18°C. This is a good 10-foot shrub for mild-winter regions, where it will get the long growing season it needs for berry set. Typically this one has glossy, nearly rectangular leaves with spines at the four corners; its berries are especially large. However, named selections vary greatly. The following all bear fruit without a pollenizer.

'Burfordii', Burford holly, has been a longtime mild-winter favorite. Its

Ilex cornuta

leaves are cupped downward and are nearly spineless. 'Dwarf Burford' ('Burfordii Nana') is a dense, smaller-leafed version eventually to about 7 feet. 'Berries Jubilee' is a small, large-leafed (and spiny) plant noted for heavy berry production. 'Dazzler' also bears heavy crops on a compact, upright plant with lightly spiny leaves. 'Willowleaf' makes a large, spreading plant (it's potentially a small tree) bearing distinctive long, narrow leaves. 'Rotunda' makes a knee-high mound with few or no berries.

I. crenata, JAPANESE HOLLY, is hardy to −10°F/−23°C. At first glance you'd hardly recognize this as a holly: the small spineless leaves look more like boxwood foliage, and the berries are black. Plants are upright, dense, usually 4 to 10 feet in height.

'Compacta' is particularly dense and compact, making it good for hedge planting; 'Convexa' is a tiny-leafed, rounded plant to 6 feet high with greater spread. 'Hetzii' is similar but with larger leaves, and 'Northern Beauty' is a more compact version. Low-growing forms include 'Glory' (a male plant), 'Green Island' (to 2 feet and spreading), 'Green Thumb' (to 1½ feet and upright), and 'Helleri' (to 1 foot and spreading).

I. meserveae is hardy to −20°F/−29°C. An English holly crossed with a species from Japan produced this group of hybrids, which combine excellent cold tolerance with "typical" holly appearance. The plants are dense and bushy, roughly 8 to 12 feet high, and have distinctive purple stems and glossy blue-green, spiny-edged leaves.

Those grown in full sun are more upright, with a bluer leaf color. Both male and female plants are needed to get the showy red berries. 'Blue Angel', 'Blue Girl', 'Blue Princess', and 'China Girl' are available female selections. 'Blue Boy', 'Blue Prince', 'Blue Stallion', and 'China Boy' are male plants for pollination. 'Golden Girl', a female plant, bears yellow fruits.

I. 'Nellie R. Stevens' is hardy to 0°F/−18°C. This fast-growing hybrid of English and Chinese hollies has glossy leaves with a few soft spines on a broadly pyramidal shrub to about 15 feet—or a small tree to 20 to 25 feet. Showy red berries will set without a pollenizer. Like its Chinese parent, this is a good plant for mild-winter, warm-summer regions.

I. opaca, AMERICAN HOLLY, is hardy to −20°F/−29°C. This North American native resembles English holly but is considerably more cold tolerant. Spiny-edged leaves may be glossy or dull green; red berries come singly or in small clusters, lacking the profusion of English holly berries. Over many years, American holly will progress from a dense pyramid to a round-topped, somewhat open small tree about 30 feet high. Well-stocked nurseries, particularly in the eastern states, offer a number of named selections, including those with yellow berries.

I. 'San Jose Hybrid' is hardy to 0°F/−18°C yet will grow well in frost-free areas. This English holly hybrid resembles another English holly offspring, *I. altaclarensis* 'Wilsonii'. Longer, narrower foliage distinguishes this plant, which is a vigorous, upright grower 15 to 20 feet high bearing copious quantities of red berries.

I. verticillata, WINTERBERRY, is deciduous and hardy to −30°F/−34°C. Native to swamps of eastern North America, this holly nevertheless grows well under ordinary garden conditions. Plants are rounded, 8 to 15 feet high and wide, bearing moderately glossy oval leaves to 4 inches long. With a pollenizer, female plants set a heavy berry crop that ripens while leaves are still green. In warmer regions, the autumn foliage colors a good yellow and then drops to leave the plant a haze of brilliant red. In coldest areas, leaves may freeze and drop before color change. 'Winter Red' is a large-fruited selection; 'Red Sprite' is a much shorter plant with abundant berries.

I. vomitoria, YAUPON, is hardy to 0°F/ –18°C. An ability to grow in alkaline soils and to endure some drought sets this species apart from most other hollies. Its appearance, too, is distinctive: shiny green leaves are narrow, 1 to 1½ inches long, with lightly scalloped edges. Bright red, tiny berries form without a pollenizer. Slender growth reaches 15 to 25 feet high, making it a candidate for a high screen or hedge. 'Pride of Houston' is an especially good form; 'Pendula' has weeping branches. 'Nana' is a spreading shrub to about 1½ feet high; 'Stokes' is a bit shorter and more compact.

Juniperus (see page 105)

Justicia brandegeana
(see page 126)

KALMIA LATIFOLIA
Mountain laurel, Calico bush
Ericaceae

Evergreen: Hardy to –20°F/–29°C
Flowers: White, pink, red; spring
Exposure: Partial shade
Water: Regular
Growth: Slow to moderate

Without a doubt, mountain laurel is one of the most elegant flowering

Kalmia latifolia

shrubs native to North America. It reveals its relationship to *Rhododendron* in both plant and foliage. Bushes are rounded, eventually 10 feet or more in height and spread. Long, handsome leaves are leathery and dark green above, yellowish green below. The flowers, too, resemble rhododendron clusters, except that each long flower stalk bears a small bud resembling a fluted turban. These buds open to 1-inch, chalice-shaped flowers with five starlike points.

Pink flowers are the norm, opening from darker-colored buds, but blooms often have a subtly different color in their throats and may boast contrasting stamens. Specialty nurseries offer an increasing range of named selections, ranging from white through pink shades to red; many sport contrasting bands of color in a single blossom. Pale pink 'Elf' is notable for being a much smaller plant, to 3 feet high and 5 feet wide.

Mountain laurel needs rhododendron conditions: well-drained, acid soil with regular moisture and a mulch for coolness. Where summer is cool, plants may flourish in full sun, but in warmer regions they need partial or light shade. These are not shrubs for dry-summer areas. The best territories are the Pacific Northwest, the eastern states south to Florida, and westward into the Mississippi Valley.

KOLKWITZIA AMABILIS
Beauty bush
Caprifoliaceae

Deciduous: Hardy to –30°F/–34°C; needs some winter chill
Flowers: Pink; spring
Exposure: Sun, partial shade
Water: Regular to moderate
Growth: Fast

Each year beauty bush lives up to its name in mid- to late spring, when its arching branches become froths of soft pink blossoms. Each ½-inch flower is bell shaped: in a typical specimen, light pink and yellow throated, though seed-raised plants show a range of color depth. After flowering has finished, pinkish brown, bristly fruits form to carry a more subtle color display into summer.

Kolkwitzia amabilis

Plants consist of many stems arching fountainlike from the ground, their tips nearly meeting it again. The ultimate height may be 10 to 12 feet, partially shaded plants growing taller than those in full sun. Ovate, gray-green leaves reach 3 inches long and may turn reddish in autumn.

Beauty bush poses no cultural challenges; it adapts to many soils and climates. Flowers come on wood formed the previous year. To encourage continued rejuvenation without sacrificing flowers, thin out the oldest stems after flowers have faded.

Lantana (see page 126)

LEPTOSPERMUM
Tea tree
Myrtaceae

Evergreen: Hardy to 20°F/–7°C; West Coast only
Flowers: Red, pink, white; winter, spring, summer
Exposure: Sun
Water: Moderate
Growth: Moderate

Diminutive foliage and flowers like small, wide-open roses hardly suggest tea. The common name derives from an antiscurvy drink made, like tea, from an infusion of its leaves. The two commonly available species differ in size, but both feature showy displays of ½-inch flowers distributed along the stems. By nature these are informal, soft-looking plants, though the leaves are a bit prickly.

Tea trees need well-drained (even sandy) soil but regular water only until they're established. Neutral to

Leptospermum scoparium **'Ruby Glow'**

slightly acid soil is best; chlorosis may develop where soil is alkaline. These are excellent choices for seaside gardens. Plants are most attractive if allowed to develop their natural form, but they can also be closely planted and clipped as hedges. If you must shape, always cut to a branch or into leaf-bearing wood; if you prune into bare wood, regrowth is unlikely.

L. laevigatum, AUSTRALIAN TEA TREE, is capable of becoming a shrub tree 30 feet high and wide with a rounded but irregular shape, drooping branchlets, and shaggy-barked, multiple trunks. Narrowly oval, 1-inch leaves are gray-green to matte green. Single white flowers appear in spring. More useful as shrubs are two smaller-growing selections. 'Compactum' is a less dense plant than the basic species and not as lavish of blossom; it reaches just about 8 feet high and a bit less across. 'Reevesii', in contrast, has slightly larger, broader, more plentiful leaves on a plant 4 to 5 feet high and wide.

L. scoparium, NEW ZEALAND TEA TREE OR MANUKA, has produced a number of named selections that are shrubs of various sizes known for their dazzling floral show. The nearly needlelike leaves are just ½ inch long; flowers may be single, semidouble, or double.

These selections have crimson to ruby red blossoms: 'Crimson Glory' (double flowers on a 3-foot shrub with bronzy leaves); 'Red Damask' (double flowers on a 6- to 8-foot shrub with red-tinted leaves); and 'Ruby Glow' (large double flowers in great quantity and dark leaves). Among the pink-flowered selections are 'Apple Blossom' (double light pink flowers on an

upright plant to 6 feet, with light green leaves); 'Gaiety Girl' (double pinkish lilac flowers on a slow-growing, 5-foot plant with reddish leaves); 'Helene Strybing' (deep pink single flowers on a 6- to 10-foot plant); 'Keatleyi' (large, pale pink single flowers on a 6- to 10-foot rangy bush); 'Nanum Tui' (single pink flowers on a 2-foot, rounded plant); and 'Pink Pearl' (double blush pink to white flowers on a 6- to 10-foot plant). For pure white blossoms, look for double-flowered 'Snow White', a spreading shrub to 4 feet high.

LEUCOTHOE FONTANESIANA
Drooping leucothoe
Ericaceae

Evergreen: Hardy to –20°F/–29°C
Flowers: White; spring
Exposure: Partial shade, shade
Water: Regular
Growth: Slow

From the woods of eastern North America comes this elegant, graceful *Rhododendron* relative once known as *Leucothoe catesbaei*. Slowly spreading clumps send up arching stems that bear opposing ranks of leathery, polished oval leaves to 6 inches long. In spring, foliage is dark green, sometimes tipped in red; but in autumn, the color changes to bronzy purple and remains so during winter. In mid- to late spring, drooping flower clusters appear on last year's growth. Each creamy white flower resembles a lily-of-the-valley blossom; the dense clusters suggest another related shrub, *Pieris.* Leaves of the selection 'Rainbow' are variegated with cream, yel-

Leucothoe fontanesiana

low, and pink; foliage of 'Scarletta' is bronzy purple.

Drooping leucothoe grows best in woodland conditions: where shade is light or dappled, in well-drained, moist, organically enriched soil.

LIGUSTRUM
Privet
Oleaceae

Deciduous, evergreen: Hardiness varies
Flowers: White; spring, early summer
Exposure: Sun, light shade
Water: Regular to moderate
Growth: Fast

The general public may automatically link "privet" with "hedge"—and many privets are indeed useful hedge plants, combining the capacity to be sheared with fast growth and a complete lack of cultural fussiness. But released from the confines of formal trimming, many species are surprisingly good-looking as specimen shrubs. Where space permits, unclipped plantings provide the desired dense separation of a hedge while allowing the natural growth habit to shine.

Privet leaves (depending on the species) are broadly to narrowly oval, light to dark green, highly glossy to nearly lusterless. The foliage, plant habit, and especially the pyramidal

Ligustrum japonicum

spikes of tiny white flowers reveal the kinship to lilac (*Syringa*, pages 136–137). Unlike lilac, however, privet's fragrance generates little enthusiasm: allergy-prone individuals may find these shrubs a horticultural hazard. Small, blue-black berries follow the flowers, offering a banquet to birds.

These shrubs will grow in virtually any soil—preferably with regular watering, though established plants often endure extended dry periods. Because flowers are a secondary feature at most, you can prune privets whenever they need shaping.

Three species and one hybrid are similar enough that your choice will be determined chiefly by hardiness, by whether you want a deciduous or nearly evergreen plant, and by whether you want green or variegated foliage. California privet, *L. ovalifolium*, is hardy to –10°F/–23°C; it's partly deciduous in all but the mildest regions. Dark green, oval leaves reach 2½ inches long. Unpruned, this shrub may achieve 15 feet, its habit upright but spreading, with several main stems rising from the ground or close to it. Removing lower limbs will create a shrub tree. This privet's root system is notoriously greedy. In *L. o.* 'Aureum' (*L. o.* 'Variegatum'), each green leaf is broadly edged in yellow.

Hardiest of these similar privets—to –40°F/–40°C—is Amur privet, *L. amurense*. Its leaves are less glossy than those of California privet, and the plant is totally deciduous except in mildest regions. Common privet, *L. vulgare*, is hardy to –30°F/–34°C and reliably deciduous. The leaves are bright green and semiglossy, the roots less aggressive than those of California privet. The selection 'Lodense' ('Nanum') makes a 4-by-4-foot mound. *L. ibolium* 'Variegata', hardy to –20°F/–29°C, is a hybrid of California privet and much like it, except that its leaves are margined in creamy yellow.

Among deciduous privets, *L.* 'Vicaryi' stands alone because of its bright yellow leaves. Unpruned, it makes a rounded, 8- to 12-foot bush hardy to –20°F/–29°C. Its color is most vivid in full sun; as shade increases, leaves become chartreuse to green.

The most widely sold evergreen species is *L. japonicum* (also sold as *L.*

texanum), the Japanese or waxleaf privet; it's hardy to 0°F/–18°C. The leaves are a distinct selling point: dark green, leathery, rounded ovals to 4 inches long, their upper surface glossy, their undersides pale to nearly white. This is a dense, compact, fairly upright shrub, achieving 12 feet if not restricted by pruning. It's a handsome plant untrimmed but can be sheared easily. Where summer is hot and dry, give plants partial shade. Among the several selections, 'Texanum' offers an especially dense foliage cover on a plant just 6 to 9 feet high. Even shorter (4 to 5 feet) is 'Rotundifolium', with nearly round leaves and stiff, upright habit. 'Silver Star' is like the basic species, except that its dark leaves are mottled with gray and edged in creamy white.

The shortest evergreen privet is the hybrid *L.* 'Suwannee River', hardy to 0°F/–18°C. Unlike other privets, it grows slowly and bears no fruits. Its ultimate height is 3 to 4 feet, the plant densely covered with leathery, dark green, oval, slightly twisted leaves.

LONICERA
Honeysuckle
Caprifoliaceae

Deciduous, evergreen: Hardiness varies
Flowers: Pink, white; spring, summer
Exposure: Sun, partial shade
Water: Regular to moderate
Growth: Fast

Like the familiar vining honeysuckles, these shrubby species are vigorous, easy to grow, and virtually trouble free.

Lonicera tatarica 'Arnold Red'

Though they lack the floral "punch" of some of the more flamboyant shrubs, their plentiful flowers promise a restrained beauty and pleasant scent; and blossoming is followed by small, berrylike fruits that attract birds. Individual blossoms are tubular, flaring into two unequal lips; most white-flowered kinds age to yellow. Typically, leaves are oval and blue-green to green; they lack autumn color.

Honeysuckles are not demanding about soil. They'll look best with regular watering (provided you don't saturate the soil) but will get by with a moderate ration. All but *L. fragrantissima* flower on new growth, so they should be pruned in late winter or early spring before growth begins (prune *L. fragrantissima* after flowering has finished). Prune each year as needed, to remove broken and dead stems and head back any wayward branches. Every 3 to 4 years, thin out oldest stems to encourage renewal growth from the ground.

L. 'Clavey's Dwarf' is deciduous; it's hardy to –20°F/–29°C. This is the least showy of the shrub honeysuckles—greenish white flowers are small, often hidden in foliage—but it makes an excellent natural or clipped hedge. Unrestrained plants grow to 6 feet tall but can easily be kept to 3 feet. Gray-green leaves densely cover the plant, obscuring most of the red berries that form after flowering.

L. fragrantissima, WINTER HONEYSUCKLE, is deciduous to partly evergreen. It's hardy to –10°F/–23°C. Though the small, white spring flowers are not especially showy, their sweet fragrance alone makes the shrub worth planting. Somewhat stiff, arching stems reach 8 feet high, bearing lusterless, dark green leaves with blue-green undersides. Red berries ripen in late spring.

L. korolkowii is deciduous; it's hardy to –20°F/–29°C. Blue-green leaves, rose pink flowers in late spring, and red berries in late summer to early autumn add up to a harmonious picture. Arching stems form a shrub 8 to 12 feet high and about 8 feet wide. The selection 'Zabelii' has rosy red flowers on a smaller plant, about 6 feet tall.

L. maackii, AMUR HONEYSUCKLE, is deciduous; it's hardy to –40°F/–40°C. This is the tallest of the group, forming a wide-spreading plant 12 to 15 feet high. White flowers in late spring form berries that ripen to dark red in autumn. As the foliage is very late to drop, the plentiful red fruits are usually set off by green leaves.

L. morrowii is deciduous; it's hardy to –30°F/–34°C. The 6-foot, mounding plants spread up to 12 feet and are covered in gray-green leaves. Cream-white flowers in late spring are followed by red summer fruits.

L. nitida, BOX HONEYSUCKLE, is evergreen. It's hardy to 0°F/–18°C. Upright growth and a dense cover of ½-inch glossy leaves suggest boxwood (*Buxus*) in both appearance and hedge potential. Creamy white, ½-inch flowers in late spring are followed by blue-purple fruits. Leaves take on bronze to maroon tones during winter. These plants will grow well in exposed seacoast conditions.

L. tatarica, TATARIAN HONEYSUCKLE, is deciduous; it's hardy to –30°F/–34°C. Upright stems with arching branches form a dense plant 8 to 10 feet high, covered in dark green to blue-green foliage. The showy late spring flowers are usually pink but may also be white; their color varies among seed-grown plants. Summer berries are red. A number of selections have been named, including 'Arnold Red', which has dark rosy red blossoms. Mature plants tend to be rather bare at their bases.

Lycianthes rantonnei
(see page 127)

MAGNOLIA
Magnolia
Magnoliaceae

Deciduous: Hardiness varies
Flowers: White, pink, red; spring, summer
Exposure: Sun
Water: Regular
Growth: Slow to moderate

Most magnolias, even if shrubby while young, eventually grow up to be trees. But these two species and their hy-

Magnolia stellata

brids can be counted on to remain bushy at all times. Give them the same culture as specified for the tree-size magnolias on pages 69–70.

M. liliiflora (M. quinquepeta), LILY MAGNOLIA, is hardy to –10°F/–23°C. Its eventual height may be 12 feet, with many stems rising from a slowly spreading clump to an even greater spread. Flowers come in midspring as leaves are emerging and may continue into early summer. The vertical buds look a bit like purple bananas, opening to six-petaled flowers like elongated tulips with white petal faces. The leaves are 6- to 7-inch lustrous ovals that turn an attractive bronzy color before falling.

Several named selections offer flower variations. 'Nigra' has blossoms a bit larger than the standard 4 inches, their petal backs dark purple and their insides creamy white overcast with pink. 'O'Neill' is slightly larger and more highly colored than 'Nigra'.

M. stellata, STAR MAGNOLIA, is hardy to –20°F/–29°C. This is a twiggier plant than lily magnolia, but it grows slowly to about the same dimensions. A lavish floral display appears very early on bare branches—late winter to early spring, depending on the climate. Each blossom opens wide, to about 3 inches across, displaying up to 18 ribbonlike white petals. The matte green, 3- to 5-inch leaves give a finer-textured appearance than other magnolias.

Among named selections, 'Rosea' features pink buds opening to blush flowers that eventually fade to white; 'Rubra' has totally pink blossoms on a plant more inclined to grow as a shrub tree. 'Dawn' also has pink flowers, but each contains up to 50 petals. 'Centen-

nial' and 'Waterlily' have larger flowers (to 5 inches) with broader petals: pink-tinted in the former, totally white in the latter. 'Royal Star' presents its 25- to 30-petaled white flowers about 2 weeks later than the others.

Hybrids between lily and star magnolias are now in the general retail trade. In appearance and flowering time, they favor the *M. liliiflora* parent; their hardiness is around –20°F/–29°C. They include 'Ann' (clear pink with darker buds), 'Betty' (rosy purple and white), 'Pinkie' (pink), and 'Randy' (rose-purple and white).

MAHONIA
Mahonia
Berberidaceae

Evergreen: Hardiness varies
Flowers: Yellow; spring
Exposure: Sun, partial shade
Water: Moderate
Growth: Moderate

All mahonias are distinguished by handsome, durable foliage. Although they're related to barberries (*Berberis*), only the bright yellow, slightly cupped blossoms suggest the connection. The foliage shares a characteristic with another relative, *Nandina:* what appear to be separate leaves are actually leaflets of a much larger compound leaf. Minor details vary among the species, but spiny or prickly ("hollylike") leaflet margins are typical. Some mahonias become branching shrubs, but several popular species are decidedly sculptural plants, forming clumps of upright, unbranched stems. All bear conspicuous clusters of flowers at branch tips, followed by blue-black or reddish berrylike fruits.

(Continued on next page)

Mahonia aquifolium

In general, mahonias are not demanding about soil. Prune as needed to shape the plants; induce branching by cutting stems back to any height.

M. aquifolium, OREGON GRAPE, is hardy to –10°F/–23°C. Clusters of dark fruits with a chalky "bloom" on their surface do suggest grapes, but the 3-inch leaflets could nearly pass for English holly foliage. Light bronze when new, the glossy leaflets mature to medium green, turning bronzy purple in winter on plants in exposed areas. Many stems rise from the ground—some upright, others spreading—to form an upright, rounded plant to about 6 feet. Usually there's enough branching to ensure adequate foliage cover. Over time, a plant's bulk increases as new stems rise from ground level and expand the clump. Showy clusters of small yellow flowers sit atop stems in early to midspring; the fruits that follow are technically edible. The selection 'Orange Flame' has brightly colored new growth and winter foliage. 'Compacta' may reach 2 feet high, spreading by underground stems into sizable patches.

The hybrid *M.* 'Golden Abundance' resembles Oregon grape but is a more densely foliaged, rounded plant of about the same height bearing a greater number of flowers and fruits. *M. pinnata*, California holly grape, also resembles Oregon grape but is hardy only to 10°F/–12°C. It differs, too, in its spinier, more wavy-edged leaflets, more brightly colored new growth, and potential height—to about 10 feet. 'Ken Hartman' is a superior selection.

M. bealei, LEATHERLEAF MAHONIA, is hardy to 0°F/–18°C. This is one of the sculptural types, the clump containing a number of near-vertical stems each crowned by a whorl of horizontal leaves. An individual leaf can be over 12 inches long, bearing up to seven leaflet pairs (plus a terminal one), each broadly oval and up to 5 inches long, with widely spaced marginal spines. Their color is a distinctive yellowish green with gray-green undersides. Upright, 6-inch spikes of flowers come in late winter or early spring, to be succeeded by chalky-surfaced blue berries. This species appreciates good, organically enriched

soil and regular water. Only in cool-summer regions will it take full sun.

M. lomariifolia is hardy to 15°F/ –9°C. This is another "conversation piece" mahonia—part of the conversation being "Ouch!" when the unwary stray too close. The nearly branchless stems rise 10 to 12 feet, bearing whorls of 2-foot leaves held almost horizontally at stem ends. Each leaf is patterned like a fish skeleton bearing up to 24 pairs of 3-inch glossy leaflets with toothed edges and needle-sharp spines at their tips. In late winter or early spring, bright flowers appear in dense clusters of narrow spikes at the top of each foliage whorl; the later fruits are blue, with a powdery surface.

In combination with a Japanese species, *M. lomariifolia* has produced a group of hybrids designated *M. media*. Selections from the cross resemble this parent but offer greater hardiness—to about 5°F/–15°C. 'Winter Sun' reaches 6 to 8 feet, each leaf carrying up to 20 spiny-tipped leaflets. Lemon yellow blossoms appear in late winter.

MYRTUS COMMUNIS
Myrtle
Myrtaceae

Evergreen: Hardy to 15°F/–9°C
Flowers: White; summer
Exposure: Sun, partial shade
Water: Moderate
Growth: Moderate

At all times of year, myrtle looks fresh and healthy. Plentiful glossy foliage accounts for much of its vibrant appearance: each leaf is ovate to lance shaped, to 2 inches long, and pleasantly aromatic when crushed. In summer, the dark green backdrop is liberally dotted with small white blossoms that look fluffy due to their prominent stamens; pea-size black fruits come later. Myrtle naturally assumes a rounded shape, growing to 6 feet or taller and just as wide; truly old plants can become picturesque shrub trees if never subjected to pruning shears.

Nurseries offer a number of named selections that vary in foliage character and in overall size. 'Variegata' adds white-margined foliage to the basic

Myrtus communis 'Compacta'

description. 'Boetica' grows especially upright, to 6 feet with thick, twisted branches and larger, darker leaves. 'Buxifolia' is a boxwood mimic with small, elliptical leaves. 'Compacta' is a slow-growing form, to about 3 feet high, with inch-long leaves. It, too, has a variegated-leaf alternative: 'Compacta Variegata'.

These are tough, easy-to-grow plants that thrive at the seashore, in the desert, and in all climates in between. Give them well-drained soil to avoid problems with chlorosis. Untrimmed plants are rounded and rather billowy, but you can trim, shear, or prune them to limit their size or to maintain them as hedges.

NANDINA DOMESTICA
Heavenly bamboo, Nandina
Berberidaceae

Evergreen: Hardy to 0°F/–18°C
Flowers: White; spring
Exposure: Sun, partial shade
Water: Regular to moderate
Growth: Moderate

The essence of heavenly bamboo can be captured in just one word: "feathery." Unbranched stems rise vertically from the ground to 6 to 8 feet, bearing—almost at right angles—large, triply pinnate leaves containing countless lance-shaped to ovate leaflets. New growth is strongly tinted pink or bronze; it takes on a fresh lettuce shade before finally maturing to dark green. Cool autumn weather brings reddish tones, and in winter the entire plant often turns brilliant red.

In mid- to late spring come tiny, creamy white flowers in airy, pyramidal clusters at stem ends. If another plant is nearby for pollination, those blooms are followed by large sprays of pea-size berries that ripen in autumn to bright red.

Named selections offer several useful variations for the landscape. 'Umpqua Warrior' is taller and has larger leaflets than the basic species. 'Royal Princess' (sometimes sold as 'Chinensis' or 'Chinese Princess') makes a more open clump, bearing finer-textured leaflets that give the effect of a see-through Chinese screen. 'Moyers Red' features broader leaflets and particularly vivid winter color.

Several selections offer shorter plants. 'Umpqua Chief' tops out at 5 to 6 feet; 'Gulf Stream' is shorter by about a foot. 'Compacta' reaches 4 to 5 feet, with a finer texture due to its narrower leaflets. 'Filamentosa' reduces its leaflets to a threadlike thickness; its plants grow slowly to 4 feet. 'Harbour Dwarf' and 'Nana' are low, spreading kinds that can be used as small-scale ground covers.

Although winter foliage is more colorful on plants grown in full sun, heavenly bamboo will grow in partial shade anywhere—and will need it where summers are hot and dry. You'll get best growth in good soil with regular water, but established plants tolerate drought and even competition from tree roots. In alkaline soil, leaves may become chlorotic. A clump's bulk will increase over the years as additional stems grow from the ground. You can increase bushiness and maintain foliage low on the plant by selectively cutting back stems to various heights to induce branching.

Nandina domestica

Nerium oleander

NERIUM OLEANDER
Oleander
Apocynaceae

Evergreen: Hardy to 15°F/–9°C
Flowers: Red, pink, cream, white; summer
Exposure: Sun
Water: Moderate to little
Growth: Fast

Colorful oleander prospers in nearly all climates within its temperature range. Only where coolness and fog persist will it appear less than topnotch. These are robust shrubs, full of vim and vigor, coarse textured but not unattractive. Many stems rise from the ground to form a rounded, 8- to 12-foot shrub bearing thick, glossy, lance-shaped leaves up to 12 inches long on the most vigorous shoots. From mid- to late spring and continuing into autumn, 2- to 3-inch blossoms are borne in showy clusters at branch ends.

Many named selections are available, the flowers single or double and often fragrant. Double-flowered kinds tend to hang on to their faded flowers, whereas single kinds are shed cleanly. Single white 'Sister Agnes' grows considerably larger than the others, reaching 20 feet under good conditions. Widely sold 'Mrs. Roeding' (double salmon pink) reaches only about 6 feet; its leaves are smaller and narrower than those of other named selections. Others in the 6-foot height category include red-flowered 'Algiers' and 'Ruby Lace', pink 'Tangier', and white 'Casablanca'. 'Little Red' and members of the 'Petite' series are even lower

growing (and less hardy)—easily kept to 4 feet with occasional pruning.

Oleanders grow well in a variety of soils, even poorly drained ones with a high salt content. Although established plants easily withstand long dry periods, you should give young plants regular to moderate watering until they're established. Oleanders will take any amount of pruning; the best time is early spring.

Yellow oleander aphids and scale are possible pests. A bacterial gall sometimes causes splitting of young stems, galls on older growth, and blackened flowers; to control it, cut off stems well below any visible infection. (*Caution:* All parts of this plant are poisonous if ingested; even smoke from burning branches can cause severe respiratory irritation.)

OSMANTHUS
Osmanthus
Oleaceae

Evergreen: Hardiness varies
Flowers: White, cream, orange; season varies
Exposure: Sun, partial shade
Water: Regular to moderate
Growth: Moderate

Dense, orderly growth and glossy foliage recommend the various osmanthus species as good "basic" shrubs. But their deliciously fragrant (though usually inconspicuous) flowers elevate them beyond the strictly useful. Plants aren't particular about soil, and once established they're fairly drought tolerant.

(Continued on next page)

Osmanthus delavayi

O. delavayi, DELAVAY OSMANTHUS, is hardy to 5°F/−15°C. Arching branches form a mounding plant up to 6 feet high with a greater spread. Plants are well covered in glossy dark green, oval leaves just an inch long. Conspicuous clusters of tubular white flowers emerge to perfume the garden in early to midspring. In hot-summer regions, plant them in partial shade.

O. fortunei is hardy to 5°F/−15°C. This is a hybrid between the next two species, inheriting the larger (4-inch) leaves of sweet olive but with the spiny margins of holly-leaf osmanthus. Small white flowers come in spring and summer, but the selection 'San Jose' bears its cream to orange blossoms in autumn. Plants are dense and slow growing, ultimately to 20 feet.

O. fragrans, SWEET OLIVE, is hardy to 0°F/−18°C. This species offers the most penetrating fragrance of all: sweet, fruity (close to apricot), and detectable from some distance. The tiny white flowers appear primarily in spring and summer but also sporadically during other seasons. Glossy, oval leaves to 4 inches clothe a plant 10 or more feet high and wide. You can prune and pinch to alter or direct growth, even training a plant as a shrub tree or using several as a hedge. Orange-flowered *O. f. aurantiacus* blooms mainly in autumn, on a plant with narrower, less glossy leaves. Give plants partial shade—especially afternoon shade—in hot-summer regions.

O. heterophyllus, HOLLY-LEAF OSMANTHUS, is hardy to 0°F/−18°C. It's no wonder this is sometimes sold as *O. aquifolium* or *O. ilicifolius,* names that indicate hollylike foliage. The spiny-edged, 2½-inch glossy leaves suggest those of English holly (*Ilex aquifolium*); but, unlike holly's, they appear opposite one another on the stems. Fragrant white flowers in late autumn and winter later form berrylike fruits that are blue-black rather than holly red. Unrestrained plants will reach 15 to 20 feet and perhaps half as wide, but like sweet olive can be directed by pruning.

The selections 'Gulftide' and 'Ilicifolius' are dense and upright, especially good for background and screen planting. 'Rotundifolius' has small, lightly spined, nearly round leaves; 'Purpureus' ('Purpurascens') has dark purple new growth and retains purple tints in mature leaves. 'Variegatus' has the typical foliage margined in ivory on a less-hardy plant that reaches 5 feet.

PAEONIA
Tree peony
Paeoniaceae

Deciduous: Hardy to −30°F/−34°C; needs some winter chill
Flowers: Purple, red, pink, lavender, white, cream, yellow, orange; spring
Exposure: Sun
Water: Regular
Growth: Slow

The magnificent tree peonies are in a class by themselves. Only some rhododendrons and reticulata camellias can replicate the silken surface of their flower petals, and no other shrub or tree—save for a few magnolias—can produce individual blossoms reaching 12 inches across. Flowers may be single (with a central tuft of stamens), semi-double, or double—the latter huge and shaggy, yet somehow still refined. Backing these floral offerings is a rounded to upright plant outfitted in graceful, doubly pinnate leaves whose irregularly toothed leaflets are bronzy green to blue-green. Branching is rather sparse and asymmetrical, making for picturesque patterns during winter's bare period.

Two species are the basis of the hybrid selections offered by both retail and specialty nurseries. Those with

Paeonia suffruticosa **'Shira Giku'**

flowers in purple, red, pink, lavender, and white may be derived entirely from the Chinese species *P. suffruticosa;* yellow, orange, and sunset-colored flowers stem at least in part from Tibetan *P. lutea.* Many of the *P. lutea* derivatives—particularly those with double flowers—have blossoms so heavy that they bend toward the ground unless staked into an upright position. The same holds true of many of the double-flowered European hybrids.

Given their preferred conditions, tree peonies are not difficult to grow. First, choose a location away from competing tree and shrub roots; dappled or light afternoon shade (in all but the coolest climates) will promote blossom longevity and will also be good for plants during summer. Shelter plants from winds and give them good, well-drained, neutral to somewhat acid soil liberally enriched with organic matter.

Most plants sold are grafted, the roots of herbaceous peonies furnishing their root systems. When planting, set the juncture of roots and stems 4 to 5 inches below the soil surface to discourage sprouting from the rootstock. In time, supplementary root systems will form from the grafted tree peony part of the plant.

Prune tree peonies only to remove dead stems in spring. Where winter temperatures reach −10°F/−23°C or lower, stems may freeze back severely—to snow cover or to the ground. New growth usually replaces frozen stems in spring. In such regions, it is a good idea to give tree peonies some sort of winter protection (as you might roses) to keep at least part of the stems alive. Botrytis fungus may damage new growth and flower buds in a humid spring.

PHILADELPHUS
Mock orange
Saxifragaceae

Deciduous: Hardiness varies
Flowers: White; late spring, early summer
Exposure: Sun, partial shade
Water: Regular to moderate
Growth: Fast

Philadelphus coronarius

The best of these shrubs release a fragrance that fully lives up to their common name. And though that might be reason enough to plant them—particularly where real oranges are out of the question—the beauty of their white flowers is a further incentive. Blossoms range from four-petaled single through semidouble to double, 1 to 2 inches across. The bountiful late-spring display comes on trouble-free plants clothed in pointed oval, thin-textured leaves having a somewhat quilted appearance. Larger-growing kinds make arching, fountainlike plants; the shorter sorts form leafy mounds.

Mock oranges will grow well in a wide range of soils with just casual care. For best appearance, though, prune plants routinely to remove played-out wood and encourage new growth. They flower on wood formed the previous year, so prune just after flowering has finished. Remove the oldest, least productive stems to the ground; then cut back stems that have flowered to where vigorous new shoots are sprouting.

P. coronarius is hardy to –20°F/ –29°C. This is the "old-fashioned," indestructible mock orange, with showy single white flowers carried on a 10-foot upright plant of great vigor. Give it ample room to accommodate not only its bulk but also its competitive root system. Autumn color is tawny yellow. Slightly less vigorous is the selection 'Aureus', which features yellow new foliage that turns bright yellowish green by midsummer.

P. lemoinei is hardy to –10°F/–23°C. The "Lemoine mock oranges" are hybrids of *P. coronarius* and a less showy but highly fragrant species. Many named selections exist, but few are currently available in nurseries. Most are arching, mounding plants in the 4- to 8-foot height range. 'Avalanche' has 1-inch flowers in great profusion on a 4-foot plant with arching, cascading stems; 'Innocence' has larger blossoms on a plant to 8 feet high.

P. purpureomaculatus is hardy to 0°F/–18°C. This is another group of hybrids (derived from *P. lemoinei*), most of which are characterized by white flowers lightly stained a rosy purple in their centers. 'Belle Etoile' is the best known of these (though it's sometimes listed under *P. lemoinei*): a 6-foot plant bearing single flowers with fringed petals to 2½ inches across.

P. virginalis is hardy to –20°F/–29°C. Under this name are sold a number of hybrids of *P. lemoinei* that offer greater hardiness. The tallest plants, to about 8 feet, are 'Natchez' (with 2-inch, single blossoms) and double-flowered 'Minnesota Snowflake' and 'Virginal'; the latter has a particularly long flowering season on plants that tend to be bare at their bases. Double-flowered 'Enchantment' reaches about 6 feet, whereas 'Glacier' (also double) grows only 3 to 5 feet high. Shortest of all is the double 'Dwarf Minnesota Snowflake', reaching just 3 feet.

PHOTINIA
Photinia
Rosaceae

Deciduous, evergreen: Hardiness varies
Flowers: White; spring
Exposure: Sun
Water: Regular to moderate
Growth: Moderate

As a group, photinias may be underappreciated, due to their overuse in commercial landscapes. Plants are sizable and bulky, densely clothed in large, elliptical to oval leaves. Brilliantly colored new growth puts on the first show in spring; then come large, flattish clusters of small white flowers. Most species go on to form red or black berries that decorate plants (and attract birds) during autumn and into winter. Evergreen kinds may suffer considerable damage if tempera-

Photinia glabra

tures remain below 10°F/–12°C for prolonged periods.

These are easy plants to grow, given reasonably good soil and routine watering. You can maintain a plant as a dense shrub, heading back any lanky, wayward stems to balance the silhouette; or you can thin out lower stems to create a multitrunked shrub tree. All species are susceptible to fireblight; *P. serrulata* is especially prone to powdery mildew, and only *P. fraseri* is really resistant to it.

P. fraseri is evergreen, hardy to 0°F/ –18°C. Brilliant bronzy red new leaves mature to 5-inch, dark green ovals on a plant 10 to 15 feet high with greater spread. Lack of decorative berries is the trade-off for disease-resistant foliage. The selection 'Indian Princess' is a smaller plant by about half, featuring orange-red new foliage.

P. glabra, JAPANESE PHOTINIA, is hardy to 0°F/–18°C. In effect, this is a smaller version of *P. fraseri*. The 3-inch ovate leaves, which emerge a lustrous copper color and age to dark green, cover a rounded shrub 6 to 10 feet high and wide. Berries are red at first, turning black as they ripen.

P. serrulata, CHINESE PHOTINIA, is hardy to 0°F/–18°C. Unrestrained plants of this species have reached 35 feet—definitely in the tree category, whether or

(Continued on page 128)

Mild-Winter Shrubs

Where frost is an infrequent visitor, gardeners can enjoy tender shrubs that are out of the question, except as container plants, in other regions. The following eight shrubs are among the best of these specialties; all are evergreen unless otherwise noted.

BRUNFELSIA pauciflora (B. calycina). BRUNFELSIA. *Solanaceae.* Evergreen or partly deciduous; hardy to about 15°F/–9°C. These are shrubs to feature in a lightly shaded location for their lavender blossoms over a long spring-summer flowering period. Most widely grown is *B. p.* 'Floribunda', commonly called yesterday-today-and-tomorrow for its changeable blossoms: first purple, then lavender, and finally white. Each 2-inch flower is tubular, with five petal-like lobes that form a circular outline; oval leaves reach 4 inches long. Growth may attain 10 feet, upright and spreading, but can be kept lower by judicious pruning.

B. p. 'Eximia' is naturally smaller growing and produces a greater quantity of smaller flowers. *B. p.* 'Macrantha'—also sold as *B. floribunda* 'Lindeniana' and *B. grandiflora*—is a more upright plant that tolerates very little frost. More distinctive, though, are its flowers and foliage: the purple blossoms are 2 to 4 inches across, and the leaves can reach 8 inches long.

All brunfelsias need good, well-drained soil and prefer it slightly acid; chlorosis may occur in nonacid soils. Give them regular watering and fertilize periodically throughout the growing season.

CALLIANDRA. CALLIANDRA. *Leguminosae.* Hardy to about 28°F/–2°C. Flowers are the feature of calliandra: spherical puffs of brightly colored stamens. Both have twice-pinnate leaves with small, oval leaflets. *C. haematocephala (C. inaequilatera)*, pink powder puff, makes a rounded shrub 6 to 8 feet tall but will grow as an informal espalier against a wall. Leaflets reach over an inch long—glossy copper when new, maturing to a metallic dark green. Puffy flowers are 2 to 3 inches across and bright watermelon pink, blooming from midautumn to early spring. Give plants well-drained, light soil and regular watering.

In contrast, *C. tweedii*—Trinidad or Brazilian flame bush—makes a more angular plant to about the same size, but the tiny leaflets compose fernlike leaves that reveal plenty of branch structure. Crimson red, fluffy flowers begin in late winter and continue into autumn. Plants aren't particular about soil quality but do poorly in alkaline soils. Although drought tolerant once established, they'll take regular watering if drainage is good.

HIBISCUS rosa-sinensis. CHINESE HIBISCUS. *Malvaceae.* Hardy to about 30°F/–1°C. Where this plant thrives, nurseries offer a number of named selections that produce the ultimate in showy flowers on plants that range from 6-foot shrubs to robust 15-foot (or more) shrub-trees. Leaves are glossy bright green, broadly oval, and pointed, against which are displayed 4- to 10-inch wide blossoms of circular, "morning glory" shape with a prominent central spike of stamens and pistil. Colors range from white through pink and red to orange, yellow, and blended or bicolor combinations. Main flowering season is summer, but flowers may appear all year in warmest regions.

Chinese hibiscus demands a well-drained soil (roots will rot if water remains long around roots) but also needs regular, deep watering. Plants need full sun and heat for best performance. In coastal regions, reflected heat from walls will help; where summer is particularly hot, give plants a bit of afternoon shade. Locate them out of the wind. For luxuriant growth and plenty of flowers, fertilize plants monthly during the spring and summer growing period. To maintain compactness and encourage new growth, prune back by about one-third in early spring, then pinch new growth as needed during the growing period.

JUSTICIA brandegeana (Beloperone guttata). SHRIMP PLANT. *Acanthaceae.* Hardy to about 25°F/–4°C. One look at a plant in flower and you'll understand the common name. The true flowers are white and tubular, but they're enclosed in rust-colored, overlapping bracts that form an elongated, curved spike 3 to 7 inches long; the color and general shape suggest a succulent shrimp. (The selection 'Chartreuse', however, has unshrimplike yellow-green bracts.) Flowers appear throughout the year.

Plants are a bit weedy, consisting of many more-or-less upright stems bearing apple green, egg-shaped leaves to 1½ inches long. They form mounds 3 to 4 feet high unless pruned lower; pinching as stems lengthen promotes compactness, as does cutting back flowering stems when flower bracts turn black.

Shrimp plant isn't particular about soil and takes moderate to regular watering if drainage is good. Partial shade (except in coastal gardens) is best to retain the bract color, but the plants themselves will grow well in full sun.

LANTANA. LANTANA. *Verbenaceae.* Hardy to about 28°F/–2°C. Lantana flowers lavishly throughout the year if not curtailed by light frosts. And even where winter is too cold for its survival, gardeners often grow it as an annual—or keep it in containers so plants can be overwintered in frost-free locations. Wherever lantana can persist from year to year in the ground, the original species—*L. camara*—will grow to 6 feet high and spread as much or more. Stems are covered in scratchy hairs; the dark green, ovate leaves (to about 3 inches long) are similarly rough textured. Small flowers are grouped in nearly flat-topped, nosegaylike clusters to 2 inches across; the innermost flowers are cream to yellow, the outer ring pink or orange.

Many named selections and hybrids have been developed from this species. Their colors vary widely—white, cream, yellow, orange, red, pink shades, and bicolor combinations—and plants range from the basic size down to 2-footers that may spread to double their height or more.

Plant lantana in full sun, in any soil. It thrives in both dry heat and humidity, and will grow well—with mildewed leaves—in cool, oceanic regions. Water deeply but infrequently: too much water (and fertilizer) reduces the amount of bloom.

LYCIANTHES rantonnei (Solanum rantonnetii). PARAGUAY NIGHTSHADE. *Solanaceae.* Hardy (with some damage) to about 20°F/−7°C. This is a vinelike shrub or shrubby vine, depending on how you want to use it. Nurseries even offer it trained in a small tree form, in the manner of "tree" roses. To keep a plant definitely shrublike (at 6 to 8 feet), you'll have to head back wandering branches frequently. Bright green, wavy-edged oval leaves to 4 inches are a backdrop to 1¼-inch, blue-violet flowers shaped like flat morning glories. 'Royal Rose' has red-violet blossoms. Bloom is continuous throughout warm weather and will go year-round in the mildest areas.

Paraguay nightshade isn't demanding about soil. Regular watering produces the fastest, lushest growth, but established plants are fairly drought tolerant.

PLUMBAGO auriculata. CAPE PLUMBAGO. *Plumbaginaceae.* Hardy to 20°F/−7°C. Where hard frosts don't "prune" plants, cape plumbago becomes a mounded, almost vinelike shrub about 6 feet high and 10 feet across—though given any support to help it along, the height can double. Oval, 2-inch leaves

are a light, almost lettuce green, completely clothing the plant in frost-free regions, partly shedding during winter in colder areas. The inch-wide flowers resemble phlox blossoms and are carried in rounded, phloxlike clusters; their usual color is blue, but white individuals do exist. Choose plants in flower to get the shade of blue you prefer.

Given well-drained soil (quality isn't important), this plant is trouble free. Heavy frost may inflict what appears to be severe damage, but regrowth is fast. In fact, you can severely cut back an overgrown plant to rejuvenate it. But where winter temperatures regularly dip into the 20s, wait until spring to plant cape plumbago.

PLUMERIA rubra. PLUMERIA, FRANGIPANI. *Apocynaceae.* Hardy to 30°F/−1°C. One whiff of plumeria's fragrance will evoke memories of a Hawaiian vacation: these are the classic lei flowers. In size (about 15 feet) these plants are shrubs, but their growth is treelike, with one or several trunks supporting an open framework of thick, sausage-like branches. Leathery, elliptical leaves 8 to 16 inches long cluster toward branch tips. Waxy flowers of heady fragrance are tubular, with five petal-like lobes, 2 to 2½ inches across. Clustered blossoms appear from late spring to midautumn. You have a choice of selections with blossoms of white, cream, yellow, pink, red, and purple. White-flowered Singapore plumeria, *P. obtusa*, has smaller leaves and tolerates no frost.

Flowering is most profuse on plants in full sun, but in low desert heat they need afternoon shade. Grow in average, well-drained soil and water moderately; keep plants fairly dry during winter.

TIBOUCHINA urvilleana (T. semidecandra, Pleroma splendens). PRINCESS FLOWER. *Melastomataceae.* Hardy to 25°F/−4°C. You might not call this a

Lycianthes rantonnei

beautiful shrub—but with those flowers, who cares? As befits royalty, blossoms are a rich, bright purple, the five petals forming a circular flower with the texture of both silk and velvet. The prominent, threadlike anther filaments are red. Clusters of these sumptuous blooms appear at branch tips intermittently from midspring to midwinter. Broadly oval leaves are strongly ribbed from base to tip and often edged in red; branch tips, buds, and new growth appear velvety due to a coating of orange and bronzy red hairs.

The plant is rangy and open, to about 15 feet tall, and needs pinching and periodic heading back if you want to impose compactness. Lightly prune after bloom cycles, but wait until winter to attempt heavier cutting back.

Princess flower does best in reasonably good, well-drained, slightly acid soil. The best locations in cool-summer areas shade the roots but allow full sun on the plant; where summer is warm to hot, choose a spot in partial shade. For maximum foliage and flowers, fertilize after winter or spring pruning and again, lightly, after each bloom cycle. Geranium budworm can destroy flowers in bud.

not you remove lower limbs. But with periodic pruning you can maintain it in a shrubby state at a 10- to 15-foot height. Dark green 8-inch leaves have prickly toothed margins, starting from glowing, copper-colored new spring growth. The berries are bright red. One selection, 'Aculeata' (often sold as 'Nova' or 'Nova Lineata'), makes a smaller, more compact plant whose leaves have midribs and main veins of cream to light yellow.

P. villosa is deciduous, hardy to –20°F/–29°C. This makes an upright plant to 15 feet high and about 10 feet wide with 3-inch, broadly oval leaves. In spring, leaves emerge a pinkish gold, maturing to glossy green. Small clusters of white flowers form showy red berries in autumn—an effective contrast to the foliage, which by then is bronzy red or yellow.

PIERIS
Pieris
Ericaceae

Evergreen: Hardiness varies
Flowers: Rosy red, pink, white; late winter, spring
Exposure: Partial shade
Water: Regular
Growth: Moderate

Not without reason are these shrubs described as elegant: at all times of year they're neat plants of refined beauty. Even the lavish flower displays are in good taste—neither garish nor

Pieris japonica

bland. And their handsome foliage would make pieris worth planting even if they never flowered. New growth is often brightly colored—pink to red or bronze—but matures to a glossy dark green. Each leathery leaf is lance shaped or narrowly oval; leaves are positioned radially on stems, often tending to group toward branch tips in a nearly whorled effect.

Individual blossoms are small and urn shaped, appearing in late winter to midspring, depending on the species, usually clustered like bunches of grapes at the ends of branches. Most plants form flower buds by autumn, so that potential flower clusters are a subtle decorative feature over winter.

Pieris need the same garden and climate conditions as the related rhododendrons: well-drained but moisture-retentive acid soil and summers that are cool to merely warm, not dry. Locate plants where they'll be sheltered from wind; give them high shade or dappled sunlight at least during the warmest afternoon hours.

P. floribunda (Andromeda floribunda), MOUNTAIN PIERIS, is hardy to –20°F/–29°C. This species differs from the others in several respects. White flowers appear in upright clusters, backed by nonglossy leaves that mature from pale green new growth. Plants are rounded to slightly spreading, up to 6 feet high. Mountain pieris tolerates sun, heat, and low humidity better than the others.

P. forrestii (P. formosa forrestii), CHINESE PIERIS, is hardy to 0°F/–18°C. This becomes a tall (to 10 feet), wide shrub outfitted in 6-inch, highly polished leaves. New growth ranges from pale pink to bright red; select nursery plants in spring when they're putting on new growth if you want a particular leaf color. Midspring flowers are white.

P. japonica (Andromeda japonica), LILY-OF-THE-VALLEY SHRUB, is hardy to –10°F/–23°C. This species makes an attractively structured plant, its dense growth appearing in layers or tiers on an upright shrub to about 10 feet. New leaves emerge pink to red or bronze and mature to 3-inch, dark green ovals. White flowers may appear as early as late winter.

Named selections offer both foliage and flower variations, usually on shorter plants than the basic species. 'Variegata' is a slow-growing shrub whose leaves are variegated in ivory (often tinted pink in spring); the leaves of 'Bert Chandler' emerge orange before changing to pink, cream, white, and finally light green. 'Mountain Fire' was selected for its vivid new growth. 'Flamingo' and 'Valley Valentine' have the darkest rose red flowers; those of 'Valley Rose' are soft pink. 'Christmas Cheer' has blossoms combining rose red and white; the white blooms of 'Dorothy Wyckoff' open from red buds. 'White Cascade' is a heavy producer of notably large flower clusters.

Several distinct hybrids have been produced from *P. japonica.* 'Forest Flame' (hardy to –5°F/–21°C) comes from a cross with *P. forrestii.* New foliage is brilliant red on a broad, dense plant to about 7 feet high. 'Spring Snow', a hybrid of *P. floribunda,* produces large, upright clusters of white flowers set off by dark, glossy leaves on a compact, rounded plant to 6 feet high.

Pinus mugo mugo
(see page 105)

PITTOSPORUM TOBIRA
Tobira
Pittosporaceae

Evergreen: Hardy to –5°F/–21°C
Flowers: White; spring
Exposure: Sun, partial shade
Water: Regular to moderate
Growth: Moderate

Pittosporum tobira

Tobira is a trouble-free shrub that combines a handsome appearance with an aura of robust health. Each leaf is leathery, glossy dark green, and narrowly elliptical to obovate, to 5 inches long; leaves radiate around stems and tend to group in whorls toward branch tips. In spring, those leaf whorls become backdrops for orange blossom–scented white flowers in nosegaylike clusters. Round green fruits about the size of garbanzo beans follow the flowers, turn tannish orange in autumn, and finally split open to reveal sticky seeds.

Plants are dense and rounded in outline, eventually reaching 10 to 15 feet if not restricted by pruning. Older specimens can be converted to small trees by removing lower branches.

Several named selections offer distinct and useful variations on the basic theme. 'Variegata' has soft gray-green leaves irregularly margined in ivory to white; the plants are also smaller, topping out at 5 to 10 feet. 'Wheeler's Dwarf' is a pocket-size edition of the species, forming a 2-foot, spreading mound of glossy leaves. 'Turner's Variegated Dwarf' is a low plant with the foliage colors of 'Variegata'.

Tobira will survive drought but looks best with routine watering. It is not particular about soil quality. Aphids and scale are potential pests.

Platycladus orientalis
(see page 105)

Plumbago auriculata
(see page 127)

Plumeria rubra (see page 127)

POTENTILLA FRUTICOSA
Bush cinquefoil, Potentilla
Rosaceae

Deciduous: Hardy to –40°F/–40°C
Flowers: Red, orange, yellow, white; summer
Exposure: Sun
Water: Moderate
Growth: Moderate

The shrubby potentillas have a wildflowerlike charm: single flowers look like wild rose blossoms, and the pinnate leaves—containing up to seven small leaflets—give a ferny effect. Many named selections are available, ranging from 2 to nearly 5 feet high and usually spreading wider; stems are upright to arching, clad in green to gray-green foliage. Flowers from 1 to 2 inches across appear profusely over a long stretch, from late spring to early autumn.

Yellow is the prevailing color, with many selections and shades to choose from. Light yellow 'Katherine Dykes' (to 5 feet) is the tallest, followed by 4-foot, bright yellow 'Jackman's Variety'. In the 3-foot range is deep yellow 'Hollandia Gold'; 2-footers are represented by deep yellow 'Gold Drop' and 'Klondike'. 'Primrose Beauty' is pale yellow. The shortest—about 1 foot tall and spreading to 3 feet—are 'Longacre' and 'Sutter's Gold'. 'Maanelys' ('Moonlight') has palest yellow flowers on a 1½-foot plant.

As for other colors, vigorous 'Mount Everest' is appropriately tall (4 feet or more) and with single white flowers; 'Snowflake' has semidouble flowers on a 2- to 4-foot plant. White 'Abbotswood' is a spreading shrub to about 2 feet high. When weather is cool, 'Red Ace', 'Sunset', and 'Tangerine' live up to their names, but in heat their flowers quickly bleach to yellow; plants of 'Red Ace' and 'Tangerine' reach 2 to 2½ feet tall, those of spreading 'Sunset' about 1½ feet. Four-foot 'Daydawn' is a mingling of light yellow and orange that registers as peachy pink.

Given well-drained soil, shrubby potentillas are trouble-free shrubs that assort well with somewhat drought-

Potentilla fruticosa

Prunus glandulosa

tolerant perennials. Prune plants occasionally, after flowering stops: remove oldest stems and head back any wayward shoots.

PRUNUS
Almond, Cherry, Cherry laurel, Plum
Rosaceae

Deciduous, evergreen: Hardiness varies
Flowers: Pink, white; spring, summer
Exposure: Sun
Water: Regular to moderate
Growth: Moderate to fast

The shrubby *Prunus* species are a mixed bag of dissimilar relatives. The evergreen cherry laurels are the greatest departure: the basic species are big, bulky, glossy-leafed shrubs with small white flowers in spikes. Among deciduous kinds, flowering almond is a fairly stiff plant, notable for its lavish early-spring blossom show. The one plum offers both colorful blossoms and foliage, whereas the shrubby cherries produce tasty fruits. None is demanding about soil.

P. besseyi, WESTERN SAND CHERRY, and *P. tomentosa*, NANKING CHERRY, are deciduous, both hardy to –50°F/–46°C. These similar plants give a good show of white spring blossoms followed by heavy crops of edible cherries. Western sand cherry grows to about 6 feet, upright and somewhat spreading, bearing black summer fruits; Hansen's bush cherry is a larger-fruited selection. Nanking cherry is a slightly larger, more rounded plant with red cherries. Both are tough plants, tolerating heat, cold, wind, and drought.

P. caroliniana, CAROLINA CHERRY LAUREL, is evergreen, hardy to 10°F/–12°C. Glossy oval leaves to 4 inches long form a dense cover on this upright shrub to 20 feet. (With training, it can become a tree to nearly twice that height.) Inch-long spikes of white flowers produce small black fruits. Selections 'Bright 'n' Tight' and 'Compacta' reach only about 10 feet. Plants are drought tolerant once established, but they may become chlorotic where soil is alkaline.

P. cistena, PURPLE-LEAF SAND CHERRY, is deciduous, hardy to –40°F/–40°C. You might call this a triple-purpose shrub: it gives a show of white to light pink flowers as leaves emerge, then covers itself in red-purple foliage, and later may offer a small crop of ¾-inch blackish purple cherry-plums. Slender stems make an upright but rounded plant to 10 feet high. 'Big Cis' is a taller (to 14 feet), pink-flowered form.

P. glandulosa, DWARF FLOWERING ALMOND, is deciduous, hardy to –30°F/–34°C. This shrub's many slender stems become wands of 1-inch flowers in early spring before leaves appear. Double-flowered selections 'Alboplena' (white) and 'Sinensis' (pink) are widely sold. Plants grow 4 to 6 feet high, the branches upright and spreading, with light green, 4-inch, willowlike leaves. Prune heavily during or after flowering to promote strong new growth for the next year's bloom. Fireblight can be a problem.

P. laurocerasus, ENGLISH LAUREL, is evergreen, hardy to 5°F/–15°C. The basic species is a bulky, fast-growing, greedy-rooted shrub to about 30 feet high, valuable chiefly as a background plant where you need a dense wall of glossy green. Oval leaves may reach 7 inches long; 5-inch flower spikes appear among the leaves in spring, later producing black fruits. Named selections 'Mount Vernon', 'Nana', and 'Otto Luyken' are more generally useful because they make rounded plants to just 6 feet, bearing smaller leaves.

'Schipkaensis', Schipka laurel, is a bit hardier than the basic species and has narrower, shorter leaves; wide-

spreading branches form a broad plant 10 to 15 feet high. In 'Zabeliana', Zabel laurel, the main branches angle broadly outward from the plant's base; in time a plant may reach 6 feet high but can be kept lower—even pegged down as a ground cover. Leaves are narrow and willowlike.

English laurel and its variants need regular water and some fertilizer for best appearance. Plant them in partial shade where summer is hot. ('Zabeliana' is more sun tolerant than the others.) Borers and fireblight are possible problems.

P. lusitanica, PORTUGAL LAUREL, is evergreen, hardy to 5°F/–15°C. Think of this as another variant of English laurel. It, too, is a large, bulky plant, but just to about 20 feet as a shrub or to 30 feet trained as a tree. Glossy, dark leaves may reach 5 inches long, yet do not obscure the 5- to 10-inch spikes of white flowers in late spring. Red to purple fruits come later. The geographic variant *P. l. azorica* makes a strongly upright, columnar plant only half as wide as its height. Compared with English laurel, Portugal laurel grows better in heat and sun; also, its roots are more drought tolerant and less competitive.

PUNICA GRANATUM
Pomegranate
Punicaceae

Deciduous: Hardy to 10°F/–12°C
Flowers: Orange, cream; summer
Exposure: Sun
Water: Moderate to little
Growth: Moderate

In one respect, pomegranates are like persimmons (*Diospyros*): even if you don't find the fruits tasty, you'll love their decorative effect. And among pomegranates, you have a choice between full-size fruiting plants and smaller-growing selections that generally bear only flowers.

The fruiting kinds (best known is 'Wonderful') make large shrubs or small shrub trees; they'll reach about 10 feet high, their upright, arching branches forming a fountain shape. Bronzy new growth matures to 3-inch, narrow, glossy leaves of bright to yel-

Punica granatum

lowish green. In autumn, the foliage puts on a good show of bright yellow except in mildest-winter regions. Flowers may reach 4 inches across, a single row of ruffled orange-red petals surrounding a central clump of stamens. Autumn-ripening fruits also reach about 4 inches in diameter: they're spherical (with a "neck" opposite the branch attachment), rusty red, and leathery skinned.

Several moderate-size to dwarf selections lack only edible fruits. 'Legrellei' ('Mme. Legrelle') is the largest, reaching 6 to 8 feet high; its cream-colored double blossoms are striped coral red. 'Nana' (often sold simply as "dwarf pomegranate") makes a dense, 3-foot mound that is virtually evergreen in mildest-winter regions; its single orange flowers are followed by small, inedible fruits. 'Chico'—the dwarf, carnation-flowered pomegranate—presents its double orange, powderpuff blossoms on dense, twiggy plants just 18 inches high.

Pomegranates are remarkably unfussy. They have no special soil needs and will even grow well in highly alkaline conditions. They revel in heat but don't demand it; established plants tolerate considerable drought. Though they need only moderate watering, they'll take regular watering given well-drained soil. For good crops of firm, unsplit fruits, locate plants in well-drained soil and give them regular, deep watering.

PYRACANTHA
Firethorn, Pyracantha
Rosaceae

Evergreen: Hardiness varies
Flowers: White; spring
Exposure: Sun
Water: Moderate
Growth: Moderate to fast

Like junipers, the pyracanthas are attractive, adaptable shrubs whose beauties have been dulled by overexposure. In spring you get a good show of sweetly fragrant white blossoms in flattish clusters along the branches. By late summer (in some kinds) to midautumn, the branches become laden with pea-size orange to red berries that make a spectacular show until polished off by hungry birds or battered off by storms. Glossy oval to ovate leaves are 1 to 4 inches long, carried on stems armed with needlelike (and needle-sharp) spines.

Growth habits vary widely: from upright (to as much as 15 feet), to tall and spreading, to under 10 feet and rounded to irregular, to low, spreading ground cover selections. Some of the taller kinds make distinctly angular plants, and some even have pendant branches (especially when loaded with berries).

Pyracanthas will grow in nearly any soil so long as they are not overwatered. Aphids, scale, and spider

Pyracantha

mites are possible pests, but the most potentially devastating problem is fireblight (see page 38), which if unchecked can kill an entire plant. In cool, foggy regions, apple scab can cause serious defoliation in spring. You can prune these shrubs to your liking—they have been used as hedges, espaliers, and even small trees in addition to specimen shrubs. Although you might head back wayward branches to regularize a plant's shape, these shrubs are generally more attractive if you let their natural irregularity prevail.

P. coccinea, hardy to −10°F/−23°C, is the hardiest of these shrubs. It makes a more or less upright plant to 10 feet high, maturing orange-red berries in midautumn. Named selections guarantee certain characteristics. 'Government Red' has bright red berries; those of 'Kasan' are the normal orange-red, but they last especially long before shriveling. Berries of 'Wyattii' turn orange-red earlier than usual. 'Lalandei', with scarlet berries, and 'Monrovia' ('Lalandei Monrovia'), with orange-red fruits, are the best choices for the coldest end of the range.

P. fortuneana (P. crenatoserrata) is hardy to 0°F/−18°C. These limber-branched plants may reach 15 feet high and as much as 10 feet across, bearing coral to orange fruits throughout winter. 'Graberi' has dark red fruits on a plant of more upright growth; 'Cherri Berri' also has deep red berries, on a 10-foot shrub.

P. koidzumii is hardy (with some damage) to 0°F/−18°C. This species from Taiwan is best known by its selection 'Victory', a 10-foot plant whose dark red berries color late in the year and persist through winter. 'Santa Cruz', on the other hand, can be used as a ground cover: its spreading stems seldom exceed 3 to 4 feet in height.

Several valuable hybrids are also available; they are hardy to about −5°F/−21°C unless otherwise noted. 'Mohave' was released by the National Arboretum as a selection resistant to fireblight. It makes a bulky 12-foot shrub covered in orange-red berries starting in late summer. 'Teton' is also fireblight resistant: it's a bolt upright plant to 12 feet, with yellow-orange

fruits. 'Watereri' is a rounded 8-foot plant yielding heavy crops of bright red berries. 'Ruby Mound' is hardy to about 0°F/−18°C; bright red berries decorate arching stems that form spreading, mounded plants.

RHAMNUS
Buckthorn
Rhamnaceae

Deciduous, evergreen: Hardiness varies
Flowers: Inconspicuous
Exposure: Sun
Water: Moderate
Growth: Moderate to fast

The various buckthorns are "basic shrubs": good-looking, easy-to-grow foliage plants useful chiefly as background and informal hedge planting. All have small, berrylike fruits. Poor soil, heat, and moderate drought don't faze the buckthorns, but they'll also thrive with decent soil and routine watering.

R. alaternus, ITALIAN BUCKTHORN, is hardy to 0°F/−18°C. Plants are dense, their upward-sweeping branches covered in bright green, glossy, oval leaves to 2 inches long. The somewhat billowy natural shape, topping out in the 12- to 20-foot range, clips well into hedge form. Pea-size fruits are black, may produce many volunteer seed-

Rhamnus californica **'Eve Case'**

lings. Leaves of the selection 'Variegata' ('Argenteo-variegata') are bright green, irregularly blotched with gray-green and broadly margined in ivory.

R. californica, COFFEEBERRY, is hardy to 0°F/−18°C. The basic species—a variably upright plant to 15 feet with 3-inch glossy, oval leaves—may be sold by western native plant specialists. More generally available are two named selections. 'Eve Case' makes a compact, rounded shrub 4 to 8 feet high; 'Seaview' spreads to 8 feet but can be kept under 2 feet tall with slight pruning. Both have broadly oval leaves to 6 inches long; cherry-size fruits turn red, then black.

R. frangula, ALDER BUCKTHORN, is hardy to −40°F/−40°C. This is also a dense shrub, initially upright but maturing to a height and spread of 10 to 18 feet. Glossy, dark green leaves are broadly obovate, to 2½ inches long; they turn yellow in autumn. Pea-size berries form over an extended period, turning from greenish yellow to red-orange, dark red, and then black.

The selection 'Columnaris', tallhedge buckthorn, is a compact, vertical plant as tall as the species but only about 4 feet wide. Just occasional trimming of the sides will maintain it as a tight hedge; the height can be managed by topping.

RHAPHIOLEPIS INDICA
Rhaphiolepis, India hawthorn
Rosaceae

Evergreen: Hardy to 10°F/−12°C
Flowers: Pink, white; winter, spring
Exposure: Sun, partial shade
Water: Regular to moderate
Growth: Moderate

India hawthorn comes close to being a perfect shrub. Plants are dense, rounded, and symmetrical, covered in leathery, glossy, oval leaves to 3 inches long. Single, five-petaled blossoms are about ½ inch across, appearing in dense clusters over a 4- to 5-month period. More subtle color comes from bronzy new growth and the blue-black berries that follow bloom.

Nurseries sell named selections that differ in flower color and plant size. Those that reach 4 feet high or more

Rhaphiolepis indica **'Pink Lady'**

include 'Clara' (5 feet, white flowers), 'Enchantress' (6 feet, soft pink), 'Jack Evans' (4 feet, bright pink), 'Pink Lady' (5 feet, deep pink), 'Spring Rapture' (4 feet, rosy red), 'Springtime' (6 feet, deep pink), and 'White Enchantress' (6 feet, white). Shorter growers are 'Ballerina' (2 to 2½ feet, deep pink), 'Charisma' (3 feet, double pink), 'Coates Crimson' (2 to 4 feet, deepest pink), and 'Pink Cloud' (3 feet, deep pink).

The plant sold as *R.* 'Majestic Beauty' differs considerably from the named selections of *R. indica*. All its parts are larger: the leaves reach 4 to 6 inches long, the light pink flowers come in 10-inch clusters, and plants can reach 15 feet. Use it as a background shrub or as a small tree.

These are not fussy plants. Give them average soil and routine watering (though established plants are moderately drought tolerant). In partial shade, growth is more open and flowering is less profuse; in the desert, they need a bit of shade during the hottest hours of the day. Fireblight and a fungal leaf spot (in cool, wet weather) are possible disease problems.

RHODODENDRON
Rhododendron, Azalea
Ericaceae

Deciduous, evergreen: Hardiness varies
Flowers: Purple, lavender, magenta, pink, red, orange, yellow, cream, white; winter, spring
Exposure: Sun to partial shade
Water: Regular
Growth: Slow to moderate

So varied are rhododendrons and azaleas that they defy generalization. Approximately 800 species are recognized, and the International Register records over 10,000 named selections and hybrids—of which perhaps 2,000 are currently available. Botanists have arranged the species into series and subseries according to the closer relationships; one of those series includes the plants we know as azaleas.

All rhododendrons and azaleas are prized for their color display, which spans a possible 6-month period from midwinter through late spring. Their flowers are basically funnel shaped and carried in tightly knit clusters, but some have practically flat flowers, and others are tubular. True blue is about the only color missing from their spectrum, and some lavender-blue–flowered species and hybrids can lend a blue effect in the garden. Foliage varies from glossy to matte, from veined and rough looking to absolutely smooth. The plants, too, are amazingly varied. In general, azaleas are more fine-textured, lightweight-appearing plants, whereas rhododendrons are more massive and dominant—but exceptions abound!

Despite the countless differences among these plants, they share basic cultural needs. Soil must be well drained, moist, cool, and acid (but see qualifications under "Azaleas"). Their dense networks of fibrous roots need both moisture and plenty of soil air at all times. Organic matter, used in quantity, will create a soil to their liking. Plant rhododendrons and azaleas so that the tops of their root balls are several inches above soil grade. Never

Rhododendron **'Else Frye'**

Rosa moyesii

let soil wash in and bury the plant bases. These shallow-rooted plants benefit from a constant mulch: pine needles, oak leaves, wood by-products (such as redwood or fir bark or chips), or even compost.

If your soil is light to medium (sand to loam), dig plenty of organic matter into the soil; then plant high. In heavy (clay) and in alkaline soils, specially prepared raised beds will offer the best conditions. Build beds 1 to 2 feet above the soil level. Liberally mix organic materials into the top foot of garden soil beneath the raised bed; then fill the bed with a mixture of 50 percent organic material (at least half peat moss), 30 percent soil, and 20 percent sand. Some rhododendron growers with claylike soils actually plant on top of amended existing soil, then apply an extremely thick mulch nearly to the plants' bases.

The amount of sun these plants can take varies among the species and hybrids and also depends on climate; most can take full-sun locations in cool-summer regions. An ideal location anywhere is beneath tall trees where sunlight is filtered and light is good. The next-best locations are the east and north sides of houses and fences. In too-dense shade, plants become leggy and bloom sparsely.

Fertilize plants when flower buds swell, and then at monthly intervals (one or two more applications) until new growth begins. Use a commercial acid fertilizer in amounts a bit less than recommended.

Rhododendrons. These evergreen plants range from treelike shrubs bearing volleyball-size flower clusters (called "trusses") to ground-hugging creepers with blossoms and leaves under an inch in size. They all need the soil conditions outlined earlier; in addition, they are at their best where the atmosphere is cool and humid.

Natural rhododendron country includes the Pacific Northwest (west of the Cascades) and down the California coast to just below San Francisco; the Appalachian highlands, from northern Georgia into New York; the Atlantic seaboard, from northern Delaware through New England; and areas westward through New York, Pennsylvania, and parts of Ohio (es-

pecially near Lake Erie). Though these regions encompass a wide range of winter temperatures, there are rhododendrons suitable for each. Visit well-stocked nurseries and public gardens to learn of successful local kinds.

Azaleas. Among the azaleas are both evergreen and deciduous plants. In the South, evergreen azaleas have been landscape staples for generations. Because they can endure more heat than rhododendrons, azaleas grow well not only in the areas mentioned for rhododendrons but also in more of California (except for desert and mountain areas) plus the middle and deep South. A number of hybrid groups have been developed, containing many named selections in each group; not only do plant and flower sizes vary, but so does hardiness.

Deciduous azaleas offer bright yellow, orange, and flame red colors in addition to the more standard white, cream, and pink flowers. Hybrid selections are the most widely sold— Exbury, Knap Hill, and Mollis, for example—but native North American species from the Southeast and West Coast are sold on a more limited scale. Hardiness varies, from about –40°F/ –40°C for the Minnesota-bred Northern Lights hybrids to around –5°F/ –21°C for West Coast *R. occidentale.* Deciduous azaleas are the least demanding of the ideal soil and climate conditions. They'll tolerate some dry heat (if they're well watered) and fairly ordinary garden soil. Most put on an autumn foliage show of yellow, orange, red, or maroon if leaves are not damaged by powdery mildew.

As recommended for rhododendrons, your best guide to locally successful azalea types and individual named selections is a visit to local nurseries and public gardens.

ROSA
Rose
Rosaceae

Deciduous, semievergreen: Hardiness varies
Flowers: Red, pink, purple, lavender, white, cream, yellow, orange; spring, summer, autumn
Exposure: Sun, partial shade
Water: Regular
Growth: Fast

What other shrub has such a widespread hold on popular affection? So ancient is the bond between humans and roses that radically different languages use variations on the same word—"rose"—for these plants.

Modern roses. Most roses sold by the tens of thousands in nurseries, in garden centers, and by mail-order houses are modern hybrid teas, grandifloras, floribundas, and climbers.

Among the hybrid tea roses and grandifloras, you'll find the plants that furnish "typical" rose blossoms— large, shapely, long-budded, often fragrant—on bushes 3 to 8 feet high, depending on the individual hybrid and the climate. Plant quality varies from one named hybrid to another. Some of them make well-foliaged, well-branched shrubs, but many are less valuable as landscape shrubs than as simple flower factories.

(Continued on next page)

Floribunda roses are usually bushy and full foliaged, growing 2 to 4 feet tall and bearing clusters of flowers smaller than most hybrid teas but often as attractive individually. Most function well as low hedge and border plants and can be mass planted for color impact.

Modern climbing roses include both natural climbers and climbing sports of popular hybrid teas, grandifloras, and floribundas. They produce long, somewhat limber canes that can be fanned out on walls and trellises, trained horizontally on low fences, or guided up onto overhead structures.

Miniature roses derive from crosses with miniature China roses and chiefly modern hybrid teas, grandifloras, and floribundas. Flowers come in the 1- to 2-inch range, singly and in clusters, on plants generally 2 feet or less in height, with proportionate foliage. Colors include all those found in modern hybrids; flower styles range from informal to the refined hybrid tea shape.

Modern shrub roses have been developed specifically to function as flowering shrubs. They usually offer disease-resistant leaves on well-foliaged plants that may be upright, mounded, or spreading (nearly to the extent of being ground covers). Flowers usually come in clusters (in some, the individual blossoms are of hybrid tea shapeliness) and may, in some hybrids, set hips that become a decorative feature in summer or autumn.

Old garden roses. This umbrella term covers the many and diverse types of roses that were popular in the centuries before the advent of modern hybrid teas; it includes species as well as species hybrids. Mail-order specialists in "old" or "heritage" roses offer an increasing array of these plants. The "old European roses"—Gallicas, Damasks, Albas, and Centifolias—flower in spring only, but the China roses and many of their derivatives bloom repeatedly.

Among such a varied group there's naturally a range of flower sizes and styles. Among the old European roses in particular, you will find fairly flat blossoms of countless petals intricately folded and packed into a circular outline. Many have a fragrance to which the word "memorable" fails to do justice. Some descendants of the China roses—particularly the teas and hybrid perpetuals—may bear flowers that appear decidedly modern. And, of course, there are countless cluster-flowered sorts, with individual flowers ranging from single to puffball doubleness. Plant sizes and growth habits also vary widely. At one end of the scale are 2-foot bushes; at the other, rampant climbers. Many form tall shrubs, often arching fountainlike from the weight of their flowers.

Success with roses can be summed up as good soil and regular water. And for the modern hybrid classes (as well as many of the old garden roses), you would add fertilizer, pest and disease control, and routine pruning. This may sound like a long list of "chores," but when you consider the rewards of a spring-into-autumn flowering season, the effort is repaid. Roses thrive in good, fertile soil given a regular moisture supply. If drainage is good, it may be difficult to overwater.

For roses that flower once in spring and put on one flush of growth afterward, the need for nutrients and water extends just to the end of the growth cycle. After that, plants can coast on moderate watering until the next year's growth begins. But with the repeat- and continuous-flowering kinds, there's no slacking off until autumn or winter chill shuts down growth.

Give all roses an application of commercial fertilizer in late winter or early spring, before growth begins. Give repeat-flowering types additional "booster" applications after each flush of bloom. In cold-winter regions, cease applications in early to mid-August, to minimize the amount of late-season new growth that would be vulnerable to freezing. Continue nutrient applications until later in milder regions.

Prune repeat-flowering roses in the dormant period, before new growth begins: from midwinter to early spring, depending on the climate. The once-flowering kinds bloom on wood formed the previous year and put on strong new growth after flowering. Prune those right after flowers fade, removing older, played-out stems and leaving healthy new growth.

Rosmarinus officinalis 'Tuscan Blue'

ROSMARINUS OFFICINALIS
Rosemary
Labiatae

Evergreen: Hardy to 0°F/–18°C
Flowers: Blue, pink, white; winter, spring
Exposure: Sun
Water: Moderate to little
Growth: Moderate to fast

Whereas some shrubs offer a dividend of flowers for cutting or drying or of fruits to eat, rosemary gives you an endless quantity of its aromatic leaves for culinary use. In the basic species, plants reach 3 to 4 feet high—rounded and a bit spreading but irregular in outline, with main branches that tend to sweep outward and upward. Narrow, almost needlelike 1-inch leaves are usually glossy green on the upper surface, grayish white beneath, and distinctly aromatic when brushed or bruised. Plants bear small clusters of ¼- to ½-inch flowers over a long bloom period that, in some individuals, can start as early as autumn. The typical flower color is lavender-blue (the shade can vary), but specialty nurseries may offer white-flowered individuals and the lavender-rose 'Mallorca Pink'.

Other named selections vary in growth habit, plant size, and shade of blue flowers. 'Collingwood Ingram' has flowers of an intense violet-blue on a spreading plant to about 2½ feet high. 'Benenden Blue' and 'Angustifolia'—perhaps the same plant under two names—offer similarly intense dark blue blossoms on a 3- to 4-foot plant with the narrowest leaves of all and a strong, almost pinelike scent. Two distinct (and easily distinguishable) plants are both sold as 'Tuscan Blue'. One has brilliant, medium-blue blossoms on a spreading plant to about 4 feet high; the other has larger, lighter blue flowers, larger and broader leaves, and becomes a 6-foot plant with strongly upright stems.

Best known of the low-growing kinds is 'Prostratus'. Its initial growth is horizontal, but secondary stems may arch upward, then curve or twist back toward the ground. One plant can cover considerable territory, rooting as it spreads and building to 1½ or 2 feet in height. Flowers are light gray-blue, the short leaves bright to dark green.

Rosemary needs well-drained soil and little else. With good drainage plants will accept regular watering, but they'll get along with little or no supplemental water in all but the hottest-summer regions. Prune as needed to shape or direct growth, remembering that all cuts should be made to side branches or into leafy stems.

SPIRAEA
Spiraea
Rosaceae

Deciduous: Hardiness varies
Flowers: Red, pink, white; spring, summer
Exposure: Sun
Water: Regular to moderate
Growth: Moderate

Spiraeas are of two distinct types. First are the familiar "bridal wreath" sorts, with clusters of white flowers cascading down arched branches in spring or early summer. The second group includes the summer- to autumn-blooming, knee-high, shrubby types that offer colorful flowers clustered at the ends of upright branches.

Spiraeas with white flowers.
Among these spring- to summer-flowering plants, the following are widely grown.

S. cantoniensis (*S. reevesiana*) is hardy to about 0°F/–18°C. Two-inch clusters of white flowers cover the arching stems in late spring to early summer, along with the 2-inch, oval to lance-shaped, dark green leaves. Plants reach 4 to 6 feet high and spread a bit wider. In colder parts of its range the leaves will turn reddish shades in autumn, but in warmer-winter areas much of the foliage will remain on the plant without changing color.

S. nipponica tosaensis is hardy to –20°F/–29°C. The most widely available plant is the selection 'Snowmound', a name that well describes the effect created when the 3-foot-high mounded plant is covered with small white blossoms in early summer. Plants are dense, with many stems; lance-shaped, 1½-inch, dark green leaves have little autumn color.

S. prunifolia is hardy to –20°F/–29°C. White flowers like ½-inch double roses appear along the upright but arching slender stems in early to midspring, before leaves emerge. Small, dark green, glossy, oval leaves turn bright shades of red, orange, and yellow in autumn. Plants are somewhat open and filmy, unobtrusive except in spring and autumn. This is sometimes sold as *S. p.* 'Plena', to distinguish it from the single-flowered form *S. p. simplicifolia*.

S. thunbergii is hardy to –20°F/–29°C. Few-flowered clusters of starry, single white flowers cover branches in early spring before leaf-out. Plants are billowy, twiggy, and gracefully arching, to about 5 feet high with slightly greater spread. Narrow, blue-green leaves turn a soft, tawny yellow to reddish brown in autumn.

S. trilobata is hardy to –20°F/–29°C. As the species name indicates, the

Spiraea japonica 'Alpina'

small leaves often have three lobes—a feature that separates it from nearly all the other species. The selection 'Swan Lake' looks like a small version of *S. prunifolia*, giving a lavish show of small double blossoms on a 3- to 4-foot plant in mid- to late spring.

S. vanhouttei is hardy to –20°F/–29°C. This is the classic "bridal wreath" spiraea. Fountainlike growth eventually makes a mounded, spreading plant to about 6 feet high by 8 feet wide or more. From mid- to late spring—and continuing into early summer in colder regions—leafy branches are studded with circular, flattened clusters of single white blossoms. Dark green, 1½-inch leaves are oval and toothed to slightly lobed; sometimes they change in autumn to shades of red.

Spiraeas with colored flowers.
Among these summer- to autumn-flowering kinds, you will find some with other-than-green leaves.

S. bumalda is hardy to –20°F/–29°C. This is the name given to a group of hybrids between *S. japonica* and another Japanese spiraea. Upright stems carry 2- to 3-inch, ovate, gray-green leaves. A number of named selections are available, the best known of which is 'Anthony Waterer'. Broad, flat-topped clusters of carmine red flowers combine well with the pinkish new leaves on a 2- to 3-foot plant with a 4-foot spread.

'Froebelii' has flowers of nearly the same color but grows about a foot taller and starts flowering a bit later. 'Goldflame' is essentially 'Froebelii' with colored foliage: leaves emerge bronze colored, turn yellow, and mature to yellowish green. 'Limemound' reaches about 2 feet high, producing pink flowers above lime green leaves that become orange-red in autumn.

S. japonica is hardy to –10°F/–23°C. In most respects, it is similar to its hybrid offspring *S. bumalda*. But the basic species is taller growing (4 to 6 feet), with flat clusters of pink blossoms above sharply toothed, oval, green leaves to 4 inches long. Named selections are generally sold.

'Shirobana' (often sold as 'Shibori') is a novelty that bears white, pink, and rosy red flowers on the same 2- to

3-foot-high plant. 'Little Princess' and 'Alpina' mound about 1½ feet high and are covered in pinkish red flowers. At the other end of the size scale, *S. j. fortunei* (sometimes sold as 'Fortunei') is a robust, pink-flowered plant with coarsely toothed leaves 4 or more inches long. 'Atrosanguinea' is a selection of it that offers red new foliage and crimson blossoms.

There is no trick to growing spiraeas. Give them average soil, routine watering, and periodic pruning to remove old stems and encourage new growth. Prune the mostly spring-blooming, arching-growth kinds after flowers have finished; prune the summer-flowering, shrubby plants in winter or earliest spring. All those with arching stems will look butchered if headed back so far that their natural grace is lost. But do remove old, unproductive stems to the ground or back to vigorous lateral growths. With the shrubby, upright kinds, you can both thin and head back.

SYRINGA
Lilac
Oleaceae

Deciduous: Hardiness varies; needs some winter chill
Flowers: Purple, lavender, blue, white, pink, magenta; spring
Exposure: Sun
Water: Regular
Growth: Moderate

Wherever there are subfreezing winter temperatures, generations of gardeners have formed a special attachment to lilacs. Common lilac (*S. vulgaris*) in particular is considered one of the essences of spring and is cherished for the beauty and fragrance of its blossoms.

The many lilac species, hybrids, and named selections make medium-size to large shrubs, virtually all of which are vigorous and easy to grow. Individual flowers are tubular, flaring into four petal-like lobes in the single sorts or into a clutch of "petals" in double kinds. The floral show comes from the number of small flowers packed into dense pyramidal to conical clusters. Depending on climate, flowering occurs from early spring (in the earliest.

kinds) to early summer, always after leaves have formed. Most lilacs have no claim to special attractiveness once flowering has finished, and few color significantly in autumn. After bloom, their landscape effect is fairly neutral.

Give lilacs fairly good, well-drained soil. They're among the few shrubs that prefer a neutral to slightly alkaline soil; if your soil is strongly acid, dig lime into it before planting (see "Acid & Alkaline Soils," page 33). Established plants are fairly drought tolerant, but they'll look and perform better with at least moderate watering during dry periods. Powdery mildew can bother many lilacs; resistant kinds include *S. patula* and *S. prestoniae*.

A bit of annual pruning also enhances performance. Lilacs flower on wood formed in the previous year, so you should prune just after bloom has finished. Remove spent flower clusters, cutting back to a pair of leaves; growth buds at that point will make the flowering stems for the next year. Thin out overabundant new stems from the base to the most vigorous. As plants age, annual new growth will come higher and farther out on the framework of existing stems. In time, therefore, you should start to remove a few older stems each year so that the plant will continually renew itself with young stems from ground level.

S. chinensis, CHINESE LILAC, is hardy to –20°F/–29°C. This is a hybrid of common lilac and (presumably) Persian lilac, *S. persica*—itself a hybrid of cut-leaf lilac, *S. laciniata*. Compared with common lilac, these are smaller, arching plants (10 to 15 feet high) with smaller, narrower leaves and more open flower clusters. Their performance is much better in regions with mild winters and hot summers. The most common form is rosy purple and fragrant, but named selections include white-flowered 'Alba' and rosy lilac 'Saugeana'.

S. hyacinthiflora is hardy to –30°F/ –34°C. This name was given to a group of hybrids derived from common lilac and a Chinese species. In plant and flower they resemble common lilac, but they bloom at least a week earlier in spring. Many named selections exist, including 'Blue Hyacinth' and

Syringa chinensis

'Clarke's Giant' (lavender-blue), 'Esther Staley' (pink, from magenta buds), 'Pocahontas' and 'Purple Heart' (purple), 'White Hyacinth' (white), and double-flowered 'Alice Eastwood' (magenta) and 'Gertrude Leslie' (white).

S. laciniata (S. persica laciniata), CUT-LEAF LILAC, is hardy to –20°F/–29°C. Fragrance immediately links this with the other lilacs, but its garden effect is quite different. It's a fairly open, arching to rounded plant, bearing 2½-inch leaves cut nearly to the midribs. Lilac-colored flowers come in small clusters in midspring. Persian lilac, *S. persica*, a hybrid of cut-leaf lilac, is distinguished by its lance-shaped leaves.

S. patula (S. palibiniana, S. velutina), KOREAN LILAC, is hardy to –30°F/–34°C. Its foliage recalls the common lilac (though it turns red in autumn), but the plant is smaller, growing fairly slowly to 6 to 8 feet in height and width. 'Miss Kim' has clusters of purple buds that open dark and then quickly fade to palest blue.

S. prestoniae is hardy to –50°F/–46°C. This group of hybrids was developed in Canada for guaranteed survival in severe winters. Flowers come on new growth, appearing after common lilac has bloomed. Bulky, dense plants resemble common lilac, but the individual flowers are smaller and lack the traditional lilac fragrance. The numerous named selections include 'Isabella' (lilac), 'Jessica' (violet), 'Nocturne' (blue), and 'Royalty' (purple). *S. swegiflexa* is a related hybrid cross; its selection 'James MacFarlane' bears bright pink flowers, at the same time as the *S. prestoniae* group.

S. vulgaris, COMMON LILAC, is hardy to –40°F/–40°C. Its devotees would object to the word "common," for a bush in flower is uncommonly lovely and fragrant. Plants typically reach 8 to 15 feet high and nearly as wide, though unpruned specimens can achieve even larger proportions. Flowers in some shade of lavender (or white, in 'Alba') are produced in clusters to 10 inches long. Broadly oval, pointed leaves are a solid medium to dark green, up to 5 inches long.

In the last 100 years, countless named selections have been sold, covering the complete range of lilac colors in both single and double flowers; some have a bicolor effect when their dark buds open to lighter blossoms. Well-stocked retail nurseries and specialty mail-order firms will offer a good selection. 'Sensation' is worth special mention for its wine red single flowers, each petal edged in white. The Descanso Hybrids were developed in Southern California to perform in regions experiencing little winter chill. 'Lavender Lady' is the best known of these, but others include 'Blue Boy' and 'Blue Skies', lavender 'Chiffon' and 'Forrest K. Smith', rosy lavender 'Sylvan Beauty', and 'White Angel' (usually sold as 'Angel White').

Taxus (see page 105)

Thuja (see page 105)

Tibouchina urvilleana (see page 127)

VIBURNUM
Viburnum
Caprifoliaceae

Deciduous, evergreen: Hardiness varies
Flowers: White, pink; spring, autumn, winter
Exposure: Sun, partial shade
Water: Regular
Growth: Moderate

The many viburnum species, and a growing number of hybrids, are among the finest of those plants

Viburnum plicatum

thought of as "basic shrubs." Most are medium-size to large plants, good for specimen and background planting; several make good unclipped hedges. Individual flowers are small, tubular, and flaring into five petal-like lobes.

The evergreen viburnums are planted especially for their good-looking foliage; their flowers (and fruits) are an attractive bonus. Many of the deciduous sorts provide a lavish floral display, set clusters of fruits that become decorative as they ripen, and put on a show of autumn foliage color. The ripe fruits—usually red, yellow, blue, or black—inevitably attract hungry birds during autumn and winter.

You'll get the best growth in good, fertile soil, but viburnums aren't particular about its pH. They do prefer regular watering, though some species tolerate a fair amount of drought. Climate adaptability is broad: hot or cool, humid or dry. Though full sun will encourage flowering, these shrubs look especially good in woodland edge plantings, where the forest forms a backdrop and casts patchy shade. Possible pests are aphids, spider mites, thrips, and scale.

Evergreen viburnums. *V. cinnamomifolium* is hardy to 0°F/–18°C. Reaching 10 to 20 feet high and wide, it is among the largest of these species. Broadly oval, glossy leaves to 6 inches long have three distinct veins running from base to tip. In midspring, flat, 6-inch clusters of tiny, white, lightly fragrant flowers open from pink buds; blue-black fruits follow.

V. davidii is hardy to 0°F/–18°C. Though springtime brings small clus-

ters of white flowers (followed by metallic blue fruits if several plants are present), it's foliage that makes this species outstanding. Like those of *V. cinnamomifolium*, its leaves are broad ovals to 6 inches long, glossy and dark green, with prominent veins running from base to tip. Its growth habit, though, is totally different. These plants make slowly spreading clumps with stems reaching to 2 feet high; the elegant foliage makes a solid cover to the ground. Best uses are as a small-scale ground cover or foundation plant.

V. odoratissimum, sweet viburnum, is hardy to 20°F/–7°C. Here is another big, bulky background plant: 10 to 20 feet high with greater potential spread. Elliptical leaves to 8 inches have a high-gloss surface and leathery texture; 'Emerald Lustre' features even larger leaves. Small, lightly scented, white flowers come in conical, 6-inch clusters during mid- to late spring; fruits that follow are red, maturing to black.

V. rhytidophyllum, leatherleaf viburnum, is hardy to –10°F/–23°C. Its leathery leaves are a conspicuous feature. Narrowly oval to ovate, to 10 inches long, they're dark green with wrinkled surfaces, pale and felted on the undersides. Small, nearly white spring flowers come in flattish, 8-inch clusters, followed (if another plant is nearby for pollination) by red fruits that blacken when ripe. Growth is upright and fairly narrow, up to 15 feet. For best foliage appearance, locate plants where they'll be sheltered from strong winter winds. (Even so, leaves will droop in cold weather.)

(Continued on next page)

Several hybrids retain the leather-leaf foliage character. 'Pragense' makes a plant 10 feet high and wide, bearing glossy, leathery, smaller leaves with conspicuously textured veins. Its flowers are white with a pink or cream tint; the fruits go from red to black. 'Alleghany' and 'Willowwood' are from a cross with a deciduous species and will retain or drop their leaves depending on the severity of the winter; both are hardy to –20°F/–29°C. 'Alleghany' is the smaller plant, to about 10 feet high and a bit wider; 'Willowwood' grows to 15 feet high and wide, becoming bare at the base as it matures. Leaves on both resemble those of the V. rhytidophyllum parent.

V. tinus, laurustinus, is hardy to 0°F/–18°C. In the West, Southwest, and South, this is one of the best shrubs for unclipped hedge and screen plantings: growth is upright, to 12 feet if not restrained, but only half as wide. The leaves are dark green, leathery ovals to 3 inches long, making a dense cover from top to bottom; new stems are wine red. Pink buds open to white flowers in 3- to 4-inch clusters from midautumn into spring; metallic blue fruits last through summer. Mildew may be a problem near the coast.

Nurseries carry several named selections. 'Variegatum' is like the basic species, but the leaves are variegated with white and light yellow. Leaves of 'Lucidum' are a bit larger than the species and more resistant to mildew. 'Robustum' has larger, coarser, mildew-resistant leaves; it's a vigorous plant that may be trained as a small tree. 'Spring Bouquet' (also sold as 'Compactum') has leaves a bit smaller and darker than the species, on a compact plant 6 to 10 feet high. 'Dwarf' makes a rounded shrub 3 to 5 feet in diameter.

Deciduous viburnums. V. bodnantense is hardy to –10°F/–23°C. This hybrid is noted for its fragrant flowers, which can appear from midautumn through winter and into early spring. Most widely sold is 'Dawn', which produces light pink blossoms (from rosy red buds) in ball-shaped clusters on an upright plant to 10 feet high and nearly as wide. Deeply veined, oval leaves reach 4 inches long, turning dark red in autumn.

V. burkwoodii is hardy to –20°F/–29°C. At the colder end of its growing range, this is a deciduous shrub, with dark red autumn color. Where winter is milder, the leaves take on purple tones but remain through winter. The plants are upright, to 12 feet high and 5 feet wide, bearing ovate, 4-inch, glossy leaves with white-felted undersides. Fragrant, pink-budded, white flowers appear in dense, rounded clusters from midwinter into spring. Two selections are more reliably deciduous. 'Chenault' grows to about 6 feet high and 4 feet wide. 'Mohawk' is a more rounded plant to 7 feet with red-budded, white flowers and red-orange autumn foliage.

V. carlcephalum, fragrant snowball, is hardy to –10°F/–23°C. The common name perfectly describes the floral show: waxy, white, scented flowers from pink buds, in globular clusters to 5 inches across. Flowering occurs in spring and early summer, after foliage has formed. The plants are upright to 10 feet high and nearly as wide, clothed in ovate, dull green, 4-inch leaves that turn red and orange in autumn.

V. carlesii, Korean spice viburnum, is hardy to –20°F/–29°C. This is a parent of the fragrant snowball and bears the same foliage on an upright, spreading plant to about 8 feet high and nearly as wide. Highly fragrant, pink-budded, white flowers come in 3-inch rounded clusters in early and midspring; blue-black fruits follow in summer. Autumn foliage is in shades of red. The selection 'Compactum' is identical but grows just 3 to 4 feet tall with equal spread.

'Eskimo', a hybrid of V. carlesii, has white blossoms in snowball-like clusters on a compact, rounded, semievergreen plant about 5 feet around. Leath-

Viburnum carlcephalum

ery, dark green leaves are semiglossy; the fruits change from dark red to black. Yet another hybrid is V. juddii, which bears foliage and flowers like those of V. carlesii but on a bushier, more widely spreading plant about 7 feet high.

V. dilatatum, linden viburnum, is hardy to –20°F/–29°C. For a spectacular display of red fruits, this species is second to none. Tiny, creamy white flowers appear in loose, flattened, 5-inch clusters in early summer. By the end of the season, red fruits have formed, and they then last into winter. Plants are broadly rounded, 6 to 10 feet high, with nearly round, hairy, gray-green leaves 2 to 5 inches long; autumn color is rusty red to purple. 'Erie' is a somewhat smaller-growing selection that produces coral-red fruits and features yellow to orange-red autumn color.

V. lantana, wayfaring tree, is hardy to –30°F/–34°C. The basic species is a large shrub (to 15 feet high) with broadly oval, downy leaves to 5 inches long that turn to red in autumn. Small clusters of tiny white flowers in late spring form berries that go from green to red to black. 'Mohican' is a superior selection, making a smaller plant just about 6 feet high with greater spread; its fruits remain red. This species tolerates more drought than most other viburnums.

V. opulus, European cranberry bush, is hardy to –40°F/–40°C. This old-fashioned favorite is still well worth planting, if you're willing to vigilantly patrol for its major pest—aphids—as new growth appears. Upright, arching plants grow 10 to 20 feet high and spread nearly as wide, bearing lobed, maplelike leaves that turn a good maple red in autumn. Midspring bloom comes in 4-inch, lace cap clusters, in which ¾-inch sterile flowers encircle tiny fertile blossoms. Large, showy red fruits decorate the branches in autumn and winter.

Several selections offer distinct variations. The best known is 'Roseum' (V. opulus 'Sterile'), common snowball, all of whose flowers are sterile (and therefore fruitless), so that each cluster is a floral ball about 3 inches across. 'Compactum' is identical to the basic species but grows just about 5 feet high and wide. 'Aureum' has golden yellow leaves on a less vigorous plant to about 10 feet high; plant it in partial shade to avoid sunburn.

V. plicatum is hardy to –20°F/–29°C. You can easily recognize this species in its various forms by its horizontal branching pattern, which gives plants a layered look. Its midspring flower clusters are carried in opposite rows on the upper sides of branches, while the leaves point or hang downward. Broadly oval, dull, dark green leaves grow to 6 inches long, prominently veined from midrib to leaf margin. Autumn color is red-purple.

Japanese snowball is *V. plicatum plicatum* (*V. tomentosum* 'Sterile'). Its 3-inch, snowball-like flower clusters resemble those of *V. opulus* 'Roseum', but aphids are far less of a pest to this species. The plant may reach 15 feet high and wide, offering autumn foliage color but no fruits.

Doublefile viburnum, *V. plicatum tomentosum*, represents the species in its basic form, with lace cap flower clusters 4 to 6 inches wide. Fertile flowers within the clusters form red fruits that gradually age to black and remain positioned on the upper sides of branches—if not consumed by birds. Plants may reach the same dimensions as the Japanese snowball. The selection 'Mariesii' features large flower clusters with larger sterile flowers; 'Pink Beauty' varies the picture with pale pink blossoms that fade to white in heat. 'Summer Snowflake' is a shorter plant, to about 8 feet tall, that begins flowering in midspring and may continue through summer. 'Shasta' is more upright (to 8 feet) and finer-textured; its sterile flowers can be over 2 inches across. 'Watanabe' will flower from spring through summer on a slow-growing plant 4 to 6 feet high with equal spread.

WEIGELA
Weigela
Caprifoliaceae

Deciduous: Hardy to –20°F/–29°C
Flowers: Red, pink, white; spring
Exposure: Sun
Water: Regular
Growth: Fast

Because of their overpowering spring floral display, you can forgive weigelas their rather ordinary appearance during the rest of the year. Plants leaf out and then explode into flower with funnel-shaped, foxglovelike blossoms coming singly or in clusters all along cascading stems formed the previous year. The plants are upright and arching to arching and spreading, depending on the individual. Leaves are semiglossy, pointed ovals to 4 inches long that take on no special autumn color.

Average soil, routine watering, and some annual pruning keep weigelas in good shape. After flowering has finished, cut back those branches to strong new growth, leaving about two pairs of new growth to each stem. Remove to the ground all older stems that are no longer putting out strong new shoots. Finally, thin out new growth from the base to just the strongest, best-spaced stems.

W. florida (W. rosea) is the typical "old-fashioned" weigela, with pink to rosy red flowers on a plant to 10 feet high and wide. Its selection 'Variegata' is a shorter plant whose leaves are irregularly margined in creamy ivory. *W. praecox* is generally similar but reaches only about 6 feet; its pink blossoms have conspicuous yellow throats.

W. middendorffiana is a spreading shrub that mounds to about 4 feet high, with wrinkled, dark green leaves and orange-marked, soft yellow blossoms clustered toward branch ends. This one prefers more moisture and coolness than the other weigelas and even likes a bit of shade.

Among named hybrids, red-flowered kinds include 'Bristol Ruby' and 'Newport Red' in the 6- to 9-foot range

Weigela florida

Xylosma congestum

and 'Eva Supreme' at 4 to 5 feet. 'Java Red', despite its name, has deep pink flowers that open from red buds; purple-tinted, dark green leaves clothe a 6-foot, mounding plant. 'Pink Princess' is another 6-footer, bearing flowers of clear pink. 'Bristol Snowflake' is a white equivalent of 'Bristol Ruby'.

XYLOSMA CONGESTUM
Xylosma
Flacourtiaceae

Evergreen (except as noted): Hardy to 10°F/–12°C
Flowers: Inconspicuous
Exposure: Sun
Water: Moderate
Growth: Moderate

What xylosma lacks in flowers it makes up for in foliage beauty and garden usefulness. Plants grow about 10 to 12 feet high and wide, are a bit angular and open, and have branches that gracefully arch or droop; some plants are spiny. Bronze-colored new growth matures into glossy, pointed oval leaves to 3½ inches long; hard frosts may cause partial or complete defoliation. This is a handsome plant for hedge, background, or screen planting, and can even be trained as a small tree. The spiny selection 'Compacta' grows rather slowly to three-fourths the size of the basic species. 'El Dorado' is lower-growing with leaves about an inch long.

Soil type or quality is not an issue. Established plants are fairly drought tolerant but look best with at least moderate watering. In alkaline soil, you may have to treat them for chlorosis. Left to its own devices, xylosma will start as a sprawling, mounding plant. Stake up the main stems to gain height more quickly.

Western Native Specialties

The Mediterranean and semiarid climates of western North America support a number of native plants that are attractive landscape components. These five shrubs are at the top of any list of native favorites.

ARCTOSTAPHYLOS. Manzanita. *Ericaceae.* Evergreen; hardiness varies. The heath family left its mark on these shrubs in the form of tiny, urn-shaped blossoms that group into small, grapelike clusters. The plants range from ground-hugging creepers to shrub tree types. Most have shiny, leathery leaves and pink to white flowers in late winter or early spring; their small fruits resemble tiny apples. Picturesque crooked branches are typical of the larger kinds, and nearly all have mahogany-colored to purplish stems that are furniture-smooth (though bark may flake off annually).

Plant manzanitas in sun to partial shade; their growth is spindly in heavy shade. Most manzanitas are sensitive to summer watering: overwatering causes root rots, then death. Shrub types are the touchiest; native coastal ground covers are generally more moisture tolerant (though less toler-

Cercis occidentalis

ant of hot, dry summers). Well-drained, somewhat acid soil is best for all kinds. Water newly planted individuals about weekly during their first summer. Thereafter, judge by the weather and your soil type. Where summer is hot, you may water plants monthly if they're in well-drained soil, less frequently in heavier soils.

Monterey manzanita, *A. hookeri,* makes dense mounds 2 to 4 feet high and spreads to 6 feet or more. The selection 'Wayside' grows to 4 feet by 8 feet or more, whereas 'Monterey Carpet' achieves a 12-foot spread on a 1-foot height.

Common manzanita, *A. manzanita,* makes the largest plant—from 6 to 20 feet high and half as wide, with handsome, purplish red limbs. 'Dr. Hurd' is a treelike, white-flowered selection reaching 15 feet; its garden tolerance is better than that of the basic species. Shrubs to 6 feet include *A. bakeri* 'Louis Edmunds' (pink flowers, gray-green leaves) and *A. densiflora* 'Sentinel' (light green leaves, pale pink flowers). Only slightly shorter—to about 5 feet—are two other *A. densiflora* selections, 'Harmony' and 'Howard McMinn'. The hybrid 'Sunset' makes a mound about 5 by 6 feet, with copper to bright green leaves and pinkish white flowers.

Bearberry or kinnikinnick, *A. uva-ursi,* may be the most widely grown ground cover species; it's native to the northern latitudes of all Northern Hemisphere continents. The plants are prostrate, rooting as they spread and making 15-foot mats of small, bright green leaves that turn red in winter. Flowers are white or pinkish, fruits bright pink to red. Selected forms include 'Alaska' and 'Massachusetts' (with greater hardiness), 'Point Reyes' (heat tolerant), and light green–leafed 'Radiant'. For a taller-growing (to 2 feet) version, choose *A. media.* The hybrid 'Emerald Carpet' makes a solid, even, 1-foot-tall cover of tiny, bright green leaves.

CEANOTHUS. Wild Lilac, ceanothus. *Rhamnaceae.* Evergreen; hardy to 0°F/ –18°C. From palest azure to deepest cobalt, ceanothus covers the blue spectrum magnificently. Though individual flowers are tiny, they group into dense heads or spikes that blanket these shrubs during early and midspring. Most have fairly small leaves: bright to dark green, glossy ovals that usually make a dense cover.

Summer heat, heavy soil, and moisture equals death by root rot. But individuals do vary in their tolerance of summer moisture. Some demand total dryness, but others (particularly the coastal ground cover types) must have occasional summer water if they're grown away from the fog belt. If possible, plant ceanothus in well-drained soil, which will allow for the occasional summer sprinkle with least risk. All young plants will need supplemental watering during their first summer to become established.

'Ray Hartman' is among the largest ceanothus: 12 to 20 feet tall with sparkling, medium blue blossoms and leaves to 3 inches long, it makes an attractive small tree. 'Gentian Plume' is capable of 20 feet in both directions, growing as a sprawling shrub and producing dark blue flowers in unusually long (10-inch) spikes.

Most species and hybrids are large shrubs. 'Sierra Blue', to 12 feet, is at the tall end; this irregular plant bears medium blue flowers. 'Owlswood Blue' (dark blue) and *C. thyrsiflorus* 'Snow Flurry' (white) grow to 10 feet high with a slightly greater spread. 'Frosty Blue' can reach 9 feet, its dark blue blossoms frosted with white for an unusual sparkle. 'Blue Jeans', also to 9 feet, is the color of faded denim. It tolerates both summer water and heavy soil. 'Concha', which also takes summer water, makes a 7-foot, rounded plant with dark blue flowers. 'Julia Phelps' is a luminous dark indigo color, growing to 7 feet high with greater spread. Six-foot 'Dark Star' has tiny leaves and deep cobalt flowers; *C. rigidus* 'Snowball' makes a dense mound to 6 feet high and 16 feet wide, bearing white flowers in round clusters. Medium blue 'Joyce Coulter' reaches 5 feet high but grows as a spreading mound up to 12 feet across.

The ground cover types do best where summer is not truly hot and dry. These include light blue *C. gloriosus* and its darker selections 'Anchor Bay' and 'Emily Brown'. The latter has dark, hollylike leaves and violet-blue blossoms on a 3-foot by 12-foot plant that will accept heavy soil and (in cool regions) summer water. Carmel creeper, *C. griseus*, presents a lush, bright green foliage cover on plants that grow to 15 feet wide but just 2½ feet high; its flowers are light blue. Selections include the rank-growing 'Hurricane Point', which spreads to 30 feet, and 'Yankee Point', which spreads just about 10 feet, bearing dark leaves and medium blue blossoms.

CERCIS occidentalis. WESTERN REDBUD. *Leguminosae.* Deciduous; hardy to –10°F/–23°C. No shrub outdisplays a western redbud in full flower. Each blossom is a thumbnail-size, electric magenta sweet pea, and during the early spring bloom period the bare branches are literally encrusted with them. As flowers finish, red-bronze new growth emerges, maturing to leathery blue-green leaves nearly circular in outline but often notched at the tip. In autumn the foliage changes to a brilliant yellow. Bare winter branches are decorated with quantities of flat, beanlike, red-brown seed capsules. Western redbud may be a many-stemmed, vase-shaped to rounded, 10- to 12-foot shrub; or it can grow into a tree to about 18 feet high.

Once established, western redbud can get along without water during the dry months, but in well-drained soil it will take moderate to regular applications (and growth will be proportionately faster). In any soil, plant in full sun for the best flower production; but expect a really good floral show only where winter temperatures drop to 28°F/–2°C or lower.

FREMONTODENDRON (Fremontia). FREMONTIA, FLANNEL BUSH. *Bombacaceae.* Evergreen; hardy to 20°F/–7°C. These are culturally fussy shrubs but so showy that they're worth a few special concessions if you have a good site for them. In spring, brilliant yellow blossoms appear along the stems; they're five-parted, circular in outline, saucer shaped, and vary from 1 to 4 inches across. Conical seed capsules follow and hang on, in a dried state, for many months. They're covered with bristly, rust-colored hairs that can cause intense skin irritation.

The plants are fast growing and sizable (6 to 20 feet high), sometimes regularly shaped but more likely asymmetrical. Some specimens become almost treelike. Dark green, leathery leaves are somewhat rough on the surface but have a feltlike coating on the undersides. They vary from rounded to lobed, depending on the species or hybrid.

Common flannel bush, *F. californicum*, gives a dazzling show of lemon yellow, 1½-inch flowers in mid- to late spring. Its geographic variant "napense" is lower and bushier, with smaller blossoms. Southern flannel bush, *F. mexicanum*, has orange-tinted blossoms to 2½ inches across; they come over a longer period but make somewhat less of a show, because they flower among the leaves. The hybrid 'California Glory' is spectacular in flower with its 3-inch yellow blossoms tinged red on their outsides. 'San Gabriel' is similar but has deeply lobed, maplelike leaves. 'Pacific Sunset' has the largest blossoms (to 4 inches wide) in a deep orange-yellow.

Fremontia is extremely sensitive to water during the normal dry period. Overwatering leads to root rot or stem canker and death. Set out young

Fremontodendron

plants in autumn or winter, so they'll need minimal watering for establishment during the following summer. Established plants are totally drought tolerant and will accept occasional summer watering only if soil is well drained. Expect leaf drop during summer. Even under the best of conditions, these are not long-lived plants.

HETEROMELES arbutifolia (Photinia arbutifolia). TOYON, CALIFORNIA HOLLY. *Rosaceae.* Evergreen; hardy to 5°F/–15°C. Handsome toyon grows as a dense, large shrub to about 10 feet high; but in time it can become a multitrunked tree to 20 feet if you encourage height and remove lower branches. Leaves are leathery, dark green, and ovate, to 4 inches long with bristle-toothed margins. Large, flattish clusters of small creamy white flowers appear in late spring and early summer. These set a heavy crop of fruits that ripen into showy, pea-size red berries in midautumn. The Channel Islands form, *H. a. macrocarpa*, has larger fruits; occasionally, a yellow-fruited form is available.

Toyon grows in nearly any soil, in full sun to partial shade. Plants tolerate considerable drought, but are better looking with moderate watering (in well-drained soil) during the dry months. In desert gardens, summer watering is a must.

An Illustrated Glossary of Descriptive Terms

Basic Leaf Shapes

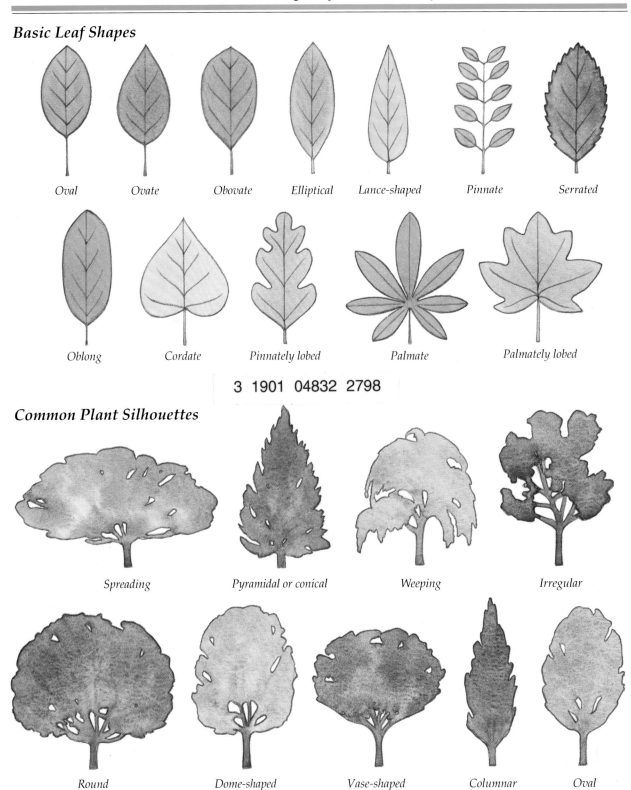

Oval   Ovate   Obovate   Elliptical   Lance-shaped   Pinnate   Serrated

Oblong   Cordate   Pinnately lobed   Palmate   Palmately lobed

Common Plant Silhouettes

Spreading   Pyramidal or conical   Weeping   Irregular

Round   Dome-shaped   Vase-shaped   Columnar   Oval

Certain botanical terms, as well as words in general circulation, precisely indicate leaf shapes and plant silhouettes or habits. Those terms, illustrated here, appear throughout the tree and shrub encyclopedias on pages 40–141.

Index